D1223051

U.S. Armored Cruisers

U.S. Armored Cruisers

A DESIGN AND OPERATIONAL HISTORY

Ivan Musicant

WITH DRAWINGS BY DAVID L. WOOD

Naval Institute Press   Annapolis, Maryland

Copyright © 1985
by the U.S. Naval Institute

All rights reserved. No part of this book may
be reproduced without written permission from the publisher.

Library of Congress Cataloging in Publication Data
Musicant, Ivan, 1943–
  U.S. armored cruisers.
  Bibliography: p.
  Includes index.
  1. Cruisers—United States—History—19th century.
2. Cruisers—United States—History—20th century.
3. United States—History, Naval—To 1900.　4. United
States—History, Naval—20th century.　I. Title.
II. Title: US armored cruisers.
V820.3.M87　1985　　　359.3′253′0973　　　85-4868
ISBN 0-87021-714-3

Printed in the United States of America

For George Musicant

Chapter opening photographs

Page 2: The fully rigged and highly transitional protected cruisers *Boston* and *Chicago*, third and fourth vessels completed in the seminal ABCD program, ride to their anchors off an East Coast port, c. 1889.

Page 14: The *New York* was the first armored vessel completed for the New Navy. In addition to her elaborate bow scroll, a distinctive feature on most of the New Navy's ships, note the torpedo aperture between her hawsepipes, her archaic ground tackle, and the projecting sponsons for her 4-inch guns. The large muzzles amidships, seemingly beneath her boats, are the open-mounted single 8-inch guns.

Page 44: An especially fine view of the *Brooklyn*, moored to a dock at the Brooklyn Navy Yard, 1899. In contrast to the forecastle deck of the *New York*, the *Brooklyn*'s has been given a coat of buff. Note her tumble home, as distinct from the boxy amidships plane of the *New York*.

Page 74: "Side cleaners over the side!" Brand new and in commission four months, the *Maryland* inaugurates the just-completed concrete and granite graving dock at the Boston Navy Yard, August 1905.

Page 146: In her building shed just before launching, the *Washington* rests on keel blocks, 7 August 1906. Note the teak backing just aft of the prow, where an armor patch has not yet been fitted.

Contents

Abbreviations

AA	antiaircraft		**KNC**	Krupp nickel chromium
AC	collier		**kw**	kilowatt
ACR	armored cruiser		**MS**	mild steel
AP	armor piercing		**NS**	nickel steel
AP	transport		**oa**	overall (length of hull)
BB	battleship		**PG**	patrol gunboat
BM	monitor		**psi**	pounds per square inch
C	cruiser		**RF**	rapid firing
cal	length of bore		**rpm**	revolutions per minute
CB	battle cruiser		**SF**	slow firing
DD	destroyer		**TB**	torpedo boat
fps	feet per second		**VTE**	vertical triple expansion
IHP	indicated horsepower		**WT**	watertube boiler

Preface

The greater part of the material in this book is drawn from official and semiofficial sources, and much care and time have been spent in evaluating and interpreting the enormous body of available information. By logical interpretation and corroboration of facts I have tried to compile the most accurate information, though as a result of often conflicting data, official and otherwise, readers may well find figures and statistics at odds with their own research. One drawback was that certain information no longer exists, a prime example being the tactical diameters of the vessels. Photographs and plans are also often at variance with official written data, and where such discrepancies appear, they have been noted.

The plans in the book are derived from official and semiofficial documents, combined and redrawn by David L. Wood. For certain vessels the official plans no longer exist. In such cases, semiofficial plans drawn by the chief constructor of the navy to illustrate private papers have been adapted by the artist.

Data concerning the movement of vessels through 1911 is taken from the annual report of the Bureau of Navigation, contained in the *Annual Report* of the secretary of the navy. The daily movements and operations of each vessel in commission, and the dates and information given citing that source, should be considered authoritative. Beginning in 1912 this information was no longer included in the *Annual Report*, and I have used, in the main, the eight volumes of the *Dictionary of American Naval Fighting Ships* to cover various dates in the ships' careers.

Much of the operational history of the armored cruisers has been culled from the writings of naval officers who were instrumental in the making of their ships' design and operational histories. Many excellent auto-biographies of the principal personalities of the New Navy exist, and I hope my use of them adds to the reader's enjoyment.

In the book's technical language I have endeavored at all times to use the common naval and engineering terminology of the times, most of which is still relevant today. As I have not provided a glossary, I would refer the questioning reader to a dictionary of American naval terms.

It has been my aim to provide a balanced book that will be of interest both to the general reader and to the expert looking for technical detail on the armored cruisers of the New Navy.

Acknowledgments

Of the many who have toiled and helped in the past three years to bring this project to completion, I would like to thank in particular David L. Wood, whose carefully drawn art is a valuable addition to this book. For guiding me to and through the primary source material, thanks are due to Ms. Maida Loescher, Mr. Robert Matchette, and especially Mr. Richard von Doenhoff, all of the Navy and Old Army branch of the National Archives and Records Service. Dr. Dean Allard of the Naval Historical Center kindly searched out obscure documents of the General Board of the navy. I would like to thank Messrs. H. A. Vadnais, Charles Haberlein, and Ms. Agnes Hoover, also of the Naval Historical Center, for their great help in assembling the photographic material. For many of the early aviation photos, thanks must be given to Mr. Grover Walker, director of the Naval Aviation Museum. I am grateful to the librarians of the Wilson and Walter libraries of the University of Minnesota and the reference and audiovisual libraries of the Minnesota Historical Society for making their resources and stacks readily available and for granting special privileges. My research assistant, Anita Rauum, lately of Augsburg College and soon of the Peace Corps, organized the bibliography. Sincere appreciation must be expressed for the assistance of Ms. Audrey Rolfing and Julie Bartell, secretaries of the Minneapolis City Council and in their off hours my stalwart typists. To my patient wife Gretchen, who read the drafts as they came out of the typewriter and can now discourse at length on the principles of metacentric height and assistant cylinders, go my heartfelt thanks.

Introduction

"The armored cruiser is hardly a distinct type of war vessel. It may be either so slightly protected and armed as to be a doubtful cruiser, or so heavily protected and armed as to be an uncertain battleship."[1] This hardly definitive statement, by no less an authority than Admiral of the Navy George Dewey, president of the General Board of the Navy, was to dog the armored cruiser as long as it was on the maritime scene. A vessel able to run down blockade-breaking merchantmen one day and on another stand in the line of battle and trade shots with enemy battleships is hard to categorize. U.S. armored cruisers had longer hulls than their battleship contemporaries, but they had somewhat smaller displacements and carried a lighter main battery. However, at the very end of the armored cruiser era, the Japanese constructed a quartet of vessels nearly indistinguishable from predreadnought battleships. Perhaps the only accurate general statement to be made about the type is that they carried far less armor than a ship their size and displacement would normally need, the weight saved being utilized to enhance speed and radius of action.

The armored cruiser evolved in the mid-nineteenth century as a response to two specific problems. First, it was realized that a relatively economic armored vessel of some force was necessary to give scouting balance to steam-driven armored battle fleets and to serve as vessels of force on the fringes of empire. Second, by the mid-nineteenth century France had reasserted the doctrine of *guerre de course*, according to which a maritime state could strategically defeat an enemy not by engaging and sinking its battle fleet but by raiding its merchant ships on the high seas. Small fast cruisers could deal with any merchantman, but in the process they were likely to encounter enemy warships protecting the trade routes, and the solution to dealing with these was obviously the armored cruiser. However, the French were not to lay down their first armored cruiser, the *Dupuy de Lôme*, until 1888, the same year Congress authorized the *New York* (ACR 2), and the type's antecedents must be sought elsewhere.

The world's first armored cruisers, the *General Admiral* and *Gerzog Edinburgski*, were laid down by Russia in 1870 and completed in 1875–77. Displacing 5,031 tons, iron hulled, and fully rigged, they carried a full 6-inch wrought-iron belt and main armament of six 8-inch and two 6-inch SF guns, all on the broadside. They were also fast for their day, their one shaft vertical compound engine designed for 13.25 knots, though the *Gerzog Edinburgski* actually exceeded this figure by nearly 2 knots. It is interesting to note that the *General Admiral* was not stricken from the Russian list until 1938.[2]

The next step in the evolutionary process was Britain's first armored cruiser, the *Shannon*, completed in 1877. Initially rated a second-class battleship, she was found unfit to stand in the line and was soon designated an armored cruiser. Although an inferior ship, the *Shannon* stands out as the first vessel to be fitted with an armored deck that ran the length of the underwater hull to compensate for an incomplete belt. This was also to be the case in the *New York* and *Brooklyn*. The *Shannon* was not a very useful ship, her 12 + -knot speed precluded a cruiser role, and most of her career was spent on foreign stations and in coastal defense duties.

During the next decade Britain and Russia laid down a number of armored cruisers, some more successful than others. Among the less successful were the British *Imperieuse* and *Warspite*, completed in 1886–88. They were the last armored vessels to be fitted with a square rig. Oscar Parkes, in his *British Battleships*, records, "The best that could be said of them was that they could take a broadside of three 9.2-inch and five 6-inch guns into action at 16 knots." In the House of Commons they were described by Admiral Sir John Commerell as "amongst the most complete failures of modern ships; badly designed; badly carried out, and absolutely dangerous."[3]

The best of the Russian lot was the *Admiral Nakhimov*, completed in 1888. Fitted with a full brig rig, she nevertheless was the first armored cruiser to carry her main battery in turrets. Her eight 8-inch guns, housed in four twin turrets disposed in a lozenge shape, gave this vessel the most powerful broadside of any armored cruiser until the early years of the twentieth century.

When France finally entered the armored cruiser race and laid down the 6,676-ton *Dupuy de Lôme* in 1888, it created a sensation. The ship, conceived for *guerre de course*, was an entirely new idea in cruiser design. For her role as a commerce raider, she was fitted with triple-shaft machinery generating 19.7 knots. Her armament, though relatively weak, consisting of two 7.6-inch SF and six 6.4-inch RF guns, was completely housed in single turrets—the 7.6-inch on forecastle and quarterdeck, the 6.4-inch on the main deck broadside. But the *Dupuy de Lôme* also carried the most extensive protection scheme of any armored cruiser to date. The ship's sides were completely armored with four inches of nickel steel from the upper deck to four feet six inches below the waterline. A complete underwater protective deck curved up from the lower edge of the belt, which was further augmented by a splinter deck over the boiler and machinery spaces.

The U.S. Navy was eventually to build twelve armored cruisers, only one of which, the *Brooklyn*, would lay claim to a stand-up fight with an opposite number. Their design and operational history belong to a great extent to the New Navy and the American naval renaissance. This was the heyday of the armored fighting ship, before submarine and aircraft superseded the classic line of battle. It was an era that also marked the emergence of the United States as a leading economic and, after 1898, imperial power in the world. As early as 1888, American political and military interest had expanded as far as Samoa, and the United States had procured its first precarious hold on the strategic shipping routes between the American West Coast and Australia. In 1893 a coup by the American "advisors" to Queen Liliuokalani of Hawaii established a provisional government "under the benevolent protection of the USS *Boston*."[4] Formal annexation would not come until 1898, but the United States was now securely in the central Pacific. With the Spanish-American War came the remains of the Spanish empire: Cuba, Puerto Rico, Guam, and the strategic albatross of the Philippines. The war justified the expense and expanse of the New Navy, and America's new territories dictated a navy commensurate with their strategic value and wealth. The enormous drag of the Philippines on the naval resources of the United States made inevitable the opening of the Panama Canal under American control, and with control of the Philippines came antagonism with Japan, by then well embarked on her doomed career of military adventurism.

It is within this context—the technological revolution, the wider span of the American naval renaissance, and the emergence of the United States as a world power—that this book is written.

U.S. Armored Cruisers

1

The American Naval Renaissance

The Last Years of the Old Navy

The years between 1866 and 1883 saw the U.S. Navy plummet from a first-class fighting force of seven hundred vessels mounting five thousand guns to a navy ranked twelfth in the world, which at its nadir had fifty-two vessels in commission equipped with less than five hundred obsolete guns.

In 1879 the fleet had sixty-seven steam vessels, of which five, built before the Civil War, were first-rate; twenty-seven second-rate; twenty-nine third-rate, only fifteen of them serviceable; and six fourth-rate, of no military value. Of twenty-two sailing vessels only five could put to sea. "Modern" vessels consisted of two experimental torpedo rams, commissioned in 1874, and one triple-turret and twenty-four single-turret Civil War monitors, of which only fourteen were rated effective. Some of the monitors remained on the navy list into the twentieth century; the *Cannonicus*, commissioned in 1864, was not broken up until 1908.

Manning the fleet, in numbers fixed by Congress in 1877, were 1,672 officers—829 line, 594 staff, 249 warrant—and 7,500 enlisted men, excluding marines. In 1879 Congress authorized the enlistment of 750 additional boys. A high ratio of officer to seamen was created by the swollen Naval Academy classes of the Civil War and effectively sealed off promotion prospects for aspiring officers. It was not unusual to find lieutenants in 1881 who had been in the same rank in 1869. The number of enlisted men was as low as that in 1830, during the administration of

Andrew Jackson. American citizens were hard to come by, and the Navy Department was compelled to draw from foreigners who frequented the ports of the world. In 1877 the executive officer of a sloop of war on the China station reported that of the 128 enlisted men on board, 47 were American citizens, 21 Chinese, 20 Irish, 9 British, and the remainder a mixture of Swedes, Danes, Germans, Scots, Greeks, Brazilians, Frenchmen, East Indians, Peruvians, Russians, Hawaiians, Welshmen, West Indians, Channel Islanders, Liberians, Newfoundlanders, and Nova Scotians.[1] In his report for 1888, David Dixon Porter, Admiral of the Navy, sourly noted, "When the *Trenton,* our best ship, lately went into commission, as fine a body of Germans, Huns, Norsemen, Gauls, Chinese, and other outside barbarians as one could wish, softened down by time and civilization, were on board. Out of the whole crew not more than 80 could speak the English language."[2]

Research and development were practically nonexistent, the prevailing professional and congressional opinion being that the United States should base its innovations on the experimentation carried on in other countries. From certain vantage points, this was not a wholly bad idea, as the period was one of great technological and tactical flux, and a fleet built upon a particular theory could rapidly become obsolete. Rear Admiral Daniel Ammen, chief of the Bureau of Navigation from 1871 to 1878, wrote "that the time is not distant when the marine ram will take the place of the enormously expensive armor-plated gun-bearing ships of today."[3] For the entire post–Civil War period of the Old Navy, only the experimental torpedo rams *Alarm* and *Intrepid,* both designs of Porter's commissioned in 1874, broke new ground.

The fleet was deployed in its traditional cruising formations of the North and South Atlantic squadrons and the European, Pacific, and Asiatic squadrons. Generally, each vessel operated independently, and even ships in a squadron rarely practiced combined evolutions. "Handling vessels in close proximity" meant little to senior officers accustomed to thinking of each ship as a solitary commerce raider rather than a unit of a fleet. A minority of officers contended that the fleet should be organized and drilled as "a unit of force acting under one head."[4] But incorrect lessons were drawn from the frigates of the War of 1812 and the Confederate raiders of the late war, both of which had inflicted great harm on enemy commerce but had not decided the war's outcome by as much as one day.

The restoration of overseas cruising squadrons after the war was complicated by the fact that the United States lacked colonies and coaling stations, and without them the navy had to depend on sail or expensive, unreliable foreign coal sources. On steam vessels, screws were altered to improve sailing and boilers were cut down for increased provision space. In a general order issued by Porter in 1869, all naval vessels were directed to be equipped with "full sail power." Regulations promulgated in 1870 expressly prohibited the use of steam except when absolutely necessary. Burning coal was a serious offense, and for many years ships' captains were obliged to enter in their logs in red ink their reasons for getting up steam. "Commanders are not to make despatch an excuse for using coal," read the order, "except under the most urgent circumstances. They must not be surprised, if they fail to carry out the spirit of this order, if the coal consumed is charged to their account."[5]

The shore establishment was terribly managed, and because of political influence in the navy yards, wholly corrupt. A congressional investigation held in 1876, while partisan in the extreme, brought to light certain indisputable facts. Before important state and national elections, hundreds of additional civilian employees swelled the navy yard work force, and as soon as the election was held and their votes cast for the politician who gave them their jobs, they were discharged. It was also common practice to assess the political contributions of civilian yard workers, and congressmen with yards in their districts exercised considerable control in the hiring and retention of workers. Corruption was so pervasive that the yards were familiarly named for their district congressmen; Norfolk was known as Mr. Platt's yard and Mare Island as Mr. Sargent's yard. Not surprisingly, during this period, and especially during the administration of President Hayes, the condition of shops, sheds, wharves, docks, and yard machinery rapidly deteriorated.

In 1869, following eight years of forceful administration by Secretary of the Navy Gideon Welles, the Navy Department was beset by a trio of secretaries unwilling to revive a declining establishment. The first, an elderly Philadelphia merchant, Adolph Borie, was appointed by President Grant on 9 March 1869 and served only sixteen weeks. It was understood in the administration and the department that the new secretary's authority was at best nominal. Touring the bureaus on his first day in office, in company with Admiral Porter, Borie was introduced to the chief of the Bureau of Ordnance, Rear Admiral John Dahlgren. Dahlgren later recalled, "Porter took me aside and told me that Grant said he should run the machine as Borie's advisor." This became official three days later in an order signed by the secretary stating, "All matters relating to the navy coming under the cognizance of the different bureaus will be submitted to Vice Admiral Porter before being transmitted to the Secretary of the Navy."[6]

The navy secretary's tenure for the next seven and a half years of the Grant administration was held by the controversial George M.

Robeson of New Jersey. Each year Robeson's annual reports conveyed the impression that the navy was steadily growing stronger, and large appropriations were authorized by Congress. Nothing could have been further from the truth; by 1877 there was little to show for the money but an antiquated collection of worthless ships and an army of enriched contractors and political retainers.

The great portion of congressional appropriations during Robeson's term was slated for repair of vessels, most of which had been added to the fleet during the Civil War and were not intended as permanent additions. They had been built rapidly of unseasoned timber, imperfect fittings, and faulty machinery. One of the best of the lot, the *Tennessee* (ex-*Madawaska* of the *Wampanoag* class), had within fifteen years of her completion repairs equaling in cost the original value of the ship. By 1883 ninety-two vessels on the navy list had cost more in repairs than their original cost of construction.

Conversely, it was under Robeson that the only new construction of the post–Civil War period was authorized. New construction came under the guise of "repair of vessels," since Robeson knew full well the impossibility of congressional appropriations for new ships. Six prewar vessels, the *Galena, Marion, Mohican, Quinnebaug, Swatara,* and *Vandalia,* were broken up as obsolete, but certain parts of theirs were retained and their names remained on the navy list. In 1872 Congress appropriated funds for the "repair" of these vessels, resulting in six virtually brand-new wooden screw-sloops.[7]

The same chicanery resulted in five new double-turret monitors. In 1874–75 over twenty single-turret monitors were sold and the proceeds used for "repair" of the *Puritan, Terror, Amphitrite, Miantonomoh,* and *Monadnock.* The original ships of the name were completely dismantled, certain portions kept, and new vessels built, though they were not completed for close to twenty years.

Robeson was followed in office by Richard M. Thompson of Indiana, appointed by President Rutherford B. Hayes. A genial Republican hack who served from 1877 to 1881, Thompson was old, slow-moving, conservative, and greatly in favor of strict economy in naval expenditures. He was also grossly ignorant of the most basic matters pertaining to his department. It was said that Thompson expressed surprise at learning that ships were hollow, and when asked at a dinner party which mast of a naval vessel should fly the American flag, "Thompson coughed and stammered a little, and said, 'I think I shall refer the question to the Attorney-General.'"[8]

Thompson advocated a strong merchant marine. He believed the United States could easily improvise a navy in an unexpected emergency. The navy under Thompson received no appropriations for new construction and during his term touched bottom.

During this period the Old Navy embarked on one major fleet operation known as the *Virginius* affair. If anything could point up the navy's shortcomings, this could, and it nearly precipitated a disastrous war with Spain. The *Virginius* was a small iron sidewheeler of fine lines, built on the River Clyde in 1864 for service as a Confederate blockade runner. In 1873, with a dubious claim to American registry, she was employed carrying arms and volunteers to Cuba. On 28 October of that year the *Virginius* steamed from Port au Prince, Haiti, en route to Cuba, full of war material, including several hundred rifles, revolvers, sabres, ammunition, saddles, clothing, and medicine. On 31 October, off the south Cuban coast, she was overhauled by the Spanish gunboat *Tornado* and taken to Santiago. The Spanish military governor declared her a pirate, and fifty-three of her officers, crew, and passengers were summarily shot, including her captain, Joseph Fry, a graduate of the Naval Academy class of 1841. The remaining 155 men on board would likely have met the same fate were it not for the timely arrival of HMS *Niobe*, under Captain Sir Lambton Loraine. Cleared for action, the *Niobe* steamed into Santiago, and under Sir Lambton's strenuous protests against the butchering of helpless prisoners, the surviving members—American, British, and Cuban—were locked up until the USS *Juniata* was available to take them to New York.[9]

This diplomatic crisis forced the navy to mobilize its resources for war. In a message to Congressman James Garfield, Secretary Robeson declared, "I have taken measures to put every iron and wooden ship of our Navy in condition for immediate duty. I have ordered all the ships of the various squadrons within reach to rendezvous at Key West."[10]

The combined squadrons, a collection of antiquated and rotting ships, steamed and sailed to Key West, where Admiral Porter took command. Robley Evans, then a lieutenant in the screw sloop *Shenandoah*, recalled, "The force collected at Key West was the best, and indeed about all we had. We had no stores, or storehouses to speak of at this so-called base of supplies, and if it had not been so serious it would have been laughable to see our condition. We remained several weeks, making faces at the Spaniards 90 miles away at Havana, while two modern vessels of war would have done us up in 30 minutes. We were dreadfully mortified over it all, but we were not to blame; we did the best we could with what Congress gave us."[11]

Owing to the efforts of Secretary of State Hamilton Fish, the *Virginius* affair ended in negotiation, with Spain eventually paying an indemnity of eighty thousand dollars.

For a quarter century the Old Navy was professionally led by Admiral David Dixon Porter. Second in rank and prestige only to Farragut, Porter came out of the Civil War a vice admiral and assumed Farragut's rank of Admiral of the Navy upon the latter's death in 1870. A crusty sea dog of the old school, Porter saw his first service in the Mexican navy as a midshipman in 1826; he was appointed midshipman in the U.S. Navy in 1829. During the Civil War he commanded the sidewheeler *Powhatan* before being elevated to command the Mortar Flotilla in the attack on New Orleans. In 1862 Porter was appointed to command the Mississippi Squadron, and as a rear admiral, the North Atlantic Blockading Squadron. At war's end he served as interim chief of the Bureau of Navigation, before receiving his long-desired appointment as superintendent of the Naval Academy. Porter completely reformed the Academy's curriculum and revitalized the entire system before being relieved in 1869. He was founding president of the U.S. Naval Institute and wrote copiously on naval matters.

For all practical purposes Porter ran the navy during Borie's tenure in office. Though his authority waned with the appointment of Robeson, Porter was given collateral duties as head of the Board of Inspection; he was to inspect and report on ships in commission, ironclads and wooden vessels laid up in ordinary, trials under steam and sail, and the condition of yards and stations. For all his talents as a fighter, Porter was not a good administrator; as Charles Paullin noted, "The Vice Admiral was too good a sailor to make a good landsman."[12] In the 1870s, when public apathy and congressional indifference to a strong navy were at their apex, Porter vigorously and insistently declared the country's need, but to no avail.

For all Porter's efforts to promote a modern fleet, he was a reactionary at heart. He believed the employment of sailors to coal ships and hoist out ashes degraded their character, and that owing to the introduction of steam, the quality of the American sailor had steadily declined since the Mexican War. In the early 1870s Porter authorized the sacking of Chief Constructor John Lenthall and Engineer in Chief Benjamin Isherwood; their push for a modern steam-driven navy opposed the admiral's misplaced whimsy for a wooden sailing fleet.

Yet, every year in his report to the secretary of the navy, Porter castigated the government for the state of the fleet. He noted to Robeson in 1874,

> There is not a navy in the world that is not in advance of us as regards ships and guns. If called upon at this time to command the naval forces of the United States, in case of hostilities, I should be put to my wit's end to succeed with such an incongruous set of

vessels as we now possess. Prudence would probably recommend that they be shut up in port and no fleet operations attempted with them. It would be much better to have no navy at all than the one like the present, half-armed, and with only half speed, unless we inform the world that our establishment is only intended for times of peace, and to protect missionaries against the South Sea savages and eastern fanatics.[13]

Birth of the New Navy

The New Navy had a pair of "fathers" and three separate "birthdays." Its first father was the capable and incorruptible General James A. Garfield of Ohio, chairman of the House Appropriations Committee who on 4 March 1881 was inaugurated as president of the United States. The times seemed propitious. Reconstruction of the nation was complete, and as the *New York Herald* put it, Garfield's election ended "the cycle in which our politics turned upon the Civil War and its immediate consequences."[14] Economically and financially, the depression caused by the Panic of 1873 had subsided, and the mining and iron industries, which had been especially hard hit, were once more producing. The federal treasury contained a surplus of one hundred million dollars, and a favorable balance of trade existed as American manufactured goods and foodstuffs captured foreign markets. For the first time in six years, one political party, the Republicans, had gained control of the presidency and both houses of Congress.

Less propitious, European powers, led by France, were exploring the possibility of a Panama canal, control of which by a hostile power would strategically isolate the United States. For a nation with a navy ranked twelfth in the world, whose only armored vessels consisted of fourteen single-turret Civil War monitors and whose most powerful ordnance was the 8-inch rifled muzzle loader, it was an ominous situation.

To insiders it was obvious the navy desperately needed rebuilding. To begin the task, and to give Southern balance to his cabinet, President Garfield appointed William H. Hunt of Louisiana to head the Navy Department. Hunt, the first of a series of competent, intelligent secretaries, was the second father of the New Navy. Bringing energy, tact, managerial skill, and a lifelong interest in naval matters to his office, Hunt surrounded himself with an able group of professional advisors, of whom Rear Admiral John Rodgers was *primus inter pares*. Hunt's first step in office was to commission Rodgers to form a naval advisory board "to present . . . a practical and plain statement of the pressing need of appropriate vessels in the service at the present time."[15] The day Hunt ordered the formation of the board, 29 June 1881, can be considered the first birthday of the New Navy.

The "Rodgers Board" recommended an enormous new construction program in two phases. The first, to begin immediately, was to consist of eighteen unarmored steel cruisers, twenty wooden cruisers, ten torpedo boats, and five harbor defense rams. The second phase, with authorizations to be made over an eight-year period, would consist of twenty-one armored cruisers, seventy-one unarmored cruisers, and twenty-five torpedo boats. No battleships were recommended, but a minority of the board advocated "construction of ships of the greatest gunpower and speed."[16] The unarmored cruisers were to be built of steel. The minority held out for iron, which was cheaper and at the time a better-quality metal. Not surprisingly, this ambitious program never got out of its congressional committee.

But matters were moving forward. On 5 August 1882 Congress sounded the death knell of the Old Navy and gave the New Navy its second birthday. Legislation was passed stipulating that no further funds be spent on the repair of wooden vessels of war that would exceed by twenty percent the new-construction cost of ships of the same class and displacement. Forty-six obsolete vessels were condemned and sold for scrap.

With the assassination of President Garfield, Vice President Chester Arthur assumed the mantle of highest office. In his first message to Congress Arthur stated that "every condition of national safety, economy, and honor . . . demands a thorough rehabilitation of the Navy."[17] Paying off a political debt, Arthur appointed William E. Chandler as secretary of the navy, and Hunt was sent to Russia as ambassador. During his three years in office Chandler came in for criticism, some well founded, much of it not, because the department fumbled reconstruction; a great deal of the fault should have been laid at the feet of Robeson and Thompson for allowing the navy to deteriorate. Chandler's big mistake in office was to award all the New Navy's initial construction to a political crony of his and George Robeson's, John Roach.

Nevertheless, Chandler should receive large credit for convincing Congress of the navy's primary needs and for seeing to fruition the appropriations for the New Navy's first vessels. As the initial step in this process, Chandler commissioned a second naval advisory board, headed by Commodore Robert W. Shufeldt, to prepare a more reasonable building program.

Profiting by the secretary's political acumen, knowing full well that Congress would never appropriate the immense funds necessary for an immediate and complete rebuilding, the Shufeldt Board recommended four partially protected cruisers, one of 4,000 tons and three of 2,500 tons, and a 1,500-ton dispatch boat. On 3 March 1883 Congress, albeit striking one of the smaller cruisers, authorized $1,300,000 for the hulls and machinery for the first ships of the New Navy. These were the famed "ABCD" ships, the *Atlanta, Boston, Chicago*, and *Dolphin*. The third of March can thus be claimed as the third birthday of the New Navy.

The building contracts for the four vessels were given to John Roach. He owned an integrated facility in Chester, Pennsylvania, which was able not only to build the ships but also to roll steel plates and erect machinery. Roach had submitted the lowest bid, and the award of the contract was legal. But he was a close political friend of both Chandler and George Robeson, and the cry "Roach, Robeson, Robbers" was soon raised by the Democrats. Only the *Dolphin* was to be completed by Roach. But the shell plating took longer than expected to roll, and when the job was completed it did not meet department standards and had to be redone. A fire then destroyed much of the building yard, while the department bureaus continually altered their specifications. The *Dolphin* was two months late for her preliminary acceptance trials, and during them she fractured her propeller shaft.

Grover Cleveland, a Democrat, had now been elected president, and his secretary of the navy, William C. Whitney, refused to accept the *Dolphin* because of her numerous deficiencies. Convincing the attorney general to void Roach's contract, work on the vessels came to a halt. Beset by creditors and threatened with a suit by the government to return the funds already paid on the contract, Roach threw his company into receivership. Secretary Whitney thereupon seized the yard, and the vessels were completed more or less under government supervision, the *Atlanta* and *Boston* receiving their fitting out at the Brooklyn Navy Yard.

The ABCD ships represented the advent of the New Navy, but they left the United States without any modern armored warships. If the nation and fleet were to be ranked first, a program of construction would have to be initiated. Neither the Rodgers nor the Shufeldt boards had recommended an armored ship, though both had considered proposals for such a vessel displacing 8,500 tons. The decision not to recommend at that time was not wholly reactionary but based on the technological and industrial capacity of the nation. Steel forgings for major-caliber ordnance were still being imported from British gun founders, and not until 1887, when the Bethlehem Iron Company of Philadelphia was awarded the first contract, was modern ordnance of all calibers manufactured in the United States. Moreover, naval and commercial yards could not yet accommodate large hulls in their dry docks; the big navy yard at Brooklyn was unable even to install the *Chicago*'s machinery.

Having no experience in the design and construction of modern armored ships, the Navy Department sponsored an international competition with a $15,000 prize for an acceptable vessel. The result, submitted by a British firm, Naval Construction and Armaments Company of Barrow-in-Furness, was the little 6,135-ton second-class battleship *Texas*.

Were it not for a change in nomenclature during construction, the New Navy's second armored vessel, the second-class battleship *Maine*, would have been the first "ship chapter" of this work. While the design search for the *Texas* proceeded, the department put its hand to its own plans, based very strongly on the British-built Brazilian battleship *Riachuelo*. Completed in 1883 by Samuda Brothers, Poplar, and mounting a battery of four 9.2-inch guns in twin en echelon turrets and six 5.5-inch SF guns on the broadside, she was, when delivered, the most powerful warship in the Western Hemisphere.

When the plans were finalized as armored cruiser no. 1, the *Maine*'s 6,682-ton hull carried four 10-inch guns in twin en echelon turrets and six 6-inch SF guns on the broadside. Her top speed was 17 knots. Her armored belt, of Harveyized steel, maintained a 12-inch thickness. Both the *Texas* and *Maine*, along with the protected cruiser *Baltimore*, were authorized in the congressional act of 3 August 1886. During construction it was conceded that the *Maine*'s speed and armored belt were more suited to battleships than to armored cruisers, and her designation was altered.

It was not until the act of 9 September 1888 that the first armored cruiser commissioned into the New Navy, the *New York*, was authorized. This piece of legislation was the largest appropriation since the Civil War; it aggregated 27,436 tons and included, in addition to the *New York*, the big protected cruiser *Olympia* (C 6); five smaller cruisers, the *Cincinnati* (C 7), *Raleigh* (C 8), *Montgomery* (C 9), *Detroit* (C 10), and *Marblehead* (C 11); and the Naval Academy practice vessel *Bancroft*.

That same year Admiral of the Navy David Porter, in his annual report to the secretary of the navy, prophetically recorded, "The days of old fashioned ships have passed away. The pot-metal guns of 25 years ago will be melted up and a new system of ordnance will rule the hour. New kinds of ships, new kinds of guns, including machine and rapid-firing guns and torpedoes, will take the place of old means of offense and defense."[18]

2

The *New York*

Introduction

The *New York* was authorized on 7 September 1888 in an act stipulating "one armored cruiser of about 7,500 tons displacement, to cost, exclusive of armament, not more than $3,500,000."[1]

The *New York* was the third armored vessel ordered for the New Navy and the first to enter service; and as such she represented a quantum leap over previous designs. Unlike the *Texas* and *Maine*, with their British-designed en-echelon turrets, suitable only for actions in line abreast, the *New York* was of an advanced configuration and placed the U.S. Navy firmly on the path of contemporary naval evolution.

Not since the *Wampanoag*-class wooden screw frigates had the nation constructed a vessel of war that was the best of its type. Secretary of the Navy Benjamin Tracy called the *New York* "an unusual combination of great offensive and defensive power, with extraordinary coal endurance, and a high rate of speed which is sufficient to enable her to escape from any more powerful ship afloat today, and to overtake the majority—certainly 95 percent—of all the ships in the world, naval or mercantile."[2]

A better vessel for the New Navy would be hard to imagine. The *Texas* and *Maine*, while first off the drawing boards, were second-class ships in both concept and actuality, with their limited coal endurance confining them to a coastal defense role. What was needed in the years before the construction of an oceangoing battle fleet were large, power-

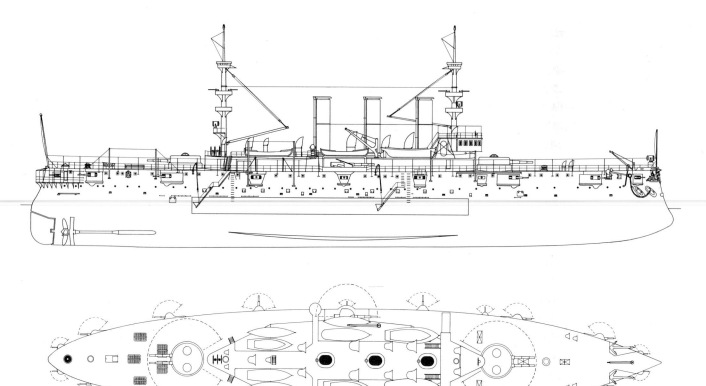

The USS *New York* (ACR 2)

ful seagoing cruisers, and the *New York* filled this gap perfectly. As Secretary Tracy noted, "She is built to keep the sea and thus destroy an enemy's commerce, and not only his commerce, but any commerce destroyer he may send out. For general purposes of service in war she is believed to have a wider field of usefulness than any other ship yet designed for the Navy."[3]

Although it was over two years from congressional authorization to keel laying, the specifications for the *New York* had yet to be made final by the spring of 1890. Ignoring the specifications laid out in the funding legislation for one armored cruiser, the Bureau of Construction and Repair had submitted preliminary plans for a large protected cruiser of 7,500 tons and 22-knot speed, based on the lines of the British *Blake* class.[4] These two units, the *Blake* and *Blenheim*, were laid down in 1888 as improved versions of the *Orlando* (1888); instead of the latter's narrow armored belt they had a complete armored deck and an enhanced engineering plant, which gave them a design speed of 22 knots under forced draft. (This was never achieved; the maximum speed of these ships was 19 knots.)

According to Charles Cramp, at the time the U.S. Navy's leading contractor, the design for the large protected cruiser was laid to rest at a conference called by the newly installed secretary of the navy, Benjamin Tracy, in late March 1890. Those present included the secretary, Cramp, and the chiefs of the Bureaus of Construction and Repair, Ordnance,

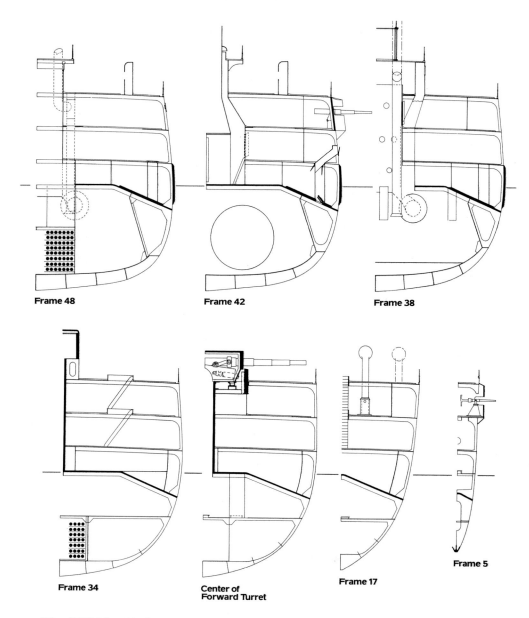

Frame 48   Frame 42   Frame 38

Frame 34   Center of   Frame 17   Frame 5
              Forward Turret

The USS *New York* (ACR 2)

The *New York* runs her builder's trials, 1892.

and Steam Engineering: Commodores Theodore Wilson, Montgomery Sicard, and George Melville, respectively. In the heated discussion Secretary Tracy advocated the construction of an armored cruiser along the general lines of the seminal *Dupuy de Lôme* while the chief constructor led the argument in favor of the protected cruiser.[5]

The Naval Policy Board of 1890 had published its recommendations for a "first-class thin-armored cruiser" of 6,250 tons and a speed of 19 knots that was strikingly similar to the *Dupuy de Lôme* but was a questionable improvement over the protected cruiser and decidedly undergunned.[6] Its hull mounted a pair of 8-inch guns in two single turrets and ten 5-inch RF (rapid-fire) guns in six small single turrets and four embrasured ports. This advanced arrangement of the 5-inch battery aside, the first-class thin-armored cruiser was an unsatisfactory design, with a weak main armament and a speed easily outclassed by several foreign contemporaries.

In June 1890 the bureau chiefs, charged by Secretary Tracy to formulate a new design, submitted plans for an "armored steel cruiser no. 2." A vessel of 8,100 tons, six 8-inch guns, and a 20-knot contract speed was presented for his approval.

The construction bids for armored cruiser no. 2 were opened on 10 June, and two classes of bids were tendered. Class 1 called for the bureau design with "hull and machinery, including engines, boilers, and appurtenances, complete in all respects, in accordance with the plans and specifications provided by the Secretary of the Navy."[7] Class 2 stipulated plans supplied by the builder. A modified class 2 bid was chosen by the navy. There were two bidders, William Cramp and Sons of Philadelphia and Union Iron Works of San Francisco; Cramp bid $2,985,000, $15,000 below the bid of its competitor, and received the contract.

On 28 August 1890 final proposals were agreed upon for the construction of the vessel according to bureau specifications for the hull and machinery but with Cramp's modifications for the rearrangement of the boilers. The *New York*'s keel was laid on 20 September. The ship was to be delivered to the navy by 1 January 1893.

Hull

With a length of 384 feet and a beam of 64 feet 10 inches, the *New York*'s flush-decked hull was the longest yet built for the New Navy. High and slab-sided, the vessel looked like a battleship, although her cruiser origins were apparent in the graceful curves of bow and stern.

The hull was constructed on 101 transverse frames, spaced four feet apart within the boiler and machinery spaces, between frames 36 and 74, and three and a half feet apart to the ends of the hull. Bolted to the frames were four complete decks—main, gun, berth, and armored—plus two platforms above the forward and after magazines.[8] Following the French practice inaugurated in the *Dupuy de Lôme*, the lower edge of the armored deck slopes joined the lower edge of the belt, thereby affording greater protection to the ship's vitals. The rudder was unbalanced and continued the shape of the underwater hull form, from the deadwood to the sternpost. The forefoot was cut away and the keel sloped upward, forward of frame 27, until it met the stempost approximately eight feet below the waterline.

The hull was divided into 184 watertight compartments. There were 11 more such compartments in the double bottom, which extended outward from the keel, 29 feet on each side, and extended 204 feet from frames 27 to 81.

The *New York* was one of the steadiest and most seaworthy vessels ever built for the navy. Her length-to-beam ratio of 5.9 to 1 gave her an easy roll, and in an era when this was a major factor in gunnery, her gunlayers scored consistently high. Initial stiffness and stability were maintained by the broad-beamed design, the boxy midship waterplane, and the 20-foot freeboard, which gave a metacentric height of 2.08 feet. Bilge keels were fitted to the hull to increase stability. These projected two feet from the ship's bottom and extended 188 feet along the hull.

The vessel's seakeeping ability was attested by Winfield Scott Schley, commander of the *New York* in 1897. The *New York* had steamed in formation with the battleship *Indiana* (BB 1), cruisers *Columbia* (C 12) and *Marblehead* (C 11), and monitor *Amphitrite* (BM 2) during a gale of "cyclonic force." Schley noted that "if the *New York* had been alone on this passage, it is doubtful if she would have been delayed. And while the sea was rough, and the wind violent, she weathered the gale without mishap of any kind, except a good shaking up."[9]

Armament

The *New York*'s armament went through several changes and was not completely decided upon until 1893. The armament of the first-class protected cruiser, proposed by the Bureau of Construction and Repair in 1890, consisted of two 8-inch guns mounted in two lightly armored gunhouses, fore and aft on the centerline, and ten 5-inch RF guns in open shields, casemates, and embrasured ports. Although the 1890 policy board stated that "her power is good, equal to that of the largest protected cruisers built or building by other nations," the ship was seriously undergunned for its 7,500-ton displacement.[10]

The battery of the first-class thin-armored cruiser was identical, although not as undergunned on a displacement of 6,250 tons. Protection for the battery was enhanced, the 8-inch turrets being designed for 3-inch armor sheathing. The secondary battery was a fairly heavy, generally well-positioned arrangement. The ten 5-inch RF guns were housed in six small single turrets, three per side on a superstructure deck. Had the plan been approved, it would have been revolutionary for the U.S. Navy, which was not to adopt independently housed secondary armament for cruisers until the *St. Louis* (CL 49) was ordered in 1936. The remaining four 5-inch guns were mounted on the gun deck behind armored embrasures, well up in the bow and stern. The outfit was completed with six 6-pdr. and eight 1-pdr. RF guns, four 37mm revolving cannon, and six torpedo tubes.

The *New York*'s main and secondary batteries reached their third and final state in the June 1890 armored cruiser no. 2 design, with the fitting of six 8-inch and twelve 4-inch RF guns.

The 8-inch 35-caliber Mark 3 gun was introduced into the navy in 1889 and saw initial service in the *Charleston* (C 2) and *Baltimore* (C 3). As the Mark 3 gun was not an RF weapon and fired unfixed ammunition, the designated rate of fire was only one round every 77 seconds. However, at the annual fleet exercises in March 1905, one of the *New York*'s 8-inch gun crews, firing at the rate of 2.8 rounds per minute, was able to score seven hits in two and a half minutes.

Four of the 8-inch guns were mounted in two Mark 5 twin turrets, fore and aft on the centerline. Steam-powered hydraulic pumps were employed for elevation and training, and auxiliary hand gear was

Her ram-shaped bow slicing through a calm sea, the *New York* proudly displays her prominent bow scroll. Note the projecting sponsons beneath the 4-inch battery on the gun deck.

provided. The two midship 8-inch guns were mounted on central pivot carriages, with hand training and elevating gear only. Ammunition hoists were electrically driven but fitted with steam and hand auxiliary power. All guns in the main battery were served by hand loading.

The turret-mounted guns fired through an arc of 300 degrees, and with their barrels 25 feet above the waterline they were given good command. The midship 8-inch guns had a theoretical arc of 180 degrees in order to deliver axial fire, but in practice this was limited to 140 degrees because of blast effects on the superstructure and deck. When compared with the batteries of her foreign contemporaries (except for the Russian *Admiral Nakhimov*), the *New York*'s five-gun main battery broadside was the heaviest of any armored cruiser in commission in 1893.

Unlike the *New York*'s heavy main armament, the secondary battery of twelve 4-inch 40-caliber RF guns was small and easily outclassed. It being an era when a strong secondary armament was essential for action against large ships and repelling attack by torpedo boats, the 4-inch gun was too light. The weakness of this battery, when compared with the ten 6-inch guns of the *Orlando* and *Blake* classes, is evident.

A good, well-practiced crew could keep a sustained fire of seven to eight rounds per minute, although during the 1905 target shoot off Culebra, Puerto Rico, one of the *New York*'s 4-inch-gun crews fired fourteen rounds in one minute and scored eleven hits.

The 4-inch guns were all mounted broadside on the gun deck in small sponsons covered with four inches of nickel steel 16.5 feet above the waterline. Continuous-chain ammunition hoists were electrically driven.

The light tertiary armament initially called for four 6-pdr. and four 1-pdr. RF guns, four 37mm revolving cannon, and four 50-caliber Gatling guns. During construction this configuration was changed to twelve 6-pdr., two 1-pdr., and four Gatling guns. When commissioned, the *New York*'s light armament comprised eight 6-pdr. guns sited in small sponsons on the gun deck, sheathed in two inches of nickel steel. The 1-pdr. guns and the Gatlings were mounted in the lower fighting tops.

The torpedo outfit consisted of three above-water tubes firing the 18-inch Whitehead torpedo. The tubes were located in the bow and on each broadside outboard of the forward 8-inch ammunition tube. The torpedo weighed 839 pounds and was equipped with a 110-lb nitrocellulose warhead. Maximum range was 1,000 yards at an approximate speed of 28 knots.

Protection

Armor was nickel steel throughout the ship, except for the end sections of the armored deck, the shields of the broadside 8-inch guns, and the gun-deck splinter screens, all of which were mild steel. Completed too rapidly to allow the fitting of Harveyized steel, which was used in the *Texas* and *Maine*, the *New York*'s protection was nevertheless adequate and equal to that of her foreign contemporaries.

The 538.46 tons of armor delivered by Carnegie had undergone vigorous testing by the Bureau of Ordnance at the Annapolis proving ground in 1894. A 10-inch nickel steel plate, representing the *New York*'s barbette armor, was struck by three 8-inch common shells at a velocity of 1,410 fps (feet per second); it cracked only on the third shot. A plate of 4-inch nickel steel, simulating the waterline belt, received twenty-four direct hits from 4-inch and 5-inch guns and suffered only random dishing.

The waterline belt was 200 feet long and 8 feet 10 inches wide overall. Abreast the boiler and machinery spaces, its 4-inch thickness was increased to 5 inches between the armored and berth decks. The belt extended to the fore and after 8-inch ammunition tubes and was not closed at the ends by armored transverse bulkheads. The hull was "soft-ended," as approximately 90 feet of unprotected hull extended outward from the ends of the belt.

The armored deck extended through the length of the hull and was constructed of two layers of 1.5-inch mild steel plate on the flats. This thickness was carried on the slopes, which were augmented with a 3-inch layer of nickel steel over the boiler and machinery spaces. At the *New York*'s mean draft of 24 feet, the flats of the armored deck were 1 foot above the waterline, and the bottom edge of the slopes 4 feet 9 inches below.

Running the entire length of the inner hull, between the armored and berth decks, was a cofferdam 3 feet 6 inches in height, packed with cocoa-fiber cellulose. This was another French innovation used on most U.S. naval vessels of the period. In theory, if the hull were pierced by shot, the cellulose would expand and plug the hole. But in practice, dampness made the cellulose soggy and worthless.

The location of the coal bunkers in double tiers against the hull, above and beneath the armored deck, gave added protection to the ship's vitals, especially against exploding shell and the upward force of an exploding mine or torpedo.

Ten inches of nickel steel shielded the fore and after barbettes, with 5.5 inches covering the turrets. The broadside 8-inch guns were mounted on 2-inch base rings of nickel steel, their crews protected by splinter shields of mild steel. The sponsons for the 4-inch guns were protected by 4 inches of nickel steel. The remaining nickel steel armor was distributed with 7.5 inches on the conning tower, 5 inches on the conning tower tube, and 7 inches on the fore and aft 8-inch ammunition tubes. Within the gun deck, 1-inch mild steel transverse splinter screens served as partial crew protection.

Machinery

In his annual report for 1894 Engineer in Chief George Melville wrote, "The *New York* has added 17 percent to the horsepower of the machinery of vessels in commission."[11] From any perspective this was astonishing. Until the *New York* entered service, the highest horsepower figures in the fleet were maintained by the protected cruisers *Baltimore* and *San Francisco* (C 5). Both were commissioned in 1890, generated

10,750 and 10,500 IHP (indicated horsepower) respectively, and had obsolete horizontal triple-expansion engines. But at double the tonnage of each of these cruisers and a contract speed of 20 knots, the *New York* required a machinery plant far more powerful and sophisticated than had previously existed in any U.S. naval vessel. The Bureau of Steam Engineering employed an innovative design with a powerful and relatively efficient plant.

In the mid-nineteenth century, when maximum speeds rarely exceeded 12 knots and the compound engine was in general use, it was a simple matter to cruise economically at low speeds with the same or perhaps greater energy efficiency than at maximum speed. But in a vessel with a 20-knot speed this was not possible. The friction created when the immense parts of a triple-expansion engine moved at low speeds deducted a large amount of the gross horsepower and left a very small fraction of the net. Large amounts of condensation in the three expansion cylinders further reduced fuel economy and horsepower output. Thus the *New York*'s proposed 16,000 IHP plant, if arranged in a standard fashion, would be extremely inefficient when run at 1,500 hp at speeds of 10 knots or less.

The bureau adopted a method first used in the Italian battleships *Italia* (1885) and *Lepanto* (1887), designing a four-engine vertical plant driving twin shafts. Two engines, each of 4,000 IHP, were coupled to each shaft in a fore-and-aft configuration, with each engine in its own watertight compartment beneath the armored deck. When steaming at low speeds, the forward engine on each shaft could be disconnected with a manual coupling, and the ship could run on the after engines alone. This system enabled the after engines to function close to full power and thus close to full efficiency while running the ship at low speeds. The increased weight and space of the four engines plus the greater number of moving parts was a disadvantage outweighed by the ship's greater efficiency.

Steam was provided by six double-ended Fox firetube boilers, each with eight fireboxes located in three pressurized, athwartship firerooms beneath the armored deck. The June 1890 bureau design called for three boilers in each of two firerooms, which would have resulted in a twin-funnel vessel. However, this was modified by Cramp under the class 2 bid permitting additional longitudinal and transverse bulkheads to be fitted in the engine and boiler spaces and thereby affording greater protection to the machinery and rendering the vessel less vulnerable to mining, ramming, and torpedo damage. Her builder, Charles Cramp, noted that

THE NEW YORK   25

when the plans were exhibited before the bids were sent in, it transpired that the boilers had been placed three abreast in the government plans, bringing them within a few feet of the side of the ship. With three boilers abreast, the ship was liable to be sunk at any time by a collision with a coal barge or passing schooner; any penetration of the side abreast of boiler, besides resulting in a speedy foundering, would certainly unship the side boiler, adding . . . an explosion to the other damage. With the boilers in pairs, it would be necessary for a ramming vessel to penetrate the side and two bulkheads and enter ten feet to do any damage.[12]

Two auxiliary single-ended boilers, each with two fireboxes, were located over the main firerooms above the armored deck, their uptakes passing through the center of the funnels.

Four main steam condensers, constructed of cast brass, were coupled one each to the main engines. Two auxiliary condensers were located in the after engine rooms.

Each fireroom contained one main and one auxiliary feed pump for the boilers, with each main pump able to feed any boiler in the plant. The main pumps drew from the feed tanks only and provided water solely to the boilers. The auxiliary pumps were designed to draw from the feed tanks, bilges, steam drains, cold boilers, and the sea; the pumps could deliver water to either the boilers, fire mains, or overboard.

Both main and auxiliary boilers were provided with forced draft utilizing the pressurized fireroom system. Twelve fan blowers, five feet in diameter, were bolted to the underside of the armored deck; one fan was located above the end of each main boiler. The auxiliary boilers were served with two three-foot fans. Each fireroom contained a two-cylinder ash-hoisting engine, although no air locks were cut for hoisting ashes while the ship was running under forced draft.

As a general rule forced draft was only employed during trials, engagements, squadron evolutions, and performance evaluations, as its use rapidly deteriorated the boiler tubes and exhausted the fireroom personnel. The best natural draft was provided by tall funnels, a system much favored by Melville. A trio of smoke pipes measuring 80 feet from the grate bars to the clinker screens were fitted, giving the *New York* a lofty battleship-like appearance.

The *New York*, a cruising vessel with an endurance of 4,800 miles at 10 knots, required a large bunker capacity. Sixty-three coal bunkers—two tiers of twenty, port and starboard, plus one amidship bunker were sited above the armored deck, and one tier of eleven bunkers per side was sited beneath—permitted a normal coal capacity of 750 tons and a maximum of 1,279 tons. Coal was delivered through adjustable chutes on the main deck that emptied into the inboard upper bunkers and through berth deck coaling ports into the outboard upper bunkers. Hinged sections of the armored deck were removed when the lower tiers were filled. Overhead trolleys running throughout the bunkers were used for trimming and passing.

The *New York*'s twin propeller shafts were made of steel and fitted in two sections. The forward section was 28 feet long, the after section 41 feet 10 inches long, with respective diameters of 16.75 and 17.25 inches. The shafts were cased only at the crank shaft bearings and the stern exit tubes.

Fitted to the shafts were a pair of three-bladed manganese-bronze screws. Each screw measured 16 feet from tip to tip and had a pitch of 22 degrees.

In addition to the major propulsion components, there was a myriad of auxiliary machinery. Right aft, beneath the armored deck, was the two-cylinder, horizontal, self-controlling steering engine. Engine room ventilation was provided by two large fan blowers bolted to the underside of the room's hatches. General ship ventilation was maintained by four fan blowers on the berth deck. These must have operated well, for as Robley Evans observed when he commanded the *New York* in 1895, "The quality of the air in the ship is as fine as the quantity is abundant."[13] Distilled and potable water was provided by two coil evaporators and two distillers, the whole capable of furnishing 10,000 gallons every twenty-four hours. One ton of ice was made each day by means of a dense-air ice maker. The decks were swept with compressed-air sweeps. The dynamo room, located just forward of the engine spaces, powered 721 incandescent lamps, the five searchlight "projectors," and the 8-inch ammunition hoists.

Trials

Government acceptance trials were held on 22 May 1893 in moderate sea and wind off the Massachusetts and Maine coasts, between Cape Porpoise and Cape Ann. Forced draft was used on the four-hour speed trial, and as was usual in vessels of the period, hand-picked coal from the Pocahontas seam in West Virginia was stoked into the fireboxes.

With a trial displacement of 8,400 tons, the *New York*'s engines performed excellently, although a freshwater hose was needed on the overheated wrist pins of the starboard forward high-pressure cylinder. A major hull defect, common to several vessels of the period, was noted. During the high-speed runs, water came through the bow torpedo tube and flooded several forward compartments, including the sick bay. This fault notwithstanding, the *New York* achieved a top speed of 21.91 knots, a world record. Average speed was tabulated at 21.09 knots, nearly 2 knots in excess of contract requirements, thus winning for her builders a performance bonus of $200,000.

On 24 May, during the *New York*'s return passage to Cramp's yard, an eight-hour coal-consumption trial was held. Using natural draft only, the forward engines were uncoupled and steam was generated solely by the after four boilers. Under these conditions the vessel burned 4.79 tons per hour, a result deemed "highly successful" by Melville.[14]

Modernization and Refits

On 31 March 1905 the *New York* was decommissioned at the Boston Navy Yard for the first of her two major refits. During twelve years of service her speed had been gradually reduced to 17.5 knots, and the old guns and turrets, which had seen much action in the war with Spain, were in need of replacement.

The entire ordnance outfit was unshipped and replaced with modern weapons. Four 8-inch 45-caliber Mark 6 guns, mounted in two balanced turrets, now formed the main battery. In 1905 both gun and turret were introduced into the service for installation in the *Virginia* (BB 13), *Connecticut* (BB 18), and *Mississippi* (BB 23) class battleships. Firing one round every 50 seconds, the Mark 6 gun had a maximum penetration of 4.4 inches of Krupp nickel-chromium steel at 9,000 yards. The faces and sides of the new turrets were sheathed in 6.5 inches of Krupp steel, with six inches covering the barbettes.

The weak and relatively ineffective 4-inch battery was replaced by a more logical arrangement of ten 5-inch 50-caliber Mark 6 RF guns mounted on central pivot carriages on the gun deck. Introduced in 1904 for service in the small "peace cruisers" of the *Denver* (C 14) class, these guns could pierce 1.4 inches of Krupp armor at 9,000 yards. The light tertiary battery was replaced with eight 3-inch RF guns in small sponsons, well forward and aft on the gun deck, and four 3-pdr. RF guns, port and starboard on the main deck in the positions formerly occupied by the midship 8-inch guns. The torpedo tubes and all torpedo-handling machinery were unshipped.

The engineering plant was given a thorough overhaul, the major work being the replacement of the old fire-tube boilers with twelve Babcock & Wilcox water-tube boilers.

A lot of work was done in the hull, and the ship was nearly rebuilt

New York City's East River and the Brooklyn Bridge, c. 1893.

internally, with the double-bottom, gun, and main decks replaced. For the added comfort and habitability of the crew, laundry and drying rooms were added.

The *New York*'s topside appearance was also changed, not for the better. A pair of skeleton searchlight platforms were placed on the boat deck, one between the first and second funnels, the second between the after funnel and the mainmast. These were fitted to carry four of the *New York*'s eight new 36-inch, electrically controlled projectors. Two spindly pole masts, high enough to accommodate new wireless antennae, were stepped. The foremast carried a lower fighting top. Perhaps the most disagreeable alteration to the ship's appearance was the raising of her funnels. With the outer casings coming to just three-quarter length, the hull had a truncated look, wholly inconsistent with its original form.

In 1917 the ship, renamed the *Rochester*, underwent her second major refit at Bremerton. The after pair of 5-inch-gun sponsons were plated over and the guns were unshipped. The tertiary battery was removed and replaced with two 3-inch AA (antiaircraft) guns on the boat deck aft. A small fire-control station was installed on the foremast.

The *Rochester*'s final alterations, prior to her decommissioning, took place at Cavite in 1932. Eight forward boilers and the fore funnel were unshipped, reducing the plant's output to 7,700 IHP.

Career

Laid down 19 September 1890 and launched 2 December 1891, the *New York* was placed in commission at the Philadelphia Navy Yard, League Island, on 1 August 1893. Hers was one of the longest life spans of any vessel of the New Navy. As one of its premiere units, the ship attracted the cream of the captains list in the early years of her career. Among her commanding officers were Jack Philip, Robley Evans, Winfield Scott Schley, and French E. Chadwick. The *New York*'s initial service was with the South Atlantic Squadron, where she remained on station for one year. On 4 August 1894 the *New York* hoisted the flag of Rear Admiral Richard Meade, commander of the North Atlantic Squadron. During this tour she landed her marines and bluejackets, in company with the landing forces of the *Columbia* (C 12), *Minneapolis* (C 13), *Raleigh*, and *Cincinnati*, to fight fires and suppress looting in Port of Spain, Trinidad. Arsonists had been at work, and according to Robley Evans, the city was only saved "after four hours of very hard and dangerous work by our men."[15]

In June 1895 the *New York* was assigned as temporary flagship to the commander of the European Squadron, Rear Admiral William Kirkland, the U.S. Navy's representative at the opening of the Kiel Canal. As the world's most powerful armored cruiser, the ship elicited much interest. She returned to the East Coast 25 July and resumed her duties as flagship of the North Atlantic Squadron, with Rear Admirals Francis Bunce and Montgomery Sicard in successive command. On 26 March 1898 Rear Admiral Sicard was relieved because of illness, and the *New York* hoisted the flag of Acting Rear Admiral William Sampson. The Spanish-American War was imminent.

When war was declared by Congress on 25 April 1898, neither the United States nor Spain maintained a fleet with the material strength to meet, let alone defeat, a strong second-class power. The nucleus of the New Navy battle fleet had hardly been afloat for five years, and the destruction of the *Maine* had reduced its line of battle by one-sixth. Moreover, at the outset of hostilities the line of battle was not at full strength, for the new battleship *Oregon* (BB 3) was operating on the West Coast. Had Spain been in a reasonable state of preparedness—and she should have been, given recent upheavals in Cuba—her fleet, whose backbone consisted of the big armored cruisers *Infanta Maria Teresa*, *Almirante Oquendo*, *Vizcaya*, and *Cristobal Colon*, could have engaged the North Atlantic Squadron with a fair chance of success before it concentrated its full resources.

But Spain's naval power proved largely illusory at the actual muster. Vice Admiral Pascual Cervera, who commanded the Cape Verdes

Cleared for action, her battle flags hoisted, the *New York* signals for a casualty report at the close of the Battle of Santiago, 3 July 1898.

Fleet and would lead it bravely to its doom at Santiago, noted in one of his letters to the minister of marine that "the *Colon* has not received her big guns; the *Carlos V* has not been delivered, and her 10cm artillery is not yet mounted; the *Pelayo* is not ready for want of finishing her redoubt, and I believe her secondary battery; the *Vittoria* has no ordnance, and of the *Numancia* we had better not speak."* The vessels mentioned by the admiral composed nearly half the Spanish battle fleet.

By the first week of April the strategic distribution of the American forces was nearly complete, and as the bulk of U.S. naval strength was being concentrated in the North Atlantic Squadron, Admiral Cervera sailed with his fleet from Cadiz on 8 April for the Cape Verde Islands,

---

*The *Colon* never did receive her pair of 11-inch main battery guns, and she sailed for active service with wooden dummies in their place.

there to await further political developments. This Spanish movement created more furor and consternation in the United States than Cervera could have possibly imagined. Absolute hysteria reigned along the East Coast, fanned by politicians and the press. It was expected that at any moment Spanish warships would appear off our ports to bombard them or hold them for ransom. The banking community of Boston moved their assets fifty miles inland to Worcester. To pacify a congressman who wanted ships to protect various ports on the New England coast, Assistant Secretary Theodore Roosevelt arranged to send a Civil War monitor with twenty-one members of the New Jersey naval militia.

Had this been the extent of public pacification, no great damage to the fleet's strategic dispositions would have resulted, but this was not the case. On 28 March the fleet was divided by the creation of the Flying Squadron under Commodore Winfield Scott Schley, flying his broad pennant in the *Brooklyn*. The mission of this force was to intercept any Spanish vessels attempting to harry American shores. At first, beside the *Brooklyn*, Schley had with him the speedy *Columbia* and *Minneapolis*. But these two vessels were detached and, with the *San Francisco*, ordered north to the New England coast to form the Northern Patrol Squadron. The battleships *Massachusetts* (BB 2) and *Texas* were taken from the North Atlantic Squadron and given to Schley, Admiral Sampson having to make do with the monitors *Puritan* (BM 1) and *Terror* (BM 4) in their stead.

Offensive operations began on 27 April, when Admiral Sampson received word that the Spanish were strengthening their defenses at Matanzas, just down the coast from Havana. Steaming from Key West with the *New York, Puritan* and *Cincinnati*, Sampson arrived at his objective and prepared to bombard the Spanish works. To the men on the *New York*'s portside 8-inch gun went the order to fire the first shot of the war. According to the *New York*'s captain, French E. Chadwick, this particular gun "was selected for the honor on account of the . . . rivalry between the crews of the two turrets, which was so intense that it was considered advisable not to give the first shot to either."[16]

War correspondent Richard Harding Davis, aboard the *New York*, left an interesting account of her fire control during this action.

> Captain Chadwick ran down the ladder from the forward bridge, and shouted at Ensign [*sic*] Boone, "Aim for 4,000 yards, at that bank of earth on the point." Then he ran up to the bridge again, where Admiral Sampson was pacing up and down. . . . The ship seemed to work and fight by herself; you heard no human voice of command, only the grieved tones of Lieutenant Mulligan, rising from his smoke-choked deck below, where he could not see to aim his 4-inch guns, and from where he begged Lieutenant Marble again

and again to "take your damn smoke out of my way." Lieutenant Marble was vaulting in and out of his forward turret like a squirrel in a cage. One instant you would see him far out on the deck, and then the next, pushing the turret with his shoulder as though he meant to shove it overboard; and then he would wave his hand to the crew inside and there would be a racking roar. . . . Meanwhile from below came the strains of a string band playing for the officer's mess. . . . This is not a touch of fiction, but the reporting of cold coincidence, for war as it is conducted at this end of the century is civilized.[17]

As the first days of May passed without any indication of the enemy's whereabouts, Admiral Sampson determined to search on his own. Cervera's ships would desperately require a port for coal and refitting, so logic dictated that either Havana or San Juan, Puerto Rico, would be Cervera's choice; of those two places San Juan was the more likely because it was farther from the main American naval presence at Key West. Calculating that the Spanish would arrive by 8 May, Admiral Sampson steamed from Key West on the fourth with the *New York* leading the *Iowa* (BB 4), *Indiana* (BB 1), and *Detroit*. Sailing east, the squadron rendezvoused off Havana, where it was joined by the *Montgomery*, monitors *Terror* and *Amphitrite* (BM 2), torpedo boat *Porter* (TB 6), tug *Wompatuck*, and collier *Niagara*.

An agonizing eight days were needed to reach the objective. The *Indiana*'s boilers were continually breaking down, and because of the low coal capacity of the monitors the *New York* and *Iowa* had to tow them at a fleet speed of eight knots. On the morning of 12 May the North Atlantic Squadron hove into sight of San Juan. One glance at the roadstead revealed two decrepit Spanish gunboats and the ancient French cruiser *Admiral Rigualt de Genouilly*. Following a conference of captains on board the *New York*, the ships were ordered to take up stations to bombard the forts.

On board the *New York* and the other ships of the squadron, "every preparation had been made which foresight could suggest; woodwork had been ruthlessly torn out and thrown overboard until the sea was strewn with the wreckage for hundreds of miles; the ship's cables were wrapped about the ammunition uptakes and the more vulnerable parts of the turret supports; chests, carpenter's benches, alcohol, and other inflammable articles were got rid of until the ships were stripped of everything not absolutely necessary for fighting purposes or to life aboard."[18]

General quarters was sounded throughout the squadron at 0500 hours, and the ships, led by the *Detroit*, advanced in column to the firing point, about 1,200 yards from the target. At 0515 firing commenced, and

In gray war color, the flagship *New York* at anchor off Tompkinsville, New York, at the conclusion of hostilities, 1898.

a thunderous roar split the air. Surprise was complete, and eight minutes passed before the Spanish gunners replied. For twenty-nine minutes the full broadsides of the North Atlantic Squadron hurled every caliber of shell from the 13-inch to the 6-pounder into the Spanish fortifications, but not a single Spanish gun was put out of action. Spanish losses amounted to twenty dead and a like number wounded. Of the North Atlantic Squadron's two casualties, one was Seaman Frank Widemark of the *New York*'s portside 8-inch-gun crew, killed when a Spanish 5.9-inch shell burst on board. Deeply disappointed at missing his quarry, Admiral Sampson returned to Key West with the squadron for much needed coal and repairs.

The first confirmed reports of the Spanish fleet's whereabouts were flashed to the Navy Department and Key West on 12 May.

Admiral Cervera's destroyers had been spotted at Fort de France, Martinique. But elusive as ever, the Spanish fleet slipped through the American patrol line and arrived on 19 May at their final destination, Santiago de Cuba. Of this the navy was unaware, and ten days were to pass before Commodore Schley's lookouts spotted the big armored cruiser *Cristobal Colon* scouting the outer roads at the harbor entrance.

On 1 June Admiral Sampson hove into view with the *New York* and *Oregon* and a close blockade of Santiago commenced. The force under his command was nothing short of overpowering, and though units had to be detached periodically for coal and repairs, it included on any given day the *New York, Brooklyn, Indiana, Massachusetts, Oregon, Iowa, Texas, New Orleans, Marblehead,* a few torpedo boats, and numerous auxiliaries. The admiral's attempt to sink the collier *Merrimac* in the narrow harbor channel on the night of 3 June was unsuccessful. A Spanish shot parted the tiller ropes, disabling her steering gear, and she settled on the bottom, only partially blocking the roadstead.

There were almost daily bombardments of the Spanish works and inner harbor. The first of these, on 6 June, is representative. In two columns the squadron, with the *New York* in the starboard van, proceeded slowly down to the forts. At 6,000 yards the *New York* opened fire and was immediately joined by other ships, the squadron advancing until the *New York* was 1,900 yards from the Morro Castle forts. From this distance it was impossible to direct heavy-gun fire against the batteries sited atop 200-foot cliffs, and general firing was discontinued. The squadron moved farther out to sea, then for well over an hour kept up a slow but deliberate pounding. The armored cruiser *Vizcaya* received hits by two heavy shells, the old station ship *Reina Mercedes* received several hits, the destroyer *Furor* one; additionally, two coastal defense guns were knocked out.

The blockade continued. The squadron lay motionless—but not at anchor for the depth was too great—in a compact semicircle at a distance of two to four miles from the harbor mouth. Once each hour the engines were turned over to keep station. Steadily the squadron ate into its coal, and steadily its bottoms grew more foul in the warm tropical water. In front of Santiago the army, which had landed on 22 June, was being decimated by disease, and unless something happened fast, large Spanish reinforcements could be expected from the north. A conference was hastily scheduled for 3 July to discuss how the navy could best aid the army in its plight. As General Shafter had a fever, Admiral Sampson would have to visit his headquarters several miles inland.

Unbeknownst to the American commanders, on 1 July Admiral Cervera had received orders from Captain General Blanco at Havana to reembark his crews and follow the first opportunity with the ships of his squadron.

In the very early hours of 3 July, while Admiral Sampson was anxiously pondering his next morning's absence from the blockade, certain ominous signs were observed by the squadron. Soon after midnight, the gunboat *Alvarado*, clearing the Spanish minefield in the channel mouth, was spotted from the *Indiana*. Additionally, the *Iowa's* officer of the watch reported six well-defined columns of smoke rising above the heights. This, however, aroused no undue suspicion, as the Spanish had raised steam on several occasions. The *Iowa's* signalmen, in any case, were ordered to be ready to hoist a signal indicating that the enemy's ships were escaping.

The *New York* as well as the rest of the blockading force was generally ready for action at one minute's notice. Her decks were clear and completely stripped of all combustible fittings. Steam was up in three boilers, one boiler was banked, one had fires out but hot water, and one boiler was cold. To prevent monumental coal consumption and unnecessary strain to both engineering force and machinery, the forward set of engines had long ago been uncoupled. Even in this state, where her engines had to be turned over but once each hour, the *New York's* coal consumption was 45 tons a day.

At 0850 hours on 3 July Admiral Sampson, in the *New York*, ordered the movements of the commander in chief disregarded, and with the torpedo boat *Ericsson* (TB 2) headed east for the nine-mile trip to Siboney and the conference with General Shafter. They had progressed about nine miles when, at 0935, Admiral Sampson spotted gunfire smoke at the harbor entrance. Without waiting to convey his order through Captain Chadwick, he had the ship's helm put hard aport and headed for the enemy. The *New York* was now ploughing through the water at 12 knots, and appeals were being sent by messenger, voice tube, and telephone for the chief engineer to rush the fires. At about 1000 the *New York* had come abreast the harbor forts on her starboard side and for some fifteen minutes was subject to their concentrated fire. Admiral Sampson, anxious to pursue the Spanish ships, denied Captain Chadwick's request for permission to return fire.

The Spanish destroyers *Pluton* and *Furor*, recently engaged by the *Iowa* and *Indiana*, were in a hot fight with the converted yacht *Gloucester*. Steaming past, the *New York* opened fire on the *Furor* with her 4-inch bow chasers, the only rounds she would loose in the battle. Suddenly the *Pluton* received a shot from the *Gloucester* in her boilers and blew up; the ex-yacht then repeated her exploit by running the *Furor* on the rocks.

As the *New York* raced after the fleet, Captain Chadwick, standing on the forecastle and waving his cap, led her crew in "wild cheers for the plucky little *Gloucester*."[19] The *New York's* engines were now pounding out 16 knots. On the bridge, Captain Chadwick remembered, "our ship

Fully modernized in 1905 and renamed in 1911, the *Saratoga* flies the flag of the commander in chief, Asiatic Fleet, at Shanghai, c. 1911. Note the new elliptical turrets, the absence of amidship 8-inch guns, the 5-inch battery on the gun deck, the heightened funnels, and the spindly pole masts.

was quivering fore and aft, and had set up the pleasant jingling of certain metallic objects on the bridge which we knew meant high speed. The chief engineer by now had reported the engines could go no faster, but the forward pair were ready for coupling should it be necessary."[20] The *Maria Teresa* and *Oquendo*, both a boiling mass of flame and smoke, with sailors jumping off their bows, had run aground on the beach and were passed to starboard.

At 1105 hours, the battle had progressed eighteen miles west of the harbor mouth. On the *New York*'s port bow were the *Oregon, Brooklyn, Texas,* and *Iowa*, bending on every fraction of a knot in order to overhaul the *Vizcaya* and *Colon*. Abruptly, the *Vizcaya* "turned in with colors down, and headed for the beach. She steamed in rather slowly, and at such short distance crossed our bows, that the crews were virtually face-to-face, and we looked at each other—victors and vanquished—the former without a cheer, the latter huddled forward, clear of the flames, without sound or movement."[21]

Many Spanish sailors were passed in the water; one of them was right in her course, shouting "*Amerigo! Amerigo! auxilio! auxilio!*" His appeal was mercifully answered. The *New York* shifted course slightly to avoid running him down, and a seaman flung him the chaplain's reading desk.[22]

Ordering the *Iowa* to stand by and take off the *Vizcaya*'s crew, the *New York* settled down to the chase. Ahead, the *Brooklyn* and *Oregon* had opened ranging shots with their 8-inch guns. Falling short, the *Oregon* shifted to main battery, and after six rounds the *Colon* hauled down her colors and slowly drove her bows onto the beach.

The *New York* hove into signaling range at 1345 and received her first message from Commodore Schley, who signaled that a great victory had been won. Admiral Sampson responded with the order to report casualties, and he was astonished to read that only one man had been killed. Spanish casualties amounted to 323 killed and 151 wounded. For the Americans it was a smashing victory almost without cost.

Meanwhile, a prize crew from the *Oregon* had been placed aboard the *Colon*, and immediate preparations were made to float her off the beach. But it was soon found that her sea valves had been opened prior to hauling down her colors, and she was rapidly taking on water. After dark the rising tide kept her afloat temporarily. In an effort to keep her from going down in deep water, the *New York*, with heavy rope fenders on her bow, was set the delicate task of pushing the *Colon* further up the beach. The *New York* slowly headed in, placed her bow against the *Colon*'s starboard quarter, and began forcing her up. Without warning, the *Colon* rolled over on her port side and was left with her starboard broadside guns pointing at the sky.

For all practical purposes the war was over, and only minor operations, at least for the fleet, were now carried out. On 10 and 11 July the *New York* and the other heavy ships of the blockading force bombarded Santiago in support of the army's advance, directly contributing to the city's fall.

On 14 August the *New York* steamed from Guantanamo. She arrived off Tompkinsville on the twentieth at the head of the victorious fleet to a tumultuous welcome.

At war's end the *New York* returned to normal duties as flagship of the North Atlantic Squadron, now under Rear Admiral Norman Farquhar. The ship trained state naval militias and showed the flag in Central American and Caribbean trouble spots. The winter of 1899–1900 was spent conducting wireless testing with the *Massachusetts*. The *New York*'s wireless officer reported to Secretary Long that the "Marconi system of wireless telegraphy is well adapted for use in squadron signaling under conditions of rain, fog, darkness, and motion of ship."[23] The report was rejected.

The *New York* left the East Coast for the Asiatic Station and arrived at Cavite on 20 May. Initial duties called for the ship to represent the United States at the unveiling of the Matthew Calbraith Perry Memorial

In the Gatun Locks, Panama Canal, c. 1925. The old flagship has been renamed *Rochester*; note that she still carries an obsolete stocked anchor.

at Yokohama. By late summer the *New York* was back in Philippine waters, operating off Samar in support of army counterinsurgency operations. From March through November 1902 the vessel cruised the far western Pacific, calling at Russian, Korean, and Chinese ports. On 29 October 1903 she was detached from the Asiatic Squadron and ordered to the Pacific Squadron.* General duties with the squadron followed, including flag showing off the Honduran, Panamanian, and Peruvian coasts. In September 1904 the *New York* was a principal player in the *Lena* affair. Because of inoperative boilers the *Lena*, a Russian auxiliary cruiser, was forced to put into San Francisco for emergency repairs. With Russia and Japan at war, these could not be completed in the time the ship was permitted to remain in a neutral port. The choice was either internment or certain foundering at sea. Under the supervision of Captain J. J. Hunker of the *New York*, the *Lena* was disarmed, interned, and her officers and crew paroled. The *New York* left the Pacific on 4 January 1905 and entered the Boston Navy Yard on 31 March for decommissioning and a thorough overhaul and modernization.

The ship was recommissioned on 22 May 1909 and joined the newly formed Armored Cruiser Squadron of the Atlantic Fleet, taking her place alongside the big new armored cruisers *North Carolina* and *Montana*. She joined her new consorts at Naples on 10 July and with them steamed for Boston on the twenty-third. After operating off the Atlantic and Gulf coasts for the next eighteen months, the *New York* was placed in reduced commission on 31 December 1909 with the Atlantic Reserve Fleet at League Island.

Recommissioned on 10 April 1910 for the Asiatic Fleet, the *New York* arrived at Manila on 3 August. On 16 February 1911 the ship was renamed *Saratoga*, the original designation going to the hull of BB 34. For the next five years she served as flagship of the Asiatic Fleet and was a familiar sight along the Chinese coasts. On 6 February 1916 the *Saratoga* went into reduced commission with the Pacific Reserve Fleet at Bremerton, there to remain until the demands of war dictated her recall.

Placed in full commission on 23 April 1917, the *Saratoga* formed with the Patrol Force, Pacific Fleet, on 7 June and saw service off the west coast of Mexico, where she intercepted and captured a steamer carrying several German agents and American draft resisters. In

---

*As a force the Pacific Squadron, which operated along the West Coast, was extremely heterogenous, consisting of the *New York*; cruiser *Marblehead*; the old ABCD cruiser *Boston*; monitor *Wyoming* (BM 10); gunboat *Bennington* (PG 4); two torpedo boat destroyers, *Paul Jones* (DD 10) and *Preble* (DD 12); and the collier *Nero* (AC 17). Rear Admiral Caspar Goodrich, who flew his flag in the *New York*, commented, "The vessels of this squadron are so dissimilar in type and maneuvering qualities as to preclude the possibility of attaining a high standard of efficiency."[23]

November the ship transited the Panama Canal for Hampton Roads, where she was assigned convoy escort duty with Division Four, Squadron Two, Cruiser Force, Atlantic Fleet. On 1 December the old ship's name was again changed, to *Rochester*, *Saratoga* being transferred to the hull of the new battle cruiser CB 3.

During her tenure as escort, the *Rochester* completed seven turnaround passages, never once touching a European port as she transferred her charges to American and British destroyers off the Irish and Biscay coasts.

The *Rochester*'s one brush with the Imperial German Navy occurred during the evening of 25 June 1918. Escorting a slow convoy of cargo vessels, zigzagging at eight and a half knots, the ship was at her station 1,000 yards ahead of the merchantmen. In the northern latitude of 55N there was a full moon twilight, and British destroyers from Queenstown were expected hourly. At 2142 the *Atlantian*, van ship of the right flank column, opened fire with her 4-inch gun as a huge tower of water shot up her starboard side, immediately followed by the dull boom of an exploding torpedo. In the *Rochester* Captain Hinds rang for full speed, ordered the crew to torpedo defense stations, and headed for the position of the submarine. To facilitate ramming and depth charging, the ship was conned by the navigator, Lieutenant Commander James, from atop the foremast. A submarine was soon sighted running on the surface, close to the *Atlantian*, 30 degrees off the *Rochester*'s starboard bow. The *Rochester* was ordered to close and ram; she swung 30 degrees only to see the submarine crash dive and launch a torpedo. The torpedo passed 30 yards ahead of the *Rochester*, sinking the *Atlantian*. The submarine escaped.

British destroyers formed up at 0120 hours on the twenty-sixth, and for a time the *Rochester* continued eastward. Soon the rear ship of the left flank column, the *War Cypress*, received a torpedo, and the *Rochester* sheered out of station in the van to pursue the enemy. The submarine was sighted on the surface, but before the *Rochester* could clear the convoy and open fire, it had submerged. Full-speed zigzagging was resumed. At 0300 six more British destroyers joined the convoy, the *Rochester* upping helm and departing westward.

On 24 January 1919 the *Rochester* was assigned to the Transport Force and fitted to carry three hundred troops of the returning American Expeditionary Force. One turnaround passage was made. The ship was detached on 4 March. The remainder of the year was spent primarily in dockyard hands at Brooklyn, Norfolk, and Boston. Her 48,750 miles of wartime steaming had taken its toll.

In May 1919 the *Rochester* hoisted the flag of Rear Admiral Ashley Robertson as flagship, Destroyer Squadrons, Atlantic Fleet. Her first duty in her new billet was command of the ocean escort for the navy Curtiss flying boats during their transatlantic flight. In 1920, in order to provide academic and service instruction to the fleet's enlisted force, the *Rochester* was organized as the navy's prototype extension school.

Her next flag assignment came in 1923, when she relieved the *Birmingham* (CS 2) as flagship of the special service squadron for keeping the peace in Nicaragua, Honduras, and Haiti. Admiral Robert Coontz, chief of naval operations, observed that the *Rochester*, though old, was assigned this duty owing to her excellent condition. In addition to regular duties, hydrographic surveys of Mexican and Honduran ports were conducted for the navy's Hydrographic Office. On 19 July 1925 the *Rochester* embarked General Pershing and the members of the plebicite commission sent to arbitrate the Tacna-Arica border dispute between Chile, Peru, and Bolivia. On 3 December she was relieved as flagship by the *Denver*.

The *Rochester* undergoing her final major refit at Brooklyn in 1932. The ship has a radically altered appearance. The after funnel and the after set of boilers have been unshipped. Note the enlarged modern bridge structure and fire control station on the foremast.

The next seven years were spent in the ever-troubled waters of Central America and the Caribbean. In 1928 she served mainly off Nicaragua in support of expeditionary forces fighting bandits. In 1929 she was again designated flagship of the special service squadron and served as President-elect Hoover's naval escort on his fact-finding mission to Corinto, Nicaragua. In that year she also transported the First Marine Brigade to Port au Prince, Haiti. After the Nicaraguan earthquake of 1931 the *Rochester* was the first relief vessel to arrive on the scene; her crew succored refugees, and her landing force was committed to the suppression of banditry. On 25 February 1932 the *Rochester* steamed from Balboa in the Canal Zone to her final duty station with the Asiatic Fleet.

On 27 April she arrived at Shanghai and served as relief flagship for the Asiatic Fleet in the lower Yangtze until the spring of 1933. On 29 April 1933 the *Rochester* was decommissioned at Cavite and steamed her last course to Subic Bay, where she tied up at Olongapo. On 28 October 1938 she was struck from the navy list and rated an unclassified hulk. In this status she remained until the Japanese invasion of December 1941, when she was scuttled to prevent her from falling into enemy hands.

New York Characteristics

Dimensions

384' oa x 64' 10" max beam x 23' 3" mean draft

Displacement

8,150 tons normal, full supply ammunition and stores, normal coal
8,679 tons full load
Tons-per-square-inch immersion at normal draft, 39
Metacentric height, 2.08' normal draft

Armament

Original: six 8-in 35-cal Mk 3; twelve 4-in 40-cal Mk 3 RF; eight 6-pdr.; two 1-pdr.; four 50-cal Gatling; TT three 18-in Whitehead; two 3-in field guns.
1905: four 8-in 45-cal Mk 6; ten 5-in 50-cal Mk 6 RF; eight 3-in 50-cal Mk 2 RF; four 3-pdr.
1917: four 8-in 45-cal Mk 6; eight 5-in 50-cal Mk 6 RF; eight 3-in 50-cal Mk 2; two 3-in 50-cal Mk 2–3 AA

Protection

Belt: 5" NS amidships; 4" NS ends
Barbettes: 10" NS
Turrets: 5" NS

Base rings: 2″ NS
Conning tower: 7½″ NS
Conning tower tube: 5″ NS
Sponsons: 4″ NS
8-inch ammunition tubes: 7″ NS
Armored deck flats: 3″ MS
Armored deck slopes: 3″ NS + 3″ MS amidships; 3″ MS ends
Cofferdam: cocoafibre cellulose

Machinery

Engines: four sets 3-cyl VTE
Boilers, original: six DE Fox firetube; two Fox firetube SE
Boilers, 1905: twelve Babcock & Wilcox WT
Indicated horsepower: 16,000
IHP generated on trials: 17,075
Trial speed: 21.09 kts
Coal capacity: 750 tons normal; 1,279 tons maximum
Steaming radius: 4,800 miles at 10 kts
Propellers: twin shaft, 3-bladed

Complement

34 officers, 535 men (as commissioned)

Contract price (hull and machinery)

$2,985,000

Total cost

$4,346,642

New York *Engineering Characteristics*

No. of engines	4
No. of cylinders, each engine	3
Diameter of high-pressure cylinder	32″
Diameter of intermediate-pressure cylinder	47″
Diameter of low-pressure cylinder	72″
Stroke of all pistons	42″
No. of main steam condensers	4
Combined cooling surface	22,240 sq. ft.
No. of boilers, firetube	6 DE, 2 SE (aux)
Heating surface per main boiler	5,167.52 sq. ft.
Total heating surface, main boilers	31,005 sq. ft.
Grate surface per main boiler	165 sq. ft.
Total grate surface, main boilers	990 sq. ft.
Ratio heating to grate surface	31.3:1
Working pressure, main boilers	160 psi

3

The *Brooklyn*

Introduction

On 19 July 1892 Congress authorized, along with the battleship *Iowa*, the construction of one armored cruiser of about 8,000 tons displacement. It was to be similar to armored cruiser number two, the *New York*, and to cost, excluding armament, not more than $3,500,000.

As an improved *New York*, the *Brooklyn* brought to a conclusion, especially in her hull form and the disposition of her armament, the French theories of warship design first proposed by the 1890 Naval Policy Board for the first-class thin-armored cruiser. The result was an excellent vessel and, like her half sister, a sought-after command and flagship. Secretary Tracy asserted that her offensive and defensive capabilities surpassed those of any similar vessel afloat or building.

The bid proposals were published on 28 September 1892 under the standard class 1 and 2 procedures. The class 1 respondents, which would build to plans and specifications supplied by the navy, included Newport News Shipbuilding and Drydock, Union Iron Works, and William Cramp and Sons. The class 2 respondents, with their own plans, were Cramp and the Bath Iron Works of Bath, Maine. The Cramp class 1 bid was chosen at $2,986,000, and the contract was formally awarded on 11 February 1893, with completion set for 11 February 1896. This contract was the last in which the bonus/penalty clause of $50,000 per quarter knot in excess of or below designed speed was included.

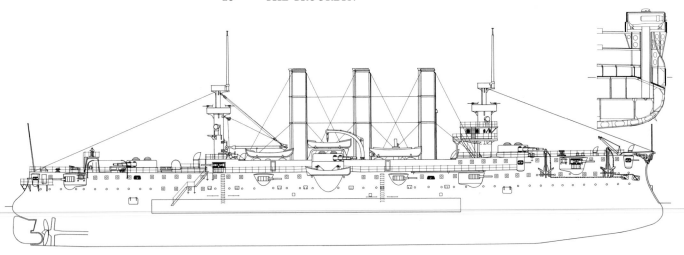

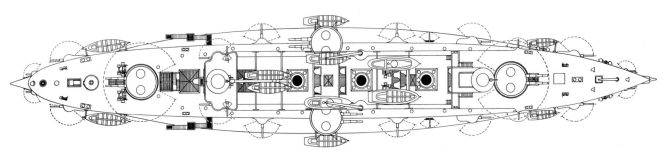

The USS *Brooklyn* (ACR 3)

Hull

The hull that slid down the ways of Cramp and Sons on 2 October 1895 was the most unusual yet seen in the New Navy. Its lines indicated a near total acceptance of French design theory. There was an extreme tumble home, a feature only hinted at in the *New York*. Beginning at the berth deck and sweeping upward and inward to the forecastle deck, it gave the wing turrets complete axial fire, which the slab-sided *New York* did not have. Additionally, a huge amount of weight was saved by carrying the freeboard in at a maximum of 11 feet at forecastle deck level. This saving compensated for the additional mass of the long topgallant forecastle, the wing turrets, and the enhanced secondary battery of twelve 5-inch guns.

It was normal for vessels constructed with an extreme tumble home to experience stability problems, but fortunately this was not the case with the *Brooklyn*, as the massive weight of the wing turrets kept the ship remarkably steady and gave her an "easier curve of stability."[1] Her metacentric height of 2.5 feet was a near perfect balance between initial stiffness in a beam sea and the easy roll necessary for accurate

Seemingly deserted, the *Brooklyn* at a Baltimore pier, c. 1895.

gunlaying. The ship's overall length of 402 feet 7.5 inches and her extreme beam of 64 feet 8.5 inches gave the hull a length-to-beam ratio of 6 to 1, which showed fine underwater lines. During builder's trials, "the wonderful steadiness of the ship while being driven under forced draught was remarked by all on board. The fine lines of the hull were shown in the way the *Brooklyn* goes through the water when being speeded. There was no great bow wave, but the vessel threw the water to each side as cleanly as a knife cuts through cloth."[2]

This effect was the result of the enormously lofty cutwater, sweeping in a graceful, concave arc 29 feet 10 inches from the waterline to the base of the jack staff. The cutwater, coupled with the increased length of the hull, enabled the *Brooklyn* to achieve a higher speed than the *New York*, although each vessel was equipped with the same propulsion machinery. The great height above water was carried to just abaft the mainmast by the addition of the topgallant forecastle, which provided commodious living spaces, kept the forward part of the ship dry in every sort of weather, and gave great command to the forward turret.

The *Brooklyn* was constructed on 106 frames, 4 feet apart between frames 35 and 82 (the boiler and machinery spaces) and 3.5 feet fore and aft. Fifteen watertight transverse bulkheads divided the hull into 242 watertight compartments, 13 of which were in the double bottom. The double bottom, 3 feet 6 inches deep and extending 29 feet outboard from the keel, was worked from frame 22, just forward of the 8-inch magazine, aft to frame 82, between the after engine room and after 8-inch-shell room. Trimming tanks were located forward between frame 15 and the stem, and aft from frame 96 to the rudder post.

The base line of the keel extended from frame 23 aft to frame 97. Forward of frame 23, the keel sloped sharply upward, terminating at the stem at frame 6. Aft of frame 97 the deadwood was cut away slightly, and the underwater framing ended at frame 101, where it met the balanced rudder. The rudder, unlike the *New York*'s unbalanced type, was only semicongruous with the after hull form. The bilge keels, which provided increased stability, extended from frame 28 aft to frame 79 and projected outward from the shell plating 24 inches.

From top to bottom the decks were designated as forecastle main, gun, berth, orlop (armored), three platforms, and the hold. The weight of the hull and fittings, excluding armor, was 3,780 tons.

The superstructure and masting were typical of the "fierce face" pattern common to French heavy ships in the last decade of the century, with the masts resembling especially those of the *Dupuy de Lôme*. These were huge cylindrical towers, fitted as the design circular noted, "with fighting tops, and to carry no sail." The foremast, whose base was anchored to the conning tower roof, was 9 feet in diameter with a height of 30 feet that reached the lower fighting top. At the level of the mahogany chart house, the back plating of the mast was removed to provide a clear view from the wheelhouse, aft. The mainmast, 6 feet in diameter, with its base at gun-deck level, also reached 30 feet from the forecastle deck to the lower fighting top. At its gun-deck base, a spiral staircase led up through it as an escape mechanism for engine room personnel.

The *Brooklyn* carried fifteen boats: two steam cutters of 33 and 30 feet, two 30-foot whaleboats, one 30-foot gig, one 33-foot sailing launch, one 30-foot admiral's barge, four 28-foot sailing cutters, two 20-foot dinghies, and two side-cleaning punts. The steam cutters, gig, barge, sailing launch, and one of the big whaleboats were carried on cradles on the forecastle deck and handled by two large goose-neck boat cranes

A fine view of the *Brooklyn*, with the *New York* to starboard, on her return to New York following the war with Spain. The bow torpedo tube is visible on her cutwater. Note also her very cluttered sides, distinctly French, and the extreme tumble home as it sweeps inboard from the amidship 8-inch sponson.

amidships and a derrick boom fitted to the mainmast. The other boats, with the exception of the punts, were suspended from davits.

Armament

The *Brooklyn*'s eight 8-inch and twelve 5-inch guns gave the ship an offensive capability unmatched by any armored cruiser at the time of her commissioning. The main battery, in four twin turrets, was arranged in a lozenge formation, adopted from the French pattern first used in the battleship *Marceau* (1891). The *Brooklyn* was the only vessel in the U.S. Navy ever to employ the lozenge arrangement, and the results were favorable. Because of the extreme tumble home of the hull and the massive sponsons, 23 feet outboard from the keel line, on which the wing turrets were mounted, the guns were able to achieve complete fore-and-aft axial fire. This was evident at Santiago, where the *Brooklyn*, firing at the head of the Spanish line, executed her famous turn and nearly rammed the *Texas*. But as her captain, Francis Cook, reported, "our tumbling-in sides enabled us to maintain continual fire while turning."[3]

The 8-inch, 35-caliber Mark 3 guns were the same type as those mounted in the *New York*, but they were fitted with the new Fletcher breech, which permitted electrical firing. The barrels for the main battery guns were delayed in manufacture. Forged by the Midvale Steel Company of Philadelphia, they were honeycombed with tiny "sand splits" caused by excessive amounts of clay and slag, dangerously weakening the metal. These, as well as the 8-inch forgings for the *Iowa*'s secondary battery, were initially rejected by the Bureau of Ordnance, and new forgings had to be ordered. But after a delay of two years they were accepted at reduced cost.* This, the most serious of many delays in the installation of the ordnance plant, prevented the *Brooklyn* from joining the fleet for nearly eleven months following the contract completion date.

The 8-inch guns were mounted on the new Mark 6 mount, which featured an improved spring-recoil cylinder and elevating gear. This latter feature was prone to jamming, and the guns were remounted in the months prior to the war with Spain. The addition of the forecastle deck gave the forward turret great command at 33.5 feet above the waterline. Secretary Tracy, no doubt thinking of sea fights in years gone by, considered this a great advantage in close-range battles. The wing turrets were sited 25.5 feet and the after turret 24 feet above the waterline. The forward and after turrets maintained an angle of train of 290 degrees, while the wing turrets were able to traverse a full 180 degrees without danger of major blast damage to deck and superstructure.

Initially all four main battery turrets were to be turned by steam, but problems with the *New York*'s steam-turning machinery raised questions at the Bureau of Ordnance, which had been conducting experiments with electric-turning machinery on board the old monitor *Montauk* at League Island. Convinced that the electric system was superior to existing systems—steam, hydraulic, and pneumatic—the

---

*Three of the *Iowa*'s 8-inch guns blew off their muzzles during a target practice in 1904.

chief of the bureau, Captain William Sampson, ordered one of the navy's smart young thinkers, Lieutenant Bradley Fiske, to study the use of electricity and its application to turret-turning machinery.*

Of the existing methods for turret turning, steam was the most widely used and reliable, but it did have significant drawbacks. The turning engines had to be given absolute protection from enemy shot and were thus located beneath the armored deck in the ammunition-handling rooms, with steam lines running through the ammunition tubes to the turret. Not surprisingly, the engines caused uncomfortably high temperatures in an ammunition area. Further, the bureau objected to the practice of leading steam pipes from the boilers through numerous bulkheads to the handling rooms. The best control was given by a hydraulic-turning system. This eliminated the danger of high temperatures and bursting steam pipes, but any leaking fluid could totally disable the machinery; it was also the heaviest and most expensive of the systems. In the pneumatic system, pipe joints were subject to bursting at high pressures.

Electricity presented none of these problems, but it did introduce others, notably the difficulty of traversing the turret while loads were changed during a ship's roll. The *Montauk* experiments were working to reduce the problem, but existing electrical machinery was as yet far too expensive and cumbersome. Still, Sampson was able to report in 1894 that while "in weight, space occupied, and cost, steam has greatly the advantage over any other power. . . the Bureau is of the opinion that with good control electricity is preferable to any other method of turning turrets."[4]

Fiske visited the General Electric Company, the prospective contractor for the turret-turning machinery, and began adapting their Ward-Leonard system for installation in the *Brooklyn*. But a major and totally unexpected setback occurred. Secretary Hilary Herbert, usually sensible, removed the research and development of electric turret-turning machinery from the Bureau of Ordnance and divided the task between the Bureaus of Construction and Repair and Steam Engineering, both of whose chiefs were opposed to its adoption. In its subse-

*Fiske, whom we will encounter in a later chapter as captain of the *Tennessee* (ACR 10), epitomized the new breed of naval officer that arose during the American naval renaissance. Graduating second in the Naval Academy class of 1874, Fiske combined a full seagoing career with intellectual curiosity and mechanical inventiveness. Included among his myriad inventions were the telescopic sight, turret rangefinder, shutter signal lamp (still in use and virtually unchanged), engine room telegraph, torpedo bomber (1912), navigational devices without number, and an electric turret-turning device. As executive officer of the gunboat *Petrel* at the Battle of Manila Bay, Fiske was also the first person ever to employ director fire control in battle.

The *Brooklyn* in New York harbor during the naval victory review following the Spanish-American War. Her 8-inch and 5-inch sponsons are visible. Note also the upper edge of the armored belt protruding above the waterline amidships and the antiquated method of securing the anchor.

quent report to the secretary, the Bureau of Construction and Repair compared the relative values of electricity and steam in the categories of reliability, accuracy, simplicity, space, weight, cost, and the time required to install the apparatus in the *Brooklyn*. As expected, steam was favored over electricity.

Captain Sampson issued an official rejoinder, composed by Fiske. The simplicity and cheapness arguments in favor of steam were admitted; but "if these were the principal things required in a warship," Fiske wrote, "we should now be building sailing ships like the *Dale* [a sloop of war commissioned in 1839] and not ships like the *Brooklyn*; from all the stand points of gunnery, the electric system has advantages over the steam which cannot be overestimated."[5] In an addendum Fiske suggested that two of the *Brooklyn*'s turrets be fitted with electrical turning gear, two with steam gear, so that "the two systems could be tried on board the same ship, by the same officers, at the same time, and under identical conditions of wind and sea."[6]

With the three design bureaus in total disagreement, the matter was left to Secretary Herbert, who eventually permitted Fiske's compromise and authorized General Electric to install their electric turret-turning gear, at their own risk, into the forward and starboard turrets. A test was ordered and subsequently conducted on 3 March 1896. The test board reported "that the electric controlled turrets could be turned from

Scraping and painting in dock at the Brooklyn Navy Yard, 1898. Note the absence of safety gear for the men on the scaffold and the emergency manual wheel abaft the *Brooklyn*'s after turret.

any point within the limits of train, and brought to rest with the object hairs of the sighting telescope with great facility, . . . the turret having a smooth and regular motion. While it was possible to arrive at the same results with the steam-turned turret, it was only done with considerable difficulty, owing to the fact that the controlling lever could not be worked with sufficient facility, and to the jerky movement of the turret.''[7]

The secondary battery was composed of twelve 5-inch 40-caliber Mark 2 RF guns, which saw initial service in the cruisers of the 1888 program—the *Olympia* and the small cruisers of the *Cincinnati* and *Montgomery* classes. Four of the guns were sited in the forecastle deck, two well forward in small sponsons and two in embrasured ports at the break of the forecastle, abreast the mainmast. Each gun maintained an arc of fire of 137 degrees, axial fire being achieved forward for the forward pair and aft for the after pair. The eight remaining guns were installed on the gun deck, well spaced from abreast the foremast to nearly right aft. The forward and after pairs were mounted in good-sized sponsons, with identical arcs and axial bearings as the forecastle deck guns. The amidships quartet, behind shuttered ports, were equally spaced outward from the 8-inch wing turret sponsons and fired through an arc of 140 degrees, but they did not bear axially.

Initial specifications called for the guns to be mounted on the Mark 4 mount, but during construction the new Mark 5 was substituted. One advantage was an improved recoil system, which placed the elevating and training gear in the hands of the gun captain rather than with separate pointers. As with most ships of the New Navy, which were veritable showrooms of Fiske's inventions, the mount was fitted with his new telescopic sight. The 5-inch mounts caused trouble at Santiago, especially the elevating gear. At the close of the action two of the guns were bulged at the muzzle, and ''several were rendered useless for battle.'' New elevating gear was recommended for the entire secondary battery.[8]

Ten ammunition hoists, all electrically driven, served the main and secondary batteries.

The light battery was composed of twelve 6-pounders, four 1-pounders, four Colt automatic machine guns, and two 3-inch field guns for the marine detachment and ship's landing party. Four of the 6-pounders were mounted in small sponsons well forward in the forecastle, the forward pair being nearly in the ship's eyes. Two were in exposed positions behind light shields on the after deckhouse astride the mainmast, four in broadside positions on the gun deck, and two right aft on the gun deck in small sponsons. The 1-pounders and machine guns were mounted in the fighting tops.

Originally the torpedo armament was to consist of five tubes, one in the bow and four broadside, firing the 14.2-inch Howell torpedo. This was a quite different weapon from the Whitehead model with which most ships of the navy were equipped. The Howell was an engineless weapon powered by the movement of an internal flywheel. It had no external rudder system for depth and direction but relied on the gyroscopic force exerted by the flywheel. During the latter stages of construction, the decision was made to replace the Howell with the Whitehead system. The Howell equipment was unshipped and not replaced with the Whitehead until after acceptance trials.

Protection

Protection was similar to that of the *New York* except that Harveyized armor was added for the belt, turrets, and barbettes. The remainder of the armor consisted of a combination of nickel steel and forged mild steel.

The Harvey process of face-hardening nickel steel plates was a significant advance in the evolution of the armored warship. When fitted to a vessel, Harveyized steel required about one-third less thickness and weight than nickel steel to achieve the same purpose. The technique, perfected in 1889 by Hayward Harvey, president of the Harvey Steel Company of Newark, New Jersey, was a relatively simple one. About one foot of carburized material, usually charcoal, was placed on the face of a nickel steel plate and subjected to superheat in a sealed furnace for about one hundred hours. The resulting plate was impervious to existing common shell.

Harvey brought his experiments to the attention of the navy, and a test was conducted by the Bureau of Ordnance at the Annapolis Proving Ground in 1890. The test plate, 6 inches thick, was treated under Harvey's supervision at the Washington Navy Yard gun foundry; it was so much better than ordinary nickel steel that further tests were ordered. As no domestic manufacturer yet had the capability of forging plates thicker than 6 inches, this second series of tests were conducted with 10.5-inch Schneider plates imported from France. In 1891 and 1892 10.5-inch plates of domestic manufacture were subject to severe testing, repeatedly struck by 6-inch and 8-inch shells with velocities of up to 2,075 foot-seconds. After a further refinement in the hardening process—the face-hardened plates were reforged after carburization—the navy accepted Harveyized armor as its standard.

Carnegie and Bethlehem received the contracts for the *Brooklyn*'s 701.73 tons of armor, and tests were made on simulated turrets and belt. On 10 April 1894 a 3-inch plate, representing the armored belt, was

A fine view of detail. Note the *Brooklyn*'s torpedo aperture, 5-inch and 3-inch guns and sponsons, bow scroll, and tumble home.

struck by three 4-inch armor-piercing shells at a velocity of 1,800 foot-seconds. The first two broke up on impact, while the third penetrated to the ogive before breaking up. Although the third shot penetrated the armor to the backing, the plate did not crack and was thus considered acceptable. In action at the Battle of Santiago, the *Brooklyn*'s armored belt was struck once by a 6-inch shell on the starboard waterline, in the immediate vicinity of the watertight door separating the forward and after engine rooms. The shell did not explode and only slightly dented the armor.

The turret armor was tested on 15 June 1895, when a 5.5-inch plate was struck by two 4-inch armor-piercing shells with velocities of 1,774 and 2,000 foot-seconds. The first round broke up, the head remaining in the impact area after penetrating 3 inches. The second round remained in the shot hole after penetrating the plate and backing for 9 inches. Again, because the plate was not cracked, the lot was accepted.

In the distribution of the 392 tons of Harveyized armor, 5.5 inches covered the main battery turrets with 1.5 inches on their crowns. Eight inches covered the front and sides of the barbettes, and 4 inches protected their unexposed rear. The largest allocation of the Harvey armor was in the armored belt, with 155 tons spread over 192 feet, abreast the boiler and machinery spaces. The belt measured 8 feet 3 inches wide, with an overall thickness of 3 inches. At the *Brooklyn*'s maximum draft of 26 feet, the belt was exposed 4 feet above the waterline and extended 4 feet 3 inches below.

The armored deck, running the entire length of the hull, was composed of two layers of 1.5-inch forged mild steel, for a total of 3 inches on the flats amidships, tapering to 2.5 inches at the ends. The slopes were built up, abreast the boiler and machinery spaces, with a 3-inch layer of nickel steel, for a total thickness on the slopes of 6 inches. As in the *New York*, the French practice of having the lower edge of the slope meet the lower edge of the belt was followed. With a seagoing trim of 24 feet, the lower edge of the armored deck slopes extended 5 feet 6 inches beneath the waterline, while the flats corresponded to the waterline level.

The sponsons and shields for the 5-inch guns were sheathed in 4 inches of nickel steel, with additional protection afforded by 1.5-inch mild steel splinter screens within the battery. Professor Philip Alger of the Naval Academy did not consider this adequate: "A sufficient number of 6-pounders on an enemy would make the *New York* and *Brooklyn*'s gun deck untenable, while their machinery is reasonably safe against the guns of a battleship."[9] The remaining nickel steel was distributed with 2 inches covering the ports of the 6-pounders, 7.5 inches on the conning tower, 7 inches on the conning tower tube, and 3 inches on the ammunition tubes leading from the magazines to the turrets. The sponsons of the wing turrets were unprotected and covered with mild steel only.

As in the *New York*, the cellulose-packed cofferdam ran the entire length of the hull between the armored and berth decks.

Machinery

The *Brooklyn*'s engineering plant was basically a copy of the *New York*'s, albeit with some improvements and modifications. Four vertical triple-expansion engines, each of 4,000 horsepower, in four watertight compartments, comprised the major component. Originally Cramp's designers had other and more far-reaching ideas, and when they submitted their plans for the vessel they presented a twin-screw, twin-engine, quadruple-expansion design. They argued that weight and space would be saved with two instead of four engines, steam would be more economically used with four circulations instead of three, and unequal wear on the propeller shafts, a consequence of coupling two engines to each shaft, would be avoided. When the ship was steaming at high speeds, all four cylinders would be in operation. For economy in cruising and at low speeds, the fourth (lowest-pressure) cylinder could be disconnected and the engines run as standard triple-expansion types. After careful study, the Bureaus of Construction and Repair and of Steam Engineering rejected the method and ordered the arrangement employed in the *New York*.

As installed, the main engines differed from those in the *New York* because of an improved shaft-disconnecting coupling and fractional differences in the cylinder diameters. The piston stroke for all twelve cylinders was 42 inches.

The arrangement of the boilers differed greatly from that in the *New York*. The five double-ended and two single-ended Fox fire-tube boilers were all installed beneath the armored deck, eliminating the danger of a projectile penetrating the ship's side and striking an auxiliary boiler. The boilers were arranged in three watertight compartments—two double-ended in the forward and after compartments, one double-ended in the center portside space. The two single-ended were placed back to back in the center space to starboard. As designed, the single-ended boilers were an integral part of the propulsion system while the ship was under way, but they reverted to an auxiliary status when the ship was berthed and fires in the double-ended boilers were banked.

Initial specifications called for steel fire tubes, as in the *New York*; however, these tended to leak badly, especially with forced draft, and iron tubes were substituted during construction.

Little changed from her original appearance, the *Brooklyn* nevertheless shows the passage of time. Note the absence of the 5-inch and 3-inch guns on the gun deck, the installation of 3-inch AA guns on the after bridge, and the raised topmast for wireless telegraphy.

Four fire boxes were located at the end of each boiler, for a total of forty-eight, and each was fitted with a Cone cast iron shaking grate, rocking on iron lugs, to ease the task of hauling ashes. As in the *New York*, forced draft was on the pressurized fireroom system; there were two Sturtevant 60-inch fan blowers in each fireroom.

Tall imposing funnels were a trademark of most vessels engineered under the aegis of Engineer in Chief George Melville, and those of the *Brooklyn* outdid them all. Rising 100 feet from the grate bars, they gave her the most distinctive look of any ship in the New Navy. Melville was convinced that they would provide great draft to the fireboxes and thus more pressure in the boilers with a minimal use of forced draft. As he adapted the engine and shafting designs from the *Lepanto* and *Italia*, so too did Melville introduce tall funnels into the navy from foreign sources. A Scottish-built ship, the *Scot*, had smoke pipes 120 feet high above the grate, and he used these as a model. But their adaptation to the *Brooklyn* did not meet with universal service approval. The future Admiral William S. Sims thought them "absurdly high" and detrimental to forced draft.[10] Seeking to allay the controversy, Secretary Herbert requested a report from the engineer in chief. The report pointed out that extremely tall funnels enabled a higher average speed without any special fittings, raising the sustained cruising speed of the

Brooklyn from 15.23 to 17.20 knots; increased boiler life owing to minimal use of forced draft; cut down on coal consumption; and lessened fatigue for coal passers and firemen. Chief Constructor Wilson concurred with the findings, and the secretary gave his approval.[11]

Normal coal capacity was 900 tons, with 1,461 tons maximum, giving the *Brooklyn* a 20 percent greater bunker capacity than the *New York* and a steaming radius of 6,088 miles at ten knots. The upper tier of thirty-six bunkers, against the cellulose cofferdam on the armored deck, corresponded in position to the double bottom. The lower tier of nineteen bunkers were positioned amidships on the double bottom and forward against the shell plating. The bunkers were provided with two coal-hoisting engines, each capable of lifting 1,000 pounds at 300 feet per minute to the firerooms. Steam fire-extinguisher pipes were fitted in each bunker, as spontaneous combustion was not uncommon.

As in the *New York*, there was one steam condenser per main engine, with a total plant cooling surface of 23,300 square feet. Three main and four auxiliary feed pumps were located in the firerooms. Each pump could supply any boiler in the plant, but there was no connection between the main and auxiliary systems. The main pumps drew from the feed tanks only—of which there was one in each forward engine room with a capacity of 2,130 gallons—and fed water only to the boilers. The auxiliary pumps could draw from the feed tanks, bilges, cold boilers, or the sea, and could feed to the boilers, fire mains, or over the side. There were two evaporators and two distillers with a combined capacity of 10,000 gallons of potable water every twenty-four hours. Ventilation in the engine rooms was provided by two 48-inch fan blowers bolted to the engine room hatch, while general ship ventilation was provided by four fan blowers, two in a compartment abaft the after engine rooms and two forward on the armored deck.

Three General Electric generators, with a 96-kilowatt combined output, each powered by a small two-cylinder engine, gave power to the *Brooklyn*'s 760 "incandescent lights," four 30-inch searchlight projectors, telephones, engine room telegraphs, bell circuits, range indicators, and ammunition hoists. The main switchboard did not power the electrical turret turning machinery, which relied on its own switchboard and dynamo, but it could patch into the system in case of a breakdown.

Propeller shafting followed the pattern set in the *New York*; it was arranged in two sections, each coupled to an engine. The forward section, of forged mild steel, measured 33 feet in length and 10 inches in diameter; the after section, made of nickel steel as it was subject to greater wear, measured 38 feet 10.25 inches in length and 17 inches in diameter. The twin screws, of manganese bronze, each had three blades and a diameter of 16.5 feet.

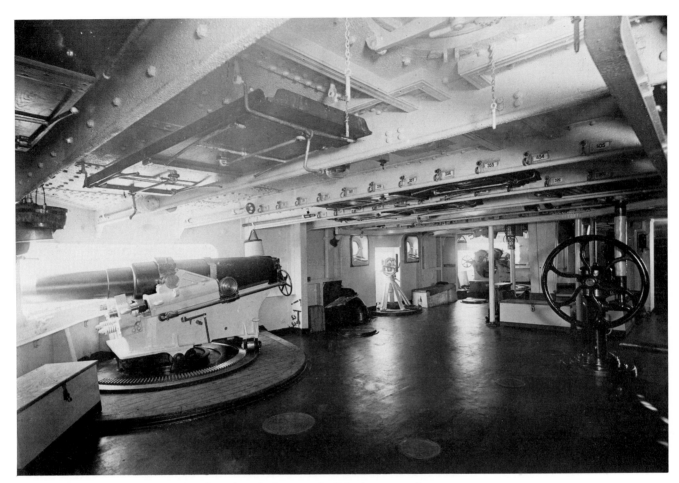

The *Brooklyn*'s gun deck, with a fine detailed view of a 5-inch gun and mount.

Trials

Builder's trials were held on 11 May 1896, seventy-five miles off the Delaware capes. The run was made under forced draft, and after three hours the *Brooklyn* reached an average speed of 21.07 knots. An observer wrote, "No stoppage for repairs was made. During the run, not a bearing or journal became hot."[12]

The Cape Porpoise–Cape Ann course was the scene for the *Brooklyn*'s acceptance trials, held on 27 August 1896. The weather was good and the sea calm. With a trial displacement of 8,150 tons and the usual hand-picked Pocahontas coal stoked into her fireboxes, the *Brooklyn* generated an aggregate of 18,248 hp. For 7 miles of the 83-mile run, the ship reached a top speed of 22.9 knots. With corrections made for wind and tide, an average speed of 21.9 knots was obtained, nearly 2 knots in excess of the contract speed. For the increase, Cramp received a bonus of $350,000, the last instance in that era of a bonus being paid to a private builder.

In his report for 1896, Melville noted with satisfaction the effect of his tall funnels: "The trial of the *Brooklyn* is worthy of special mention on account of the fact that she is the first vessel tried that has been fitted with tall smoke pipes. The results obtained on the official trial give every promise that the fitting of these tall pipes will be attended with economy, and that the *Brooklyn* will be able to steam continuously at a satisfactory speed without having to use her forced draught blowers."[13]

Modifications and Refits

Not as drastically modernized and altered as the *New York*, the *Brooklyn* did receive her share of refits during her quarter century of service. Her first post-commission modification in 1899 resulted from a department-wide directive ordering the removal of bow and stern torpedo tubes from all vessels because the flats were being continually flooded.

In the months prior to the Spanish War major revisions were made to the battery. The elevating gear of the 8-inch guns was replaced, as was one 5-inch gun that had burst, and the entire secondary battery received new top carriages and recoil slides.

At Santiago the Spanish ships, with large amounts of wood in their upperworks, proved highly combustible. As a result of this lesson, much of the wood in U.S. vessels was removed or made fire resistant. Fully half the joiner work in the *Brooklyn* above the armored deck was treated with fire-proofing materials. When the wood paneling in the wardrooms and cabins was sheathed with asbestos, the clubby atmosphere of those compartments was reduced, and objections to fire proofing were "frequently strong, . . . at times almost unreasonable."[14]

In the spring and summer of 1899 the *Brooklyn* underwent a general overhaul at the Brooklyn Navy Yard. Special attention was given to her electrical and interior communications systems.

Difficulties with the secondary battery occurred again in 1901, as twelve new 5-inch guns and pedestal mounts were shipped to Cavite and fitted on board. The new mounts, of all-steel construction, were far stronger than the older models, which contained considerable amounts of bronze and were difficult to adjust. "The Bureau is satisfied that there will be no more difficulty," noted Rear Admiral Charles O'Neil, chief of the Bureau of Ordnance.[15]

Returning to the United States in 1902, the *Brooklyn* underwent a complete machinery overhaul at New York, during which her boilers and condensers received new tubes. On 3 September 1902, during a fleet problem, the *Brooklyn* ran aground off New Bedford, Massachusetts. She was able to steam to New York under her own power but was placed in dock and taken out of commission. The damaged plates on the inner and outer bottoms were replaced, the midship frames refitted, new decks installed, the ventilating system overhauled, the fore bridge enlarged, and the spars fitted for use with wireless telegraphy. The wireless itself was installed in 1904.

By this time the *Brooklyn* could no longer be rated a first-class vessel of her type, and major refits were necessary. "The *Iowa, Brooklyn, Olympia, Monterey* and *Monadnock* have all become ancient in the matter of batteries," declared Rear Admiral Mason in 1906, "and unless equipped with modern guns, mounts, and sights, can no longer be

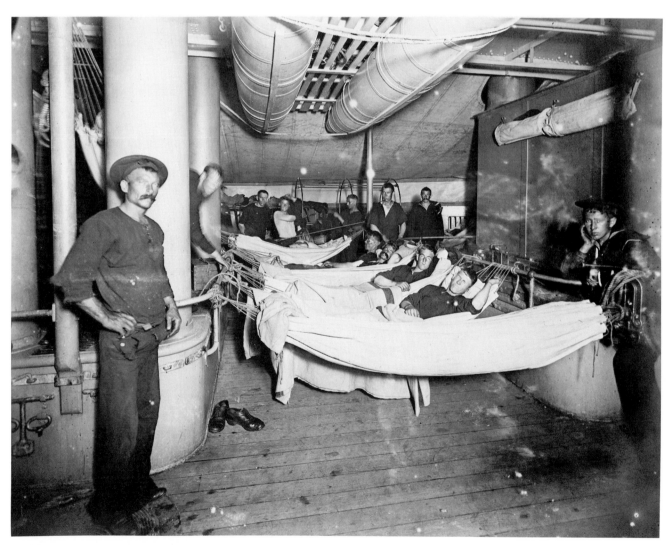

Berthing space in the *Brooklyn*.

considered efficient vessels fit for service."[16] In 1909 the *Brooklyn* was placed out of commission at League Island for a major refit.

The vessel emerged from dockyard hands more or less unaltered in appearance, but significant changes had been made. Two-stage ammunition hoists were fitted to obviate the danger of flashback into the magazines, all turrets were fitted with modern electrical turning engines, and updated fire-control devices were installed. The remaining torpedo tubes were unshipped, as were the flying bridge, after bridge, and bow scroll. The light battery was reduced to four 6-pounders, and as with all vessels, the white and buff color scheme of the New Navy was replaced with the gray war color.

The *Brooklyn* was refitted for the last time in 1918, as the four 5-inch forecastle guns were removed and two 3-inch Mark 2 AA guns were sited on the topgallant deck.

Career

The *Brooklyn* was laid down at William Cramp and Sons, Philadelphia, on 2 August 1893, launched on 2 October 1895, and commissioned at League Island on 1 December 1896 with Captain Francis Cook commanding. Her first service, as befitted the navy's newest vessel, was to represent the United States at the great naval review at Spithead, highlighting Queen Victoria's Diamond Jubilee in the spring of 1897. Upon her return to New York in July, she was assigned to the North Atlantic Squadron under Rear Admiral Montgomery Sicard. On 7 September the squadron assembled at the drill ground off the Virginia capes to perform its evolutions for Assistant Secretary of the Navy Theodore Roosevelt. Following the exercises, Mr. Roosevelt repaired on board and inspected the still controversial electric turret machinery.

The *Brooklyn* cruised the East Coast until 6 February 1898, when she departed from Hampton Roads for a month of Caribbean and West Indies steaming. This assignment was probably a reaction to the explosion of the *Maine* four days earlier. On 6 March, while the *Brooklyn* was anchored in the roads off La Guaira, Venezuela, Captain Cook received a cable from Secretary Long about deteriorating U.S.-Spanish relations: "The situation is getting worse. Proceed without delay to Hampton Roads."[17] Captain Cook ordered steam raised immediately, and the *Brooklyn* arrived at her destination on 14 March. On the twenty-eighth she hoisted the broad pennant of Commodore Winfield Scott Schley, who had been appointed to command the newly formed Flying Squadron.

The Flying Squadron, consisting initially of the *Brooklyn* (flag), the battleships *Massachusetts* and *Texas*, the very fast commerce-raiding cruisers *Columbia* and *Minneapolis*, and the recently purchased British-built *New Orleans*, remained at Hampton Roads on coastal defense duty until 13 May, when it was ordered south to the war zone.

On 18 May, at Key West, Commodore Schley conferred with Rear Admiral Sampson on board the *New York* and received orders to take the Flying Squadron to the south coast of Cuba and begin the blockade of Cienfuegos, where the Spanish squadron had erroneously been reported. The Flying Squadron steamed from Key West on 19 May, the day Admiral Cervera led his four armored cruisers and two destroyers into the harbor of Santiago de Cuba. The command, minus the *Columbia*, *Minneapolis*, and *New Orleans*, all of which had been detached, arrived off Cienfuegos on the twenty-second. Schley's effort was wasted. Receiving orders to steam for Santiago on the twenty-fifth, he lifted the blockade and arrived after a highly questionable delay off Santiago three days later with his bunkers nearly empty.

From that day until the day of battle on 3 July, the *Brooklyn* remained with the blockading fleet. The ships, nearly every major unit of the North Atlantic Squadron, were drawn up in a semicircular formation three miles from the harbor mouth. The fleet flagship, the *New York*, was stationed on the eastern flank, the *Brooklyn* at the western, and the battleships and small cruisers in between. It was tedious duty, and as Commodore Schley observed, "there were many weary and monotonous days of waiting and hoping for activity. To those splendid fellows before the furnaces and standing ready at the engine throttles below decks, where the heat was almost unsufferable, the task of duty was most severe."[18]

The Spanish harbor fortifications were bombarded on the sixth and sixteenth of June. The *Brooklyn* participated in both actions.

At 0930 Sunday, 3 July, came the great moment in the life of the *Brooklyn*. It was "Sunday routine" in the fleet, and the ships were made ready for commanding officers' inspection. In the *Brooklyn*, Captain Cook had ordered "white mustering clothes for the crew and all white for the officers." He was just about to don his own white coat when he "heard the ringing voice of the executive officer calling, 'Clear ship for action!' [He] knew at once from the tone that it meant business."[19]

Although her forward engines were uncoupled, the *Brooklyn* was still the speediest major vessel in the blockading fleet. With her after engines alone she was able to bend on 16 knots during the battle. For the American force this was fortunate, as the Spanish route of escape led straight to her position.

The *Brooklyn* opened fire on the leading ship with her port battery. At this point, both to avoid being rammed by the Spanish flagship *Infanta Maria Teresa* and to set a course westward, parallel to the Spanish, the *Brooklyn* executed her famous 360-degree turn in the midst of the battle and nearly rammed the *Texas*. "As the *Texas* veered westward," wrote her captain, John Philip,

> the *Brooklyn* was plowing up the water at a great rate in a course almost due north, direct for the oncoming Spanish ships. The smoke from our guns began to hang so heavily and densely over the ship that for a few minutes we could see nothing. We might as well have had a blanket tied over our heads. Suddenly a whiff of breeze and a lull in the firing lifted the pall, and there, bearing toward us and across our bows, turning with port helm, with big waves curling over her bows and great clouds of black smoke pouring from her funnels, was the *Brooklyn*. She looked as big as half a dozen *Great Easterns*, and seemed so near that it took our breath away.[20]

The *Texas* was able to back her engines and avoid the catastrophe, which might well have enabled the Spanish to escape; to where was another matter, but they might have lived longer than the few hours now left to them.

With the *Brooklyn* leading, the fleet kept a parallel course to the Spanish ships as one by one the *Infanta Maria Teresa*, *Almirante Oquendo*, and *Vizcaya*, their upperworks a mass of flames, drove themselves onto the beach. In the end, the *Brooklyn* and *Oregon* pounded the *Cristobal Colon* as she "turned into the beach, fired a lee gun, ran ashore, and hauled down her colors."[21] The action which had begun at 0930 was over at 1315. In his report to Admiral Sampson, Commodore Schley noted of the *Brooklyn* that she had been struck "about twenty-five times and she bears in all forty-one scars. The speed cone halyards were shot away, and nearly all the signal halyards. The ensign at the main was so shattered that [when it was hauled] down at the close of the action it fell to pieces."[22] With the exception of two hits on the starboard side belt, one a 6-inch shell that did not explode, and seven hits on the starboard shell plating, which included a 6-inch penetration forward at berth deck level, all the hits and fragments were on the superstructure, funnels, and upperworks. The fleet suffered only two casualties, both in the *Brooklyn*. Chief Yeoman George Ellis, of Commodore Schley's staff, was decapitated as he took the range atop the fore turret and a fireman first class was severely wounded.

At the close of the battle an unidentified vessel, thought to be the *Pelayo*, was reported to the east, and Admiral Sampson ordered the *Brooklyn* and *Indiana* to investigate. The intruder, however, was the

Austrian cruiser *Kaiserin und Königin Maria Theresia*, on her way to Santiago to embark Austrian neutrals. For all practical purposes the naval war had ended. The *Brooklyn* remained in the waters south of Cuba until 14 August, departing from Guantanamo on that date for New York.

The *Brooklyn* served with the North Atlantic Squadron through 16 October 1899, when she left Hampton Roads for her new assignment as flagship of the Asiatic Squadron. Steaming via Gibraltar, Suez, and Singapore, she cast anchor in Manila Bay on 16 December and hoisted the flag of Rear Admiral George Remey. Rear Admiral Kemp Tolley has described what the *Brooklyn* looked like there, a "fat mother hen and a great flock of tiny chicks," the "chicks" being twenty-four gunboats, all but six ex-Spanish ships, prizes of war.[23] There was much activity in the Philippines during this period, as the United States was engaged in a major effort to suppress a nationalist insurrection, a little-known struggle of consummate viciousness that in three years was to take over two hundred thousand lives. On 28 February 1900 the *Brooklyn*'s marine detachment was instrumental in rescuing 522 Spanish troops held prisoner by the insurgents.

For the next four months the *Brooklyn* transited the station until the problems in northern China culminated in the Boxer Rebellion. On 26 June the *Brooklyn* steamed to Taku, anchored off the bar, and landed 318 marines to reinforce the allied force assembling to assault Tientsin. She remained in the area until 11 October and returned to Cavite on 3 November.

The *Brooklyn* had local duty in Philippine waters until mid-April 1901, during which time the ship carried the commission for a naval site in the Philippines to Olongapo and Iloilo to survey the proposed new base. It was at this time that Lieutenants William S. Sims and Yates Stirling joined the *Brooklyn*. Sims was then formulating his theories on "continuous aiming" as the most effective method of hitting a target, one that would eventually be adopted by the navy. That a revision in target practice was necessary was very evident to Stirling. "On arrival in Manila," he noted in his memoir, *Sea Duty*, "I had the forward turret of 8-inch guns. One of my gun pointers was a remarkable shot. He kept destroying the target until I received word not to let him shoot. Target practice was always hurried and not interesting. There was no competition and no incentive to get good results."[24]

On 10 April 1901 the *Brooklyn*, with Admiral Remey on board, cleared Cavite to represent the United States at the opening of the first Australian parliament at Melbourne. Following the ceremonies and a tour of Australian, New Zealand, and Dutch East Indies ports, the *Brooklyn* tied up at Cavite on 7 August. On 26 September she completed her duty with the Asiatic Squadron as Admiral Remey steamed through the northern reaches of his command, touching at Russian, Korean, northern Chinese, and Japanese ports. On 1 March 1902 the ship was detached and returned to the United States, where she rejoined the North Atlantic Squadron.

Her first duties were largely ceremonial. She steamed into Havana harbor on 20 May to participate in the transfer of Cuban sovereignty. The ship was dressed overall, national salutes were fired, the marine guard was paraded, and courtesy calls were paid between the foreign warships present. With Cuba finally an independent state, Governor-General Leonard Wood took passage in the *Brooklyn* and returned to the United States.

On 30 June 1902, under the impetus of Rear Admiral Henry Taylor, chief of the Bureau of Navigation, the North Atlantic Squadron was reorganized into the North Atlantic Fleet; the *Brooklyn* was designated flagship of the Second Squadron, under Rear Admiral Charles Sigsbee. Further ceremonial functions followed in July, as the ship carried the remains of the late British ambassador, Lord Pauncefote, to Southampton.

Major fleet exercises were scheduled for the summer of 1902 off the New England coast, and from 31 July through 7 September the fleet, with Admiral Dewey in command, was put through a great variety of evolutions, including night landings, coastal bombardment, and the forcing of fortified harbors. On 4 September, during an attack on Fort Rodman, the *Brooklyn* touched ground but did not suffer serious damage and was able to continue with the exercise. The ship put into New York for repairs and was taken out of commission on 7 October.

Recommissioned on 7 June 1903 for the newly reformed European Squadron, the *Brooklyn* joined the command and steamed on the twenty-fifth for the Azores and points east. The squadron cruised the station until February 1904, when it was recalled to the drill ground off the Florida coast for target practice. Just before the recall, Rear Admiral C. S. Cotton, commanding the squadron, requested his relief due to ill health, and the command temporarily fell to Captain Harry Knox of the *Brooklyn*.

A further reorganization of the North Atlantic Fleet assigned the *Brooklyn* as flagship of the South Atlantic Squadron, commanded by Rear Admiral French E. Chadwick. Upon assuming her new duties, the *Brooklyn* led the squadron, consisting of the gunboats *Machias* (PG 5), *Castine* (PG 6), and *Marietta* (PG 15), on a cruise to the Canary Islands. When the ships arrived at Teneriffe on 14 May, orders were received to fill with coal and proceed at top speed to Tangier, where the curious Perdicaris Affair was taking place. This farce, in which an American of

On the quarterdeck of the *Brooklyn*. The triple manual wheel was used for emergency steering only.

Greek citizenship, Ion Perdicaris, was kidnapped by a Moroccan bandit, Mouley Achmet Mohammed al Raisuli, was concluded when the French paid ransom to the Sultan of Morocco, who turned it over to al Raisuli; the French were then reimbursed by the United States. The *Brooklyn* and the squadron lay anchored at Tangier until 27 June, when steam was raised for the Azores. For the remainder of the year the *Brooklyn* steamed both sides of the Atlantic, much of the time alone, and paid good will visits to west African and South American ports.

On 1 April 1905 the major Atlantic commands were again reorganized into the Atlantic Fleet, consisting of the First, Second, Third, and Coast Squadrons. Now the *Brooklyn* hoisted Rear Admiral Sigsbee's flag as commander of the Third Division, Second Squadron, comprising the cruisers *Chattanooga* (C 16), *Galveston* (C 17), and *Tacoma* (C 18). On 12 May Admiral Sigsbee led his force to Cherbourg to claim the remains of

John Paul Jones; he returned to Annapolis on 23 July, escorted by eight battleships of the Atlantic Fleet.

January 1906 again saw the *Brooklyn* in the Mediterranean, where on 6 April she received a distress call from the fleet auxiliary *Glacier* (AF 4) and assisted in recovering the floating dry dock *Dewey*. Following the effort, carried out in gale force winds, the *Brooklyn* escorted the *Glacier* and her charge to Port Said.* The *Brooklyn* returned to the United States on 8 May and was placed in reduced commission at League Island. In full commission on 7 July, she spent the next several weeks cruising off the New England coast with units of the Massachusetts naval militia. On 2 August she was again placed in reserve at League Island for one month, being recommissioned on 2 October for service in Cuban waters to protect American interests. On 20 November the ship returned to League Island and remained in reserve through 12 April 1907. The summer and fall of that year were spent at a tercentenary exhibition in Jamestown. The *Brooklyn* upped anchor on 2 December and with the monitor *Miantonomoh* (BM 5) in tow steamed to League Island for decommissioning. She would remain there until 1914.

The *Brooklyn* reentered service in reduced commission as part of the Atlantic Reserve Fleet and served as receiving ship at Boston until mid-March 1915. Placed in full commission, she engaged in neutrality patrols off the northeast coast with Lieutenant Commander Harold Stark, future chief of naval operations, as her engineering officer. In November 1915 she left the Atlantic for the Asiatic station.

On 4 October 1917 the threat of a Bolshevik rising in Vladivostock prompted the United States consul to request a visit by units of the Asiatic Fleet. Rear Admiral Austin Knight, in his flagship *Brooklyn*, arrived in the port on 25 November. According to him, "the men of the *Brooklyn* were given liberty freely. Their bearing was in all respects admirable and the example set the Russian sailors and soldiers, especially in the punctiliousness with which officers of both nations were saluted, had a marked effect on the manners of the Russians themselves."[25] The Soviet view of the visit was somewhat different, as a contemporary Soviet historian has written: "In the heat of the election campaign for the Constituent Assembly, the American cruiser *Brooklyn* anchored in Vladivostock harbor and trained its guns on the city. This was designed, as the Americans saw it, to prevent a Bolshevik victory in the elections."[26]

In July 1918 the *Brooklyn* was again at Vladivostock, this time as

---

*The *Dewey*, a mammoth floating dry dock, was towed by fleet auxiliaries from Solomons, Maryland, halfway around the world to her duty station at Olongapo, a task taking six and a half months.

part of a large interventionist force. Huge stockpiles of war materiel sent by the United States to the Russian imperial forces had accumulated in the city's warehouses, and the *Brooklyn*'s marines were landed to keep the supplies from falling into the hands of the revolutionaries. The *Brooklyn* performed another service when her medical department attended to large numbers of Czech and Russian wounded.

On 9 December, while the ship was coaling at Yokohama, a spontaneous combustion of coal dust caused a serious fire resulting in ten deaths and forty-four injured among the crew. Nine days later at Kobe a gasoline engine exploded aboard, killing seven.

The *Brooklyn* left the Asiatic station in January 1920 for her final duty as flagship, Destroyer Squadrons, Pacific Fleet, in which capacity she served until 15 January, 1921. On 9 March 1921 the *Brooklyn* was decommissioned at Mare Island and stricken from the navy list. She was sold to the breakers on 20 December 1921.

Brooklyn Characteristics

Dimensions

402' 7½" oa x 64' 8½" max beam x 24' mean draft

Displacement

9,125 tons normal, full supply ammunition and stores, normal coal
10,068 tons full load
Tons-per-square-inch immersion at normal draft, 41.80
Metacentric height, 2.5' normal draft

Armament

Original: eight 8-in 35-cal Mk 3; twelve 5-in 40-cal Mk 2 RF; twelve 6-pdr.; four 1-pdr.; four 30-cal mg.; two 3-in field guns; TT, four 18-in Whitehead
1918: eight 8-in 35-cal Mk 3; eight 5-in 40-cal Mk 2 RF; two 3-in Mk 2 AA; four 6-pdr.

Protection

Belt: 3" Harvey
Barbettes: 8" Harvey, front and sides; 4" Harvey, rear
Turrets: 5½" Harvey circumference; 1½" Harvey roofs
Conning tower: 7½" NS
Conning tower tube: 7" NS
5-inch sponsons: 4" NS
8-inch ammunition tubes: 3" NS

Armored deck flats: 3″ MS amidships; 2½″ MS ends
Armored deck slopes: 3″ NS + 3″ MS amidships; 3″ MS ends
Cofferdam: cocoafibre cellulose

Machinery

Engines: four sets 3-cyl VTE
Boilers: five DE Fox firetube; two SE Fox firetube
Indicated horsepower: 16,000
IHP generated on trials: 18,425
Trial speed: 21.9 kts
Coal capacity: 900 tons normal; 1,461 tons maximum
Steaming radius: 6,088 miles at 10 kts
Propellers: twin shaft, three-bladed

Complement

41 officers, 550 men (as commissioned)

Contract price (hull and machinery)

$2,986,000

Total cost

$4,423,790

Brooklyn *Engineering Characteristics*

No. of engines	4
No. of cylinders, each engine	3
Diameter of high-pressure starboard forward cylinder	31.94″
Diameter remainder high-pressure cylinders	31.97″
Diameter intermediate-pressure port forward cylinder	46.97″
Diameter remainder intermediate-pressure cylinders	46.94″
Diameter low-pressure starboard forward cylinder	71.94″
Diameter low-pressure starboard after cylinder	72″
Diameter low-pressure port forward cylinder	71.97″
Diameter low-pressure port after cylinder	71.94″
Stroke of all pistons	42″
No. of main steam condensers	4
Combined cooling surface	23,300 sq. ft.
No. of firetube boilers	5 DE, 2 SE

Heating surface per DE boiler   4 at 4,594 sq. ft.
     1 at 5,268 sq. ft.

Heating surface per SE boiler   2,335 sq. ft.

Total heating surface, all boilers   33,432 sq. ft.

Grate surface per DE boiler   4 at 168.6 sq. ft.
     1 at 173.2 sq. ft.

Grate surface per SE boiler   84.3'

Total grate surface, all boilers   1,016 sq. ft.

Ratio heating to grate surface   32.91:1

Working pressure, all boilers   160 psi

4

The
Pennsylvania Class

Introduction

The first three vessels of this class—the *Pennsylvania* (ACR 4), *West Virginia* (ACR 5), and *California* (ACR 6)—were authorized under a congressional act of 3 March 1899. The latter three—the *Colorado* (ACR 7), *Maryland* (ACR 8), and *South Dakota* (ACR 9)—were authorized under an act of 7 June 1900. Both appropriations stipulated vessels of about 12,000 tons, "carrying the heaviest armor and most powerful ordnance for vessels of their class."[1] Cost, excluding armament and armor, was limited to four million dollars per ship. In each bill Congress specified that one vessel be built on the Pacific coast.

The contracts for the East Coast hulls, the *Pennsylvania* and *Colorado*, were awarded to William Cramp and Sons, the bids being $3,890,000 and $3,780,000 respectively; Newport News Shipbuilding and Drydock won the *West Virginia* and *Maryland* at $3,885,000 and $3,775,000. Union Iron Works of San Francisco, with bids of $3,800,000 and $3,775,000, received the contracts for the *California* and *South Dakota*. The disparity between construction costs in the building yards was due to the design circular ordering the first three hulls to be sheathed and coppered.

The first ship of the class, the *Pennsylvania*, was originally to be named *Nebraska*, and the second battleship of the *Virginia* class (BBs 13–17) was to receive the former designation. On 7 March 1901 the names were exchanged.

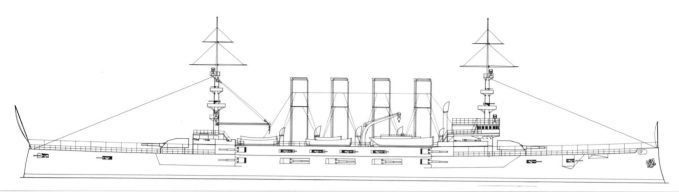

The USS *Pennsylvania* (ACR 4). The *Pennsylvania* showing her original boat-handling gear. The gaff boom was replaced by two gooseneck cranes.

The *Pennsylvania* represented a new generation of U.S. cruiser design which eschewed French concepts of hull form and main armament in wing positions for an all-centerline installation and provided a secondary battery commensurate with the weight and dimensions of the hull. It can be said that the class was the progenitor of the battle cruiser, and for this reason was subject to a fair amount of criticism. The armament and protection of the *Pennsylvania*-class ships were considered insufficient for hulls of their dimensions.

In concept the mission of the armored cruiser had changed since the laying down of the *New York*. In U.S. theory its primary role was no longer that of flagship on distant stations or destroyer of commerce raiders; instead it was intended to form the van of the battle fleet in high-speed squadrons. In this role the cruiser had to be large and seaworthy and maintain a relatively strong battery to drive in an enemy's scouts and van and engage his line in the opening phases of a fleet action. The *Pennsylvania* class more or less met these criteria, but at a large sacrifice in protection and a moderate one in main armament.

When completed, the six vessels maintained a deep-load displacement of 15,138 tons, only 900 tons less than the *Virginia*-class battleships. Yet as cruisers they were nearly 63 feet longer—the extra length was necessary for greater speed—and carried a crew of 832 officers and men, 20 more than the battleships carried. Although the offensive capability of the two types cannot be fairly compared because their roles were completely divergent, it is worth noting that the *Virginias*, on a marginally larger displacement, mounted four 12-inch, eight 8-inch, and twelve 6-inch guns, whereas the *Pennsylvania* class carried four 8-inch and fourteen 6-inch guns. Protection was also much weaker in the cruisers, which had a maximum main belt thickness of 6 inches, while the battleships had an 11-inch main belt. It was here that the main compromise was made to achieve the 22-knot contract speed, 3

The *Pennsylvania* immediately after commissioning. Note that she has yet to receive her secondary battery. The high ventilator cowl immediately abaft the bridge served the dynamo rooms and was a topside feature of the *Pennsylvania* and *Colorado* only.

knots more than the speed of the *Virginia* class. The *Pennsylvania*s represented, therefore, a series of compromises where certain "cruiser" features such as speed, great radius of action, and moderately heavy battery were stressed at the expense of "battleship" qualities, i.e., the heaviest armament and most comprehensive scheme of protection to be expected on vessels the size, weight, and cost of the class.

A leading critic of the *Pennsylvania* design, Commander David W. Taylor, later rear admiral and chief constructor from 1914 to 1922, compared the merits of the two types and came soundly down on the side of the battleship: "The question at once arises whether it is worth while to continue to build armored cruisers inferior to battleships in so many respects and superior to them in so few. . . . It would appear that the time is now about ripe for the settlement of the question whether the type shall survive or be merged into the battleship proper."[2]

But they were fine ships nevertheless and served well throughout their careers. The *Pennsylvania* and *South Dakota* remained in commission until 1931 and 1927, respectively. Until 1914 the class formed the backbone of the Pacific Fleet and projected the United States' growing involvement in Asian and Latin American affairs. All were fitted as flagships and all served at one time or another in that role. With the exception of their role in World War I, their service was that of preserv-

Eugene Ely lands aboard the USS *Pennsylvania*, 18 January 1911. (Naval Aviation Museum)

ing the peace by keeping a strong presence in the Pacific at a time of Japanese expansion.

Hull

The *Pennsylvania* "is designed upon noble lines," wrote the special correspondent to the *Army and Navy Register*.[3] And indeed she was. For until the launching of the *Tennessee,* the *Pennsylvania* and her sisters presented the longest hulls yet to slide down the ways for the New Navy.

The hull length between perpendiculars was a standard 502 feet, the load waterline breadth designed at 69 feet 6 inches. However, a decision during the early phases of construction not to sheathe and copper, plus the individual peculiarities of three different building yards, caused variations in these measurements. Thus the *Pennsylvania* and *Colorado* maintained an overall length of 504 feet 0.5 inch and an extreme beam of 69 feet 6.5 inches; the *West Virginia* and *Maryland*, 503 feet 10.25 inches x 69 feet 6.5 inches; and the *California* and *South Dakota*, 503 feet 11 inches x 69 feet 10.5 inches. Normal- and full-load displacements were also at variance by up to 100 tons. Normal draft for all vessels was 24 feet 1 inch, with a full load draft of 26 feet 6 inches.

Original specifications and the congressional appropriations bill of the 1899 session called for the hulls of the *Pennsylvania, West Virginia,* and *California* "to be sheathed and coppered."[4] The three vessels authorized by the 1900 Congress were to be unsheathed. However, in January 1900 the Board on Construction, with Rear Admiral Charles O'Neil, chief of the Bureau of Ordnance, Chief Constructor Philip Hichborn, Engineer in Chief George Melville, and the chiefs of the Bureau of Equipment and the Office of Naval Intelligence, advised Secretary Long to rescind the sheathing and coppering specifications and petition Con-

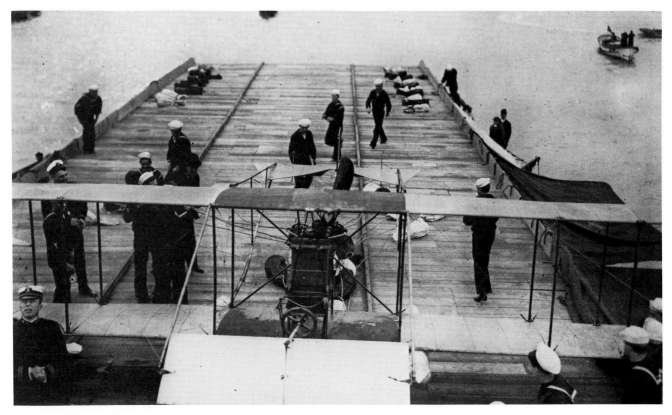

Ely's aircraft immediately after landing on the *Pennsylvania*. Note the sandbags dragged aft by the undercarriage. (Naval Aviation Museum)

gress to amend the appropriations bill with an incidental saving of nearly a half million dollars.

Sheathing and coppering the hulls had been proposed by the chief constructor to retard marine growth on the ship's bottoms and thus allow a ship to dock less frequently. This was common practice in vessels fitted for extended or tropical cruising but quite rare in large armored hulls. The board, with the chief constructor objecting and filing a minority report, listed its concerns to the secretary. Besides the savings in cost these included the difficulty of installation, with which the shipbuilders had little or no experience; the difficulty and expense of performing underwater repairs; the additional weight of 400 tons that could be better used for enhancing protection, ammunition allowances, or bunkerage; the necessity of having to pierce the armored belt; and finally, the fact that the best wood for sheathing, East India teak, was not grown in the United States. The bill and specifications were amended, and all vessels were completed unsheathed.

The flush-decked hulls comprised 124 frames, spaced four feet apart throughout, except at the extremities of the vessel, forward of frame 6 and aft of frame 117, where the frames were spaced two feet apart. The double bottom extended from frame 20 aft to frame 102 and contained eight compartments for reserve feedwater.

Watertight integrity was maintained by 279 watertight compartments, with critical spaces such as firerooms, engine rooms, and magazines sealed by the new Long-Arm door system. It was pneumatically operated and electrically controlled from the conning and after signal towers, and the ship could be sealed in a matter of seconds. During final acceptance trials, when the vessels had been in commission for up to a year, it was found that the control armatures tended to burn out, and the worm and rack on the door itself was prone to jamming. The

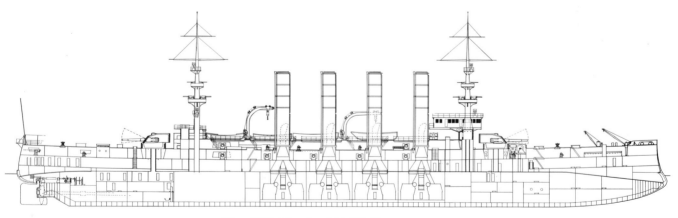

The USS *Maryland* (ACR 8)

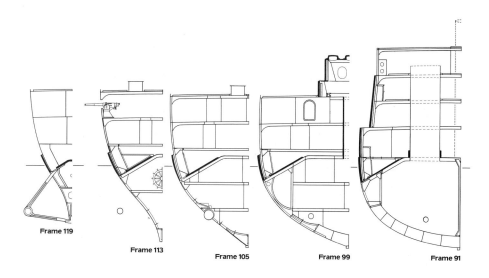

Frame 119   Frame 113   Frame 105   Frame 99   Frame 91

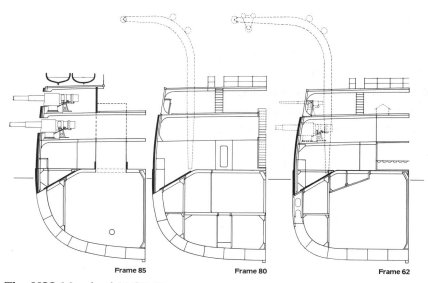

Frame 85   Frame 80   Frame 62

The USS *Maryland* (ACR 8)

manufacturers strongly disagreed with this conclusion and placed the blame squarely on the crews for mishandling the equipment. "This tendency developed in the *West Virginia, Maryland,* and *Pennsylvania* during the first week or two of their service," wrote the president of the Long-Arm System Company to William Cramp and Sons. "Our experts found over a bushel of material, including socks, dime novels, scrubbing brushes, cakes of soap, jumper shirts, overalls, and waste rags

Ely taking off from the *Pennsylvania*. (Naval Aviation Museum)

stowed back of the door plates in the firerooms."[5] Captain J. H. Dayton, president of the trials board, found no reason to alter its conclusions.

Much of the ship was fireproofed. All joiner work above the armored deck was fireproofed wood, as well as all of the woodwork that was not portable and could not be dispensed with in time of war. The teak armor backing, the woodwork of the chart and pilot house, and the woodwork below the protective deck were not fireproofed. But even this amount of fireproofing was considered insufficient, and the wooden planking on the boat deck was thought "a serious . . . defect in design . . . which should not exist in any modern vessel built for military purposes."[6]

In 1900 a suggestion was made to fit the class with the new stockless anchor now coming into service with the British and German navies. But the ground tackle was the old stocked type that had been in use for centuries. The bower anchor, weighing 8.5 tons, with chain links 2.6 inches thick, was handled by the windlass located just beneath the muzzles of the fore turret and two cathead derricks on the forecastle.

As befitted vessels designated flagships, the *Pennsylvania*s were finished with two complete bridges at either end of the superstructure, each maintaining its own armored control station—a conning tower forward and a signal tower aft. The trials board of the *Colorado* found the conning tower design a serious impediment to ship handling.

The ships carried full complements of twenty-one boats, composed of one 50-foot picket boat, two steam cutters of 36 and 33 feet, two 36-foot launches, five 30-foot cutters, one 30-foot admiral's barge, two 30-foot whaleboats, one 30-foot whaleboat captain's gig, two 20-foot dinghies, two dinghies of 16 and 14 feet, one 12-foot sidecleaning punt, and two Carley floats. The outfit was worked by two 15- and two 10-ton gooseneck cranes and eight sets of main deck davits.

The ships were good seakeepers, although their 7.2:1 length-to-beam ratio, matched with their metacentric height of 2.66 feet, made them roll somewhat. On her way from New York to Boston the *Colorado*, encountering 6-foot-high, 200-foot-long swells, completed 50 degrees of roll in 11 seconds. Her pitching, it was noted, could submerge her forward to the line of the main deck. Near the stem she took on a great deal of spray, though the sea had little effect on her speed. Her overall performance was considered excellent.

Armament

The lessons of the Spanish-American War proved the suitability of the 8-inch gun as the primary caliber for large cruisers. In numbers it had dominated both fleet actions of the war, and it had kept up a rapid rate of fire commensurate with its weight; moreover, its bursting charge caused frightful damage. At Manila Bay, when Admiral Montojo sortied with his flagship, *Reina Christina*, into the teeth of the American fire, he was subjected to such pounding that he immediately ordered the helm put hard over. Just as he did so, an 8-inch shell from the *Olympia* struck the *Reina Christina* squarely in the stern and drove through the length of the ship, rending through every obstruction, wrecking the aft boiler, and blowing open the deck in its explosion. This one shell proved the flagship's fate.

At Santiago the Spanish ships were larger, heavier, more modern vessels. Their destruction was not so much due to the accuracy of American gunnery, which was dreadful—only 123 hits of all calibers were achieved and six thousand rounds were fired—but to the raging fires on the Spanish upperworks and battery decks caused by the profusion of wood and other flammables that had not been jettisoned. However, of the hits scored—discounting those from 5-inch guns and smaller—eleven were from the 8-inch guns of the *Brooklyn* and *Oregon*.

When it came time to design the armament of the *Pennsylvania* class, the decision to mount an 8-inch battery came quite naturally. Not only did the battery perform relatively well in action; it was also a weapon common in the U.S. Navy, being already mounted in its various modifications and calibers on ten cruisers and six battleships (not counting the five concurrently designed *Virginia*-class ships, each of which carried eight 8-inch guns as an intermediate battery). When presented to Congress for authorization, the circular called for "four 8-inch guns, in pairs, in two electrically controlled elliptical, balanced turrets, having inclined port plates, one forward and one aft, on the line of the keel, and having an arc of fire of not less than 270 degrees."[7] The chief constructor, Philip Hichborn, thought this arrangement represented the latest and best practice in warship design.[8]

Glenn Curtiss and aircraft being hoisted aboard the *Pennsylvania*. The angles of the various strakes of vertical armor are clearly defined. Note especially the outer portion of the citadel in wake of the main deck 6-inch gun. (Naval Aviation Museum)

Given the high freeboard of the class, the battery had good command; both forward and after pairs had horizontal axes 26 feet three inches above the waterline. Problems with blast effects were standard, and tests aboard the *Colorado*, just prior to commissioning, resulted in cautions against axially firing the after turret at zero elevation. The guns, fired three times in salvo, sprang the quarterdeck planking, caused measurable structural vibration, and might have damaged the deck beams had firing continued. When the after turret was fired at its extreme angle of forward train, the after bridge was damaged. In identical tests with the forward turret, axial firing at zero elevation sprang the deck planking but caused no other damage, as the forecastle had been strengthened with stouter scantlings to accommodate the anchor windlass and ground tackle. However, the turret in its extreme angle of after train did much damage to the bridge and chart house. Hull stress was measured when the full 8-inch battery was electrically fired in five simultaneous broadside salvos. The hull bore up well, and no undue stress was noted. During this firing several racks holding hand grenades were torn from their bulkheads and scattered their contents, which broke up on impact but did not explode. New racks of a stronger construction were installed immediately after the *Colorado* returned to the yard. In its report, the Board of Inspection and Survey gave the following summary: "If one 8-inch gun is trained more than 2½ points forward or abaft the beam in the direction of the superstructure, considerable minor damage results. When extreme angles of train are reached, considerable damage [is done] to metal doors, air ports are blown into adjacent spaces and compartments wrecked."[9]

But the Mark 5 8-inch and 40-caliber gun had serious design flaws. Following the war with Spain, the navy began replacing its old-style fast-burning black powder with the new slow-burning "smokeless" brown type. Because of its slower combustion, the new propellant permitted a much higher muzzle velocity that increased range and hitting power. The pressures built up in the bore during ignition increased as the projectile traveled its length, and the charge was not finally blown out until the projectile cleared the muzzle. To handle the new powder, guns would have to be strengthened, and the old method of hooping the barrel short of the muzzle was not sufficient. On 22 June 1907 this lesson was driven home at the target range off Chefoo, when the *Colorado* blew off the muzzle of one of her 8-inch guns. The Bureau of Ordnance attributed the accident to "wave pressure" whose cause was unknown. But the Pacific Fleet commander, Rear Admiral Joseph Hemphill, explained the problem as "imperfect ignition of charge, . . . driving [a] considerable portion of [the] powder up the bore until it ignited at [the] muzzle."[10] All Mark 5 guns were subsequently removed from the class, rehooped to the muzzle, and placed in reserve; the vessels were refitted with the stronger Mark 6 45-caliber weapon.

The main armament was mounted in two Mark 12 balanced turrets with inclined faces, a great invention of Chief Constructor Philip Hichborn's. The *Pennsylvania*s were the first U.S. cruisers to adopt this advance in turret design. The old cylindrical type, mounted in the *New York, Brooklyn, Olympia,* and eight battleships, including the old *Maine,* had the disadvantage of the enlarged gun ports peculiar to turrets with a vertical face. With the short barrels of the earlier 30- and 35-caliber pieces, any reduction in port size would materially decrease elevation and consequent range. The inclined face of the Mark 12 turret and its successors through the post–World War II period permitted a gun port only slightly larger than the diameter of the piece, with a far greater increase in elevation. The "balance" of the turret was provided by its elliptical rather than its cylindrical shape, the after portion of the turret, overhanging the barbette, giving balance to the great weight exerted by

Pennsylvania during overhaul at Bremerton, late 1911. Her military foremast has been unshipped, and the new lattice mast is yet incomplete. The vessel moored alongside is the protected cruiser *Charleston* (C 22). As she is still in white and buff and displaying a bow scroll, she is probably in a decommissioned state.

the turret guns when trained abeam. When the turret guns were trained outboard in earlier low-freeboard ships, especially the three *Indiana*-class battleships, the hulls heeled considerably, frequently dipping muzzles into the sea and causing uneven stress on the roller path. These problems were virtually eliminated by the balanced turret. In tests conducted at the naval proving ground at Indian Head, Maryland, its performance was noted as very satisfactory.

The turrets were maneuvered electrically and by hand. In tests aboard the *California*, 15 minutes were needed to bring the turret through its 270 degrees using hand power, 45 seconds using electrical power. Electricity also served the ammunition hoists, rammers, and elevating gear.

Each vessel carried five hundred rounds of 8-inch ammunition, which was delivered at the rate of one complete round of powder and shot to each gun every 50 seconds.

The secondary battery of fourteen 6-inch 50-caliber Mark 8 RF guns comprised an extremely potent outfit and in total weight of both broadsides, 1,470 pounds, outclassed the intermediate and secondary batteries of most contemporary battleships.

The Mark 8 gun was a new weapon, fitted not only in the *Pennsylvania* class but in the *Virginia* class and the protected cruisers of the *St. Louis* class (C 20) as well. Four guns were mounted in the corners of the main deck superstructure casemate, sponsoned out for axial fire, and pointed through an extreme angle of 55 degrees in opposite train. At just 23 feet above the waterline, they could be worked in any sort of weather, an advantage over most British-designed contemporaries, which had notoriously low waterline batteries. The ten remaining guns were mounted in broadside on the gun deck, behind embrasured ports 14 feet 4 inches from the waterline and pointing through 110 degrees of train.

The 6-inch guns were installed on the Mark 10 mount introduced in the *Maine* class (BB 10). "It is simple and strong," reported Rear Admiral Charles O'Neil, chief of the Bureau of Ordnance, "all parts are accessible, it has elevating gear on both sides and friction brakes in both the elevating and training gear, it works easily, one man being able to train and elevate the gun with facility."[11] But apparently it was not an easy mount to manufacture: Fully 33 percent of the Mark 10s were rejected by the bureau because they had faulty recoil slides.

Ammunition stowage permitted twenty-eight hundred rounds. These were supplied to the guns by electric hoists, which provided one complete round every ten seconds to each gun.

Both 8-inch and 6-inch guns were fitted with the telescopic sight, an invention that can largely be attributed to Bradley Fiske. Some other types were also installed. None of these, however, met the approval of the conservative Bureau of Ordnance, which also fitted the old open bar sight perfected by Sir Philip Broke, RN, one hundred years before. According to the bureau, the bar sight was far more effective than the telescopic sight. Admiral O'Neil granted the telescopic sight was "ideal under ideal conditions," but he doubted if it was as "serviceable for quick firing in action as the open bar sight." It was left to individual commanding officers to select the method of gunlaying in battle.[12]

Target practice and gunnery training with subcaliber gear was encouraged. Each 8- and 6-inch gun was supplied a 1-pounder barrel with attachments, and "great latitude in the expenditure of ammunition for subcaliber practice" became bureau policy.[13]

Officially, the antitorpedo armament of the class consisted of eighteen 3-inch 50-caliber RF guns, twelve 3-pounders, four automatic 1-pounders, and four single-shot 1-pounders. The statistic of eighteen

3-inch guns is given initially in the design circular and repeated in every departmental publication and all commercially produced data; in actuality, only sixteen 3-inch guns were carried. Four were mounted in pairs on each gun deck broadside, well forward and aft. The outboard guns were in small sponsons, the inner pair behind hinged ports. The remaining eight pieces were mounted four per side in the main deck casemate. As for the missing pair of guns, a sketch of the *California* in the 1900 *Annual Report* shows three guns forward on the gun deck, as does the 1905 *Jane's Fighting Ships*. Various other departmental and semi-official sources depict the guns behind shields on either side of the lower forebridge. An examination of photographs shows that there was no additional piece on the gun deck and that the guns on the lower forebridge were a pair of 6-pounders. The latter are nowhere listed as part of the class armament, yet their existence is unquestioned.

The 3-pounders were positioned at the corners of the boat deck, six at either end. Two automatic 1-pounders were placed in each lower fighting top, while the upper tops contained the single-shot 1-pounders. Two 3-inch field guns and two machine guns were the province of the marine detachment for use with the ship's landing force.

The decision to equip the class as well as nineteen battleships then building or authorized and the *Tennessee* class with a torpedo outfit was not made until 1904. Great things were expected of the locomotive torpedo when it was introduced by Sir Charles Whitehead in the mid-1870s, and its first successful employment by the Russian torpedo launches *Sinop* and *Chesma*, when they ran the defenses of Batum on 26 January 1878 and sank the Turkish steam frigate *Intibakeh*, seemed to bear out the claims of its enthusiasts.

Practical U.S. experience with the locomotive torpedo was nil. In the war with Spain, U.S. torpedo boats were mainly employed as dispatch vessels. Torpedo outfits had been fitted in large ships since the time of the old *Maine* and *Texas* and had been provided in every battleship as well as the *New York, Brooklyn, Olympia,* the big commerce-raiding cruisers *Columbia* and *Minneapolis,* and several small cruisers. None had fired a torpedo in the war, and in all cases where a bow tube had been fitted the torpedo flat had been almost constantly flooded. All bow tubes were subsequently unshipped and the exit ports plated over. By 1903 the Bureau of Ordnance could report that torpedoes were most effective on vessels specifically designed for them, such as torpedo boats and submarine boats. Their value in large vessels was "problematical."[14]

Exercises were conducted at the Naval War College in 1903 using two simulated fleets of eight capital ships steaming in parallel columns, with ship intervals of 400 yards. It was concluded that the fleet armed with torpedoes possessed a decided advantage over its opponent. Critics led by the chief of the Bureau of Ordnance opined that "in war games an arbitrary and possibly a fictitious value is given to torpedoes, and that vessels having them are rated as superior to those not having them, other things being equal."[15]

A compromise was eventually reached, and the class was equipped with two submerged torpedo tubes of the British Elswick pattern. The flat was located in one athwartships compartment, just forward of the forward 8-inch magazine, between the platform and the armored deck. Each vessel carried eight Mark 2, 5-meter, 18-inch Whitehead torpedoes having a range of 4,000 yards.

Protection

The protection scheme for the ships of this class as well as for all contemporary armored cruisers displacing more than 12,000 tons was roundly criticized as being insufficient. Because of their role the design equation for these ships had been skewed in favor of speed; none made less than 21 knots. As the type developed in the early years of the century, its role broadened from trade protection and flagship on distant stations to concentration in squadrons as the high-speed van of the battle fleet. In many ships displacements nearly doubled until they reached battleship tonnage, necessary for the hulls to carry extremely powerful engineering plants. The idea that very high speed in lieu of adequate protection was a satisfactory compromise had been criticized as far back as 1895 by Lieutenant Albert Niblack in reference to the 23 + knot *Columbia* and *Minneapolis*.

By 1910 the armored cruiser had reached the zenith of its development. All first-line vessels displaced in excess of 12,000 tons, exceeded 22 knots in speed, and had relatively powerful batteries; but with very few exceptions all were fitted with armored belts of six-inch thickness or less, and none maintained an armored deck thicker than four inches on the slopes.

In World War I the type was to pay dearly for this lack of protection. On 1 November, at the Battle of Cape Coronel, the British armored cruisers *Good Hope* (1902) and *Monmouth* (1903), silhouetted against the setting sun, were sent to the bottom with all hands by the 8-inch guns of the armored cruisers *Scharnhorst* (1908) and *Gneisenau* (1908). On 8 December 1914, in the First Battle of the Falklands, these ships were in turn sunk by the overwhelming superiority of the battle cruisers *Invincible* (1908) and *Inflexible* (1908). The battle cruiser, offspring of the armored cruiser and progenitor of the fast battleship, had arrived.

When the designs of the *Pennsylvania* class had been firmed, criti-

Speed trials of the *West Virginia*, November 1904. Her 3-inch guns and minor calibers are not yet fitted.

cism was not long in coming. The eminent theoretician and chief constructor of the Royal Danish Navy, Commander William Hovgaard, considered "the armored area restricted."[16] Rear Admiral David Taylor, in his comparison of the merits of the *Maryland* and the battleship *Virginia*, stated that the side armor on the former "is not only thinner, but has less extent, absolutely, and very much less extent, relatively, considering the size of each vessel. From the waterline to the main deck the *Maryland* has 4,355 square feet, [i.e.,] 45 percent [of her is] covered by armor; the *Virginia* has 4,775 square feet, [i.e.,] 60 percent [of her is] covered by armor. The total weight of armor on the *Maryland* is a little over 2,000 tons, as compared [to] more than 3,400 on the *Virginia*."[17]

The armor contracts for the six vessels, as well as for the three *Maine*-class battleships, five *Virginia*-class battleships, and three *St. Louis*–class protected cruisers, were signed on 28 November 1900 for a total of 37,690 tons of Krupp and Harveyized armor. Carnegie received the contract for the *Pennsylvania* and *Colorado*, Bethlehem for the *California* and *South Dakota*; they shared the *West Virginia* and *Maryland*. At $420 per ton for Krupp armor and $400 per ton for Harvey, they were lucrative contracts.

As the combined manufacturing capacity of Carnegie and Bethlehem was only 7,500 tons per year, it was a foregone conclusion that delays in manufacture and delivery would result. "At the insistence of the Department," reported the chief of the Bureau of Ordnance, "the manufacturers are making preparations to increase their output from 10,000 to 12,000 tons per year, in order to complete deliveries under the present contracts, and for additional vessels to be appropriated."[18] The promises remained just that. It was evident by 1901 that the armor contractors would not deliver in time, and William Moody, in his first report as secretary of the navy, announced that "the Department's attention has been specifically called to the probability of two years' delay in the completion of the five battleships of the *Virginia* class and the six armored cruisers of the *Pennsylvania* class. . . . The capacity of the manufacturers of armor is insufficient to provide the amount of armor required for these vessels within the period of time allotted for their completion."[19]

The shipbuilders also came under fire. "Considerably more armor could have been delivered under these contracts," reported the chief of the Bureau of Ordnance, "had it been possible to get the armor drawings from the shipbuilders, to whom frequent application has been made. The vessels were contracted for 18 to 20 months ago, and in some instances no armor drawings have yet been received, and in others only those for a trifling quantity."[20]

The delay could be partially explained by the methods used to manufacture Krupp armor, which had replaced Harveyized as the main component of protection. Requiring only 5.75 inches of thickness—as opposed to 7.25 inches of Harvey, 12 inches of compound, or 15 inches

Newly commissioned, the *West Virginia* flies the two-star flag of Rear Admiral Willard Brownson. It is curious to note that she carries a new stockless anchor, when later photos show the old stocked type.

of common iron—as proof against 6-inch armor-piercing shell, Krupp armor was forged under license by every armor manufacturer in the world.

In two tests of the Krupp armor in 1901, the results met expectations. A 6-inch Carnegie-manufactured plate, representing a 250-ton side armor patch for the Russian battleship *Alexander III* (1903), for which Carnegie supplied the armor, was tested at Indian Head. Three 6-inch armor-piercing rounds with muzzle velocities ranging from 1,910 to 1,930 fps were fired. None penetrated farther than 2 inches, and all broke up into fragments.

At the Krupp test range at Meppen, in Hanover, a 5.9-inch plate for the Dutch coastal defense ship *De Ruyter* (1902) was struck by three 5.9-inch armor-piercing shells at muzzle velocities of 1,854 to 2,362 fps. Only on the last shot and at maximum velocity did the shell penetrate the plate, and that without fracture.

In its distribution in the *Pennsylvania* class, all armor 5 inches thick and more was Krupp armor and all thinner than 5 inches a combination of Harveyized and untreated nickel steel. The armored belt ran the entire length of the hull, having a uniform width of 7 feet 6 inches and protruding 12 inches above the waterline at the ship's deep draft load of 26 feet 6 inches. For a distance of 244 feet, abreast the boiler and

The *West Virginia*, c. 1909. The white and buff of the New Navy is replaced by grey war color. In this photograph she carries an old stocked anchor.

machinery spaces, it maintained a maximum thickness of 6 inches, tapering to 5 inches at the lower edge. Forward of frame 30 and aft of frame 95 the belt narrowed to a uniform thickness of 3.5 inches of Harveyized steel to the extremities of the vessel. Side protection on the belt amidships was carried upward to the main deck in a uniform thickness of 5 inches and covered the 6-inch battery. The side armor was closed at the ends, frames 42 and 92, by transverse bulkheads of 4-inch Harveyized steel extending down to the armored deck, forming an armored citadel. Inboard of the citadel corners, the 5-inch protection was extended up to boat deck level, forming individual bastions for the main deck 6-inch guns.

The face plates of the Mark 12 turrets were sheathed in 6.5 inches of Krupp armor, their sides in 6 inches. The roofs were 1.5 inches of nickel steel. The shallow barbettes, which were carried only to the main deck, were covered with 6 inches of Krupp steel, the ammunition tubes with 3 inches of Harveyized steel. This arrangement, leaving the installation weakly protected at its base, was severely criticized by Rear Admiral Francis Bowles, who had relieved Philip Hichborn as chief constructor in 1902. He felt that

> the 8-inch guns are not sufficiently . . . protected. The barbette is only carried to the main deck, below which . . . it is only continued in a narrow armored ammunition tube. Moreover, the small diameter of the ammunition tube leaves the entire structure, which carries the barbette and the roller path, and thus the guns and hood, entirely unprotected. A shell bursting against the armor tube or anywhere underneath the barbette can hardly fail to break down or dislocate the roller path.[21]

On the gun deck the 6-inch guns were separated by 2.5-inch nickel steel splinter screens. The 3-inch guns in the main deck casemate were protected by 2 inches of nickel steel and separated by 1-inch nickel steel screens.

Two control towers were fitted. The conning tower forward was covered with 9 inches of Krupp armor at its circumference, with 1.5 inches of nickel steel on the roof and 5 inches of Krupp forming the conning tower tube. The signal tower at the after end of the boat deck had 5 inches of Krupp armor on its sides and 1.5 inches of nickel steel on the roof.

The flats of the armored deck, running the entire length of the hull, were 1.5-inch nickel steel, the slopes 4-inch nickel steel.

Continuing the policy adopted in the 1890s, 66 tons of corn pith cellulose packed the cofferdam inboard of the belt.

A view of the *West Virginia*, c. 1914. The military foremast and wooden bridgework have been replaced by a modern lattice structure, and the after bridge and boat cranes have been unshipped.

Machinery

The propulsion machinery in the *Pennsylvania* class was the most powerful afloat and outclassed anything yet fitted in a U.S. man-of-war. If George Melville was able to report a decade earlier that the propulsion plant of the *New York* had added 17 percent to the horsepower of the fleet, he could have reported in 1902 that the six vessels of the class added a full 26 percent to the horsepower of the fleet; and if the figures tabulated on the ships' trials were used, the percentage would increase to nearly 32 percent.

The very high 22-knot contract speed was achieved with two inverted, four-cylinder, triple-expansion engines, sited in separate watertight compartments on either side of a centerline bulkhead. The four-cylinder engine, which was the ultimate improvement in triple-expansion technology, was first installed in the battleship *Missouri* (BB 11). It made use of two low-pressure cylinders, which increased the power of the engine, decreased vibration at high speeds, and balanced the distribution of stress along the length of the crankshaft. The engines in the *Pennsylvania* class had a combined output of 23,000 IHP at 120 rpm, and it was not until the battleships *Delaware* (BB 28) and *North Dakota* (BB 29) joined the fleet in 1910 (the *North Dakota* was powered with Curtis steam turbines) that more powerful plants were fitted.

As ordered, the engines and propellers of the *Pennsylvania* and *Colorado* were to have outboard turning, while the remaining four vessels were ordered with inboard-turning machinery. The controversy of outboard- versus inboard-turning engines had simmered since the advent of the twin-screwed vessel in the late 1870s. As George Melville saw it, "The question as to which form of installation gives the best maneuvering power has been touched upon several times during the past 20 years. There is no information extant, that for deep-draught vessels, there is any resulting advantage for either form of installation."[22] However, each method had its adherents, and those who favored the inboard-turning screw could point to fractionally higher speed as an advantage. The opposing outboard-turning school countered with the fact that inboard-turning vessels lacked maneuverability at low speeds and were difficult to dock without the aid of tugs.

In the event, only the *West Virginia* and *Maryland* were completed with inboard-turning screws, while the *California* and *South Dakota* were modified for outboard turning when well under construction. Their hulls were launched without their engines in place.

Very early in their careers the *Maryland* and *Colorado* experienced serious problems with their high-pressure cylinders and pistons. A new deep-water trials course off Rockland, Maine, had to be tested, and the *Maryland* was selected to run a second set of speed trials. However, she was prevented from doing so after developing a crack in one of the high-pressure crank pins, and the *Colorado* was chosen instead. On the day of the trials, one of that vessel's high-pressure cylinder heads was found to be defective, and as no spares were available a cylinder head was removed from the *Pennsylvania* and fitted in the *Colorado*.

The engines were given automatic lubrication. Storage tanks holding 3,000 gallons of lube oil were put at the after end of each engine room, the oil being pumped into small 25-gallon feed tanks and thence to the oil boxes on the main engines; the actual lubrication was accomplished by gravity feed. During the trials of the *California* the system refused to operate as designed, and both she and the *South Dakota* were retrofitted with injection devices.

The new water-tube boilers were a great advance over the fire tube

One of the few known photos of the *Huntington*'s operating aircraft. The aircraft taking off from her catapult is a Curtiss "F" type.

or "Scotch" boiler in use for so many years. In the latter, combustion gasses were passed through large tubes, which heated the water in the boiler drum. In the water-tube boiler, water was fed into the tubes and the combustion gasses were circulated throughout the drum and into the uptakes. This system saved feedwater and fuel and permitted a much higher steam pressure than before.

Water-tube boilers made their appearance in the U.S. Navy in 1886, when two Thornycroft small-tube express boilers of British design were authorized for the torpedo boat *Cushing* (TB 1). Beginning with the three *Maine*-class battleships, authorized in 1898, the water-tube boiler entered regular service. Most new construction was fitted with the proven Babcock & Wilcox type, but experiments were run with several other plants with varying degrees of success and failure. The most notorious failure was the *Maine*. Fitted with twenty-four French-designed Niclausse boilers of an early mark, she was the worst coal eater in the fleet and had to be left behind at San Francisco during the Great White Fleet's cruise across the Pacific because it was feared her bunkers would be emptied at sea.

In the design circular for the *Pennsylvania* class, thirty water-tube boilers of a nonspecified type were ordered. This scheme was never adopted, and the *Pennsylvania* and *Colorado* were fitted with thirty-two improved Niclausse boilers, manufactured by the Sterling Company of Chicago; the other ships of the class were fitted with sixteen Babcock & Wilcox boilers. The Niclausse plant was aligned in pairs in six watertight compartments, three on either side of the centerline bulkhead. According to the trials report, these firerooms were spacious, and there was ample room around the steam drums and uptakes. The forward and after firerooms contained six boilers each, in one bank of four and one bank of two, and the center compartments held two banks of two boilers each.

To carry the combustion gasses through the boilers and into the uptakes, the drums were fitted with "dry pipes" and baffles of common iron and zinc. Forced draft was provided by sixteen 60-inch Sturtevant fan blowers bolted to the underside of the armored deck and discharging directly into the firerooms. Air for the blowers was furnished by

Convoy escort, 1918, with the *Huntington* in camouflage. Her gun-deck batteries have been unshipped, and she is fitted with extra Carley floats on her forecastle and forebridge.

trunks extending upward to the main deck ventilator cowls. As in most ships designed by George Melville, the funnels were lofty, and the quartet in the *Pennsylvania* class rose 100 feet from the grates to the caps.

Although the Niclausse boilers in the *Pennsylvania* and *Colorado* were an improvement over those installed in the *Maine*, they were not completely effective and gave trouble in service. The drums leaked, the tubes were difficult to inspect and replace, and as the tubes were a special type, replacements were almost impossible to obtain on distant stations. As with other vessels using the Niclausse system, the plants were replaced with more efficient Babcock & Wilcox types during the course of their service.

"Steam for all uses" in the *West Virginia, Maryland, California,* and *South Dakota* was supplied by sixteen Babcock & Wilcox water-tube boilers located in eight watertight compartments, four on either side of the centerline bulkhead. As in the *Pennsylvania* and *Colorado,* these firerooms were also "convenient, and spaces around and above the boilers roomy."[23]

Forced draft in the *West Virginia* and *Maryland* was the same as that in the Cramp-built ships, but the *California* and *South Dakota* used the Howden method of one 69-inch fan blower placed directly over each boiler.

The boilers for all vessels in the class were fed by four main and eight auxiliary pumps. The main pumps, feeding the boilers only, were placed two per engine room and drew from the main feed tanks. The tanks, which had a capacity of 13,000 gallons, were placed outboard from each engine room and received the discharges from all main and auxiliary pumps and the traps and drains of all steam lines. Their main intake came from the evaporators and distillers. A hotwell pump for each main feed tank delivered water to a heater charged with steam from an auxiliary line that bypassed the main engines; the heated water was then fed into the main feed pump suction and into the boilers. The steam drums in the Babcock & Wilcox ships were connected to a line of 8-inch overhead piping (the Niclausse vessels had 14.8-inch piping) running aft to deliver steam to the engines. The steam lines joined in a groin fitting between the forward firerooms, where branch lines fed the dynamos and auxiliaries.

Each vessel in the class was equipped with two main condensers, one per engine room.

Coal was carried in twenty-eight bunkers, twelve above the armored deck and sixteen below. This gave the class a normal bunker capacity of 900 tons and a full capacity of 2,000 tons. However, the capacity differed throughout the class by as much as 250 tons, depending on the building yard. The vessels all maintained a very wide steaming radius, the *Pennsylvania* and *Colorado* having an endurance of 6,800 miles at ten knots, the rest of the class able to steam 5,000 miles at ten knots.

There were five hoisting engines, able to lift 300 pounds of ash from the fireroom floor to the gun deck in five seconds, where the refuse was dumped into overhead trolleys and discharged over the side. The location of the engines in the trunk of the forced-draft blowers made it impossible to hoist ashes while running under forced draft.

As befitted vessels the dimensions of this class, shafting and propellers were huge, but they were not of uniform size because the hulls and engines of the ships differed. The original sheathed and coppered hull plans of the *Pennsylvania, West Virginia,* and *California* called for twin shafts 48 feet long, with a diameter of 18.5 inches. The hulls were never sheathed, and the shafts were not foreshortened, being delivered and installed as ordered. In the *Colorado, Maryland,* and *South Dakota,* the shafting was cast and milled for unsheathed hulls and measured 45 feet 1 inch in length.

The diameter of the propellers also varied depending on whether the shafts were outboard or inboard turning. In the former case, the *Pennsylvania, Colorado, California,* and *South Dakota* were fitted with screws measuring 18 feet in diameter; the inboard-turning *West Virginia* and *Maryland* measured 17 feet 3 inches. All were pitched to a maximum of 23 feet 6 inches.

The *Huntington* recovering a Curtiss ''F'' hydroplane. Clearly shown are the extensions fitted to the boat booms. (Doubleday)

Problems developed early on with the *Maryland*'s propellers. For unknown reasons they were not ground smooth and tinned, as was common practice, and no attempt was made to grind off the casting flash or fair the blades to a true helicoidal surface. This resulted in a discovery in dock trials that due to these inequalities the starboard engine ran faster and used less power than the port engine. The situation was remedied by the builder prior to acceptance trials.

The electric plants of the class, the largest ever installed in U.S. naval vessels, consisted of seven dynamos situated on two levels just forward of the boiler spaces. The upper compartment contained three 50kw dynamos plus the switchboards for the entire plant; in the lower compartment were three 100kw dynamos and one 50kw. With the exception of the *California* and *South Dakota*, whose outfits were built by Union Iron Works, all were manufactured by General Electric. The plant had a generating capacity of 4,000 amps at 125 volts and powered all machinery except the propulsion plant and the anchor windlass. The switchboards for light and power were separate but linked, and the power of any generator could be channeled for any electrical purpose. The number of electric lights varied from vessel to vessel. In the *West Virginia* and *Maryland* there were 2,529 incandescent lamps of 5 and 16 candlepower (CP), fourteen 500CP arc lights for boiler and engine rooms, and six 30-inch hand-operated 21,000CP searchlight projectors. All ships in the class, with the exception of the *South Dakota*, were equipped with six 30-inch electrically controlled projectors. The latter vessel, the last commissioned, was fitted with eight 36-inch electrically controlled projectors.

All vessels had wireless equipment installed during construction or shortly after commissioning; the bids for the sets in the *Colorado* and *West Virginia* were the first tendered for U.S. naval vessels. The contracts stipulated a communicating distance of 250 miles, but this was not obtainable with the primitive sets installed. In these early electronic years, the *Colorado* and *West Virginia* held the fleet record by maintaining a transmission over a distance of 185 miles, and radio history was made in 1905 when the *Colorado*, at a distance of 100 miles from Nantucket Light Ship, sent a message to the Bureau of Navigation.

Trials

The completion and trials of all vessels in the class were seriously delayed by construction clogs, machinery and equipment changes, tardy manufacture and delivery of armor and other critical components, and lack of skilled labor.

The *West Virginia*, whose contract had been extended by thirteen months until 6 February 1905, was the first to undergo trials. She

Convoy duty, winter of 1917–18, the fore turret of the *Huntington*. (Doubleday)

departed Newport News on 29 October 1904 for the Cape Ann course, having on board 517 officials, observers, and crew. It is interesting to note that of this number, 315 were in the engineering divisions and 109 in the chief steward's department.

Speed trials were held on 2 November. The ship displaced 13,720 tons on a mean draft of 24 feet 1 inch. The trials were successful. The *West Virginia* easily made her contract speed, averaging 22.146 knots with 274 psi on boilers generating 25,726 hp. The coal was handpicked New River.

During the ship's fitting out, the Bureau of Steam Engineering decided to compare the smoke emissions of vessels equipped with Niclausse boilers to those fitted with the Babcock & Wilcox type. The *West Virginia* had the latter. The emissions were recorded during speed trials by a photographer stationed abaft the stacks who took one picture every ten minutes. The photographs from the *West Virginia* and *Maryland*, which was similarly tested, depict dense black smoke. When the same procedure was used on the Niclausse-equipped *Pennsylvania* and *Colorado*, "gray smoke of satisfactory condition" was reported. The bureau concluded that the dense smoke was not due to the coal-eating tendencies of the Niclausse boiler but to the quality and composition of the coal.

On the *West Virginia*'s run from Newport News to Boston, it was observed that the port engine averaged three to four rpm, less than the starboard engine; to compensate, the ship carried one degree of port helm. During the speed trials, an equalization was attempted by feeding steam from the main line directly into the port engine low-pressure cylinders, which resulted in a 1,502.7-hp boost for the port engine but did not affect the inequality of the revolutions.

At the conclusion of speed trials the ship underwent maneuvering evolutions. With engines stopped and helm amidships, the ship was allowed to drift until dead still with her head to the wind. At this point the port engine was started full ahead, the starboard engine full astern. Taking 14 minutes 23 seconds, the ship steamed a full 360 degrees. Reversing the order of ahead and astern, the time to turn full circle was reduced to 13 minutes 37 seconds. Both these times compared favorably with the times of the *Colorado*, whose outboard-turning screws clocked 15 minutes at their best.

Upon the *West Virginia*'s return to Newport News, she was docked and the pitch of her propellers measured. The port screw was pitched about six more inches than the starboard screw, either because of faulty measuring or because the ship fouled with a rope cable when backing away from the dock. The pitch was corrected, and the vessel had no further trouble with unequal engine revolutions. The *West Virginia* was accepted on a preliminary basis on 23 February 1905.

The *Colorado*, whose contract had been extended ten months by the Navy Department, underwent successful dock trials on 21 June 1904 and builder's trials off the Delaware breakwater from 30 June to 3 July.

Speed trials were conducted on the Cape Ann course on 24 October 1904 in smooth seas and good weather conditions. The vessel's draft was her standard mean of 24 feet 1 inch on a displacement of 13,785 tons. According to the report, the machinery was satisfactory, "there were no hot bearings, and the boilers made all the steam the engines could use."[24]

Steam pressure on the Niclausse boilers was set at 250 psi; the safety valves, blowing off steam for most of the run, were set 50 psi higher. Department observers agreed that the boilers steamed freely and economically and made more steam than the engines could use.

To coal the boilers as efficiently as possible, twenty-one shipyard boys equipped with stopwatches were assigned to the firerooms to call out the intervals for firing. The *Colorado*'s speed averaged 22.224 knots, and her engines generated 26,154 hp. Coal was handpicked Pocahontas. The ship was accepted on 10 January 1905.

The class leader, the *Pennsylvania*, whose contract had been prolonged by eleven months to 10 December 1904, underwent her dock trials on 15–16 September 1904. In the interests of time, builder's trials were dispensed with, and she departed from Cramp's for the Brooklyn Navy Yard on 12 November for docking, scraping, and painting. After

Convoy duty, winter of 1917–18, the forecastle of the *Huntington*. (Doubleday)

taking on her load of handpicked Pocahontas in 100-lb bags, the *Pennsylvania* steamed for the Cape Ann course, where speed trials commenced on 23 November.

The trials of the *West Virginia* and *Colorado* had shown the engineering plant to be far more powerful than anyone expected, and with their fine hull lines the ships had made their contract speed of 22 knots with comparative ease. In any ship in the class the engineers could have reached a speed of 24 knots with little trouble, and would have had bonus clauses been included in the contracts. But rather than risk the breakdowns commonly experienced with triple-expansion machinery, the ships were only worked to within a respectable half-knot in excess of contract requirements, the *California* making 22.756 knots on builder's trials and the *Pennsylvania*, the official leader, 22.436 knots on her acceptance trials.

The trials of the *West Virginia* and *Colorado* also showed that the boilers, both the Niclausse and the Babcock & Wilcox, were generating so much steam that fuel and feedwater were being wasted. The Bureau of Steam Engineering decided to raise the boiler pressure in the *Pennsylvania* from the design circular figure of 250 psi to 300 psi and to set the safety valves at 315 psi. The *Pennsylvania*, with higher pressure in her boilers, consumed 30.77 tons of coal per hour (the *West Virginia* consumed 40.57 tons) and averaged 22.436 knots on a displacement of 13,817 tons, on a mean draft of 24.14 feet.

The *Pennsylvania*'s engines during the trials ran with very little vibration, and none of the bearings overheated. In a series of crash turns, which followed the passing of the last stake boat on the speed trials, 20.5 seconds at 20 knots were needed to put the helm over from hard astarboard to hard aport; it took 18 seconds for the opposite maneuver. The maximum angle of heel for both was 4.5 degrees.

The report found all major propulsion components in excellent condition. The boiler tubes, while bending somewhat in the lower tiers, were considered normal and suffered no leakage. Preliminary acceptance came on 9 March 1905.

The last of the ships built on the East Coast, the *Maryland*, was the fourth of the class ready for trials, her contract having been extended sixteen months to 18 April 1905, which was also the date of her preliminary acceptance. On 21 January 1905 the *Maryland* raised steam and left Newport News for Boston and the Cape Ann course.

The trials commenced on 27 January. The ship displaced 12,749 tons on a mean draft of 25 feet 4.25 inches. The sea was rough, and the ship's steering was somewhat erratic because several marker buoys had been cast adrift. In the firerooms, an electric stoking indicator took the place of the boys in the Cramp ships.

Almost as soon as the *Maryland* crossed the starting line, the port hotwell pump broke down and was temporarily out of operation; water had to be directly fed into the boilers without passing through the heaters. Boiler pressure was lowered to 278 psi, generating 27,571 hp. The vessel's speed was unaffected, and she came in clocking 22.406 knots.

The prolonged construction of the West Coast–built *California* and *South Dakota* rivaled the desultory methods of France or Russia, the *California* taking five years and seven months from contract signing to commissioning and the *South Dakota* requiring a full seven years. Nearly every piece of the *California* and *South Dakota* had to be shipped by rail or sea from Eastern manufacturing centers to San Francisco. Further compounding the delays, a series of crippling general strikes was directed against the Union Iron Works in 1901, 1904, and 1907. Of course, no one predicted the San Francisco earthquake, which extended the thrice-revised contracts for the two ships.

The *California* underwent a successful series of dock trials between 30 January and 8 February 1906 and commenced builder's trials in the Santa Barbara Channel on 4 October. Although the ship reached a top speed of 22.756 knots, serious flaws in the engine lubricating system developed. For inexplicable reasons the gravity feed refused to function when the vessel steamed at high speeds. This overheated the crank pin brasses and melted their white-metal bushings. The brasses pounded continuously and nearly wrecked the crank shaft. A second trial was

Laundry hung up to dry on the *California*. She shows the typical clutter of the ships of the predreadnought era, c. 1908. The vessel to port is a *St. Louis*–class protected cruiser.

held on 11 October with refitted brasses, but after two and a half hours the problem started again. A third attempt was made on 26 October. The ship got up a full head of steam, reaching 22 knots before the run was halted. It was then decided to retrofit the system with a centrifugal injection feed, which solved the problem.

Government speed trials were held on 12 November. The *California* displaced 13,750 tons on a mean draft of 24 feet 1.875 inches. Throughout the trials, a combination flashing light and gong indicator was used to time the boiler firing. The Babcock & Wilcox plant, noted the trials report, "supplied steam so easily that the work of the firemen was light, and the air in the firerooms was very comfortable and not laden with dust."[25] Boiler pressure was measured at 275.5 psi, generating 29,658 hp and 22.2 knots. Handpicked and bagged Harris Navigation coal was shipped from Cardiff, Wales. The vessel was accepted on a preliminary basis on 20 July 1907.

The last vessel of the class authorized, the *South Dakota*, underwent successful dock trials from 20 to 27 March 1906 and builder's trials in San Francisco Bay on 18 December. Speed trials were scheduled for the Santa Barbara Channel on 22 December. The ship, displacing 13,750 tons on a mean draft of 24 feet 1 inch, began her run in smooth seas. Using Harris Navigation coal, the engines produced 28,158 hp. Speed averaged 22.24 knots. Again, the boilers provided more steam than the engines could consume, and the trials report noted that "the firemen seemed to be spending most of the time leaning on the handles of their shovels."[26]

Post-trials inspection showed the boiler tubes to contain some dirt and mill scale, but otherwise they were in satisfactory condition. The maneuvering trials were canceled because of faulty engine throttle valves, which were replaced by the builder. The *South Dakota* was accepted on a preliminary basis on 19 November 1907.

Modifications and Refits

Class-wide modifications and improvements were made to the ships at various points in their careers. The first, made between 1907 and 1909, resulted in a near complete rearranging of the turrets. All electrical apparatus that might emit sparks was removed from the turrets and ammunition spaces and placed in benign compartments beneath the armored deck. Apparatus that was absolutely necessary was made flameproof. In 1908 automatic shutters were fitted in the ammunition tubes to lessen the danger of flashbacks from the turret chamber down the ammunition tube and into the magazines. Further improvements in the ordnance were made in 1909, when longitudinal splinter bulkheads were fitted in each turret to separate the guns in individual compartments. The 8-inch electric ammunition hoists and rammers were unshipped and replaced with handworked gear. This separated turret chambers from handling rooms, made the turrets less liable to breakdowns, and increased the rate of fire.

Between 1908 and 1910, as a result of the accident on board the *Colorado*, all Mark 5 8-inch guns were removed and replaced with the new model Mark 6, which had been hooped to the muzzle and thus strengthened. The Mark 5s were sent to the naval gun factory in Washington, D.C., for rehooping and placed in reserve. The 6-inch and 3-inch broadside mounts also received new friction training gear.

In March 1909, upon the return of the Atlantic Fleet from its around-the-world cruise, there was a fleet-wide modification of fire control in all major vessels. In all the *Pennsylvania*s except for the *Maryland*, the military foremast was removed and replaced with the new and distinctively American lattice mast and fire control top.* The new equipment made possible the electric transmission of ranges and deflections for visual display to sight setters at each gun, ending centuries of traditional gunlaying. All flying bridges, wooden chart houses, and after bridges were removed and replaced with a modern forebridge.

In 1916 new Vickers fire director systems were installed on the forebridge and foremast and two 3-inch 50-caliber Mark 2 or 3 AA guns on the after bridge deck. It is interesting to note that just five years before the Bureau of Ordnance had merely been considering the design and manufacture of guns to be used against and on aircraft. The board at that time doubted whether service conditions would ever demand such guns.

The last of the major modifications occurred in 1918–19, as the class was stripped of its gun deck battery of ten 6-inch and eight 3-inch guns to provide berthing spaces for the returning soldiers and marines of the American Expeditionary Force from France.

In 1916 preliminary plans were discussed to completely modernize the *Pennsylvania*s and the later *Tennessee*s. This was the result of the Navy Department's awareness that the battle fleet was woefully short of modern cruisers. As an interim measure to fill the cruiser gap, at least until the new *Omaha* class (CLs 4–13) joined the fleet in 1923–24, it was suggested in 1919 that a number of the *Pennsylvania*- and *Tennessee*-class ships be modified and modernized. The proposal was first made in a

---

*The Russian battleships *Imperator Pavel* and *Andrei Pervosvanni* (1911) and the Argentine battleships *Rividavia* and *Rio Moreno* (1914, U.S. built) carried lattice masts, but those in the Russian vessels were much lighter.

The *California*, c. 1914. Note the strakes of the vertical armor abaft the 6-inch guns.

memorandum to Albert Gleaves, commander of the Cruiser and Transport Force, from Captain E. S. Kellogg, commanding officer of the *Huntington* (ex-*West Virginia*). He suggested that the major modifications include removal of all armor plate above the gun deck, including turret armor but not barbettes. The turrets would be replaced by splinter- and weather-proof gunhouses of mild steel, similar in type to those of the later U.S. treaty cruisers and the *Omaha*s. All 3-inch guns would be unshipped and replaced in the main deck superstructure by eight new 6-inch or twelve 5-inch guns—ten in the superstructure and two on the boat deck in "sky mounts." Anticipating the shore-bombardment role for large ships as well as a novel ASW device, Kellogg advocated the mounting of two 12-inch mortars, one each on the forecastle and quarterdeck, with a range of 300 to 3,000 yards; the shell could explode on impact or at any depth to 300 feet. The engineering plants would be converted to oil and have a steaming radius of seven thousand miles. Major topside modifications would include a drastic reduction in the number of boats and the elimination of the cage mast, which was distinctively American and therefore a military disadvantage. Kellogg recommended the cage mast be replaced by either a pole or tripod mast, both of which were employed in subsequent U.S. cruisers.

Admiral Gleaves forwarded these recommendations to the CNO, Admiral William Benson, hoping they would be carefully considered by the Navy Department. Modernization, however, never went beyond the generally cosmetic alterations to the armored cruisers that remained in active service beyond 1919. Curiously, the *New York/Saratoga/Rochester* was so completely transformed that offensively she could almost match a unit of the *Pennsylvania* class. Long after she passed into strategic obsolescence, she was retained on the list in lieu of newer tonnage decommissioned or scrapped under the Washington naval treaties.

The Pennsylvania

Of the six vessels in the class, the *Pennsylvania*, renamed the *Pittsburgh* on 27 August 1912, maintained the longest record of active service and underwent a far greater series of refits than her sisters. During the summer of 1911, in company with the *Colorado*, the *Pennsylvania* went into dock at Bremerton for a complete machinery overhaul. The Niclausse boilers on both vessels were poor performers, and the plants

The *Colorado* off Tompkinsville, Staten Island, in 1905.

were to be entirely replaced with new Babcock & Wilcox boilers. The new plants, however, were not installed, and the Bureau of Steam Engineering contented itself with modifying the eight boilers in the forward firerooms with Babcock & Wilcox headers and tubes, leaving intact the original Niclausse drums.

On 4 January 1911 the *Pennsylvania* tied up at the Mare Island yard for an unusual temporary fitting, prosaically described as "erection of platform in connection with aviation meet."[27] The platform, which on 18 January Eugene Ely would use in the first airplane landing on and takeoff from a ship, extended 133 feet 7 inches from the mainmast to just over the fantail; 31 feet 6 inches wide, it was angled upward from the stern and over the after turret and secured to the mainmast. At its after end it was angled down 30 degrees over the stern for a length of 14 feet 3 inches. Bulwarks of 2-inch planking extended up the sides for about 2 feet to prevent the aircraft from falling into the sea. Running the length of the platform, parallel guide rails of 2-by-4-inch scantling, placed 12 feet apart, confined the aircraft to the center of the landing deck. The arresting gear consisted of parallel lines of twenty-two pairs of 50-lb sandbags athwart the deck, each pair connected by a twenty-one-thread line, hauled taut across the guide rails. The bags, accurately weighed to prevent the machine from sluing, were placed 3 feet apart and covered 75 feet of deck. As a fail-safe measure, two canvas screens, 20 feet high and 6 feet apart, were fitted just abaft the mainmast. (See Careers section below for an account of the flight.)

After many years of almost continuous active service, the *Pittsburgh* and *Colorado* were again placed in dockyard hands in 1914. The twenty-four remaining Niclausse boilers were finally unshipped and replaced with twelve Babcock & Wilcox types. The eight composite boilers in the forward firerooms, while nearly useless, remained in place.

Although the *Pittsburgh* was scheduled to undergo a major refit at Philadelphia in 1921, the Board of Inspection and Survey decided otherwise. Rear Admiral Joseph Reeves, president of the board, wrote, "Considering the age and military value of this vessel and the shortage of funds for repairs, also the work required to keep more modern vessels in service, the Board does not recommend that any work be done on the *Pittsburgh* by the Navy Yard at this time."[28] However, it was probably at this time that six 6-inch guns were refitted on the gun deck. They were installed in the number one, two, and five positions, port and starboard, giving the ship an ugly gap-toothed appearance, especially as the empty gun ports had not been plated over.

In 1926 the decision was made to refit the *Pittsburgh* for service as the Asiatic Fleet's flagship. She was given a new, fully enclosed bridge and a new fire control system employing the Bausch & Lomb 20-foot Mark 17 and 3-foot Mark 14 rangefinder. Both antiaircraft guns were removed, and the captain recommended the 8-inch guns be replaced, but this was not approved by the Bureau of Ordnance. The entire 6-inch battery was unshipped, their spaces on the gun and main decks made over for tropical berthing.

The *Pittsburgh* was given a major overhaul, and the eight composite boilers, their foundations rotted away and ready to collapse, were finally extracted. As the ship could still make 20 knots on her remaining plant, they were not replaced. The number one funnel was now superfluous, and it too was removed, giving the *Pittsburgh* an entirely new and somewhat unsatisfactory profile, which she maintained for the remaining five years of her career.

The West Virginia

As flagship of the Fourth Division, Second Squadron, North Atlantic Fleet, the *West Virginia* was the first of the class to undergo alteration. Upon completion of her acceptance trials in July 1905, she was ordered to the Brooklyn Navy Yard to be fitted with a flying bridge for the use of admiral and staff.

From June through August 1905 both the *West Virginia* and *Maryland* were docked at Union Iron Works' Hunter's Point Yard for the major task of converting their inboard-turning engines to outboard-turning ones. In January 1910 the *West Virginia*, in company with the *Maryland* and *South Dakota*, inaugurated the new dry dock at Mare Island for a general overhaul. Until this time, dry-docking on the Pacific

The *Maryland* on her speed trials, 27 January 1905.

coast was carried out either at Bremerton or Hunter's Point. The greater part of this overhaul was accomplished by ships forces. "By keeping them in commission and utilizing the ship's force," reported Engineer in Chief Hutch I. Cone, "it will be possible to materially reduce the cost of work, and at the same time have the vessels ready for duty with the fleet in much shorter time than if they had been put out of commission."[29]

Following her service in Mexican waters during the Vera Cruz crisis, the *West Virginia* was placed in reduced commission as part of the Pacific Reserve Fleet at Bremerton, and between the summer of 1914 and January 1916 she underwent a series of refits. The boilers were completely overhauled. Because of the frequent changes of engineering personnel, her engine cylinders were not properly maintained, and she could make no more than 16 knots.

Major improvements were made to the turrets. When the *West Virginia* was first commissioned, the electric leads to the turrets were not properly connected by the builder, which resulted in only two speeds of train, go and stop. The installation was completely rewired by the ship's force, after which it obtained five or six speeds in either direction.

The *West Virginia* received new 60-foot topmasts to facilitate radio communications and a new 8-inch fire director system. Additionally, the control for the searchlights was changed from electric to mechanical, as the original installation had proved inadequate. Improved torpedo-hoisting gear was shipped, for the old jury-rigged apparatus consisting of a line purchase from the bridge wing put great strain on the structure, and the torpedoes frequently fouled the ship's side.

The *West Virginia* cleared Bremerton on 20 September 1916 for further service in Mexican waters. She was renamed the *Huntington* on 11 November. In early February 1917 she tied up at Mare Island for increased refits. The steering gear was overhauled, as "it was impossible for two men at the wheel on the bridge to operate the gear."[30] Two 3-inch AA guns were installed on the after bridge deck, and a radio direction finder was fitted. Minor matters were also rectified; for example, the Board of Inspection and Survey ordered the leather cushions in the captain's and admiral's sea cabins reupholstered because they were "vermin infested."[31]

It had been just six years since Eugene Ely proved that aircraft were capable of taking off from a ship at sea. Now it was the *Huntington*'s turn to play the role of pioneer, and the Mare Island riggers were ordered to install an "aeroplane launching device." This, one of the first catapults afloat in the navy (the *North Carolina* mounted the first) consisted of a narrow, level platform and track extending from the mainmast over the after turret to the stern. The aircraft was placed on a trolley sled attached to a cable running the length of the track. The trolley was released by compressed air, hurtled down the track, and dropped over the stern into the sea as the aircraft became airborne. The trolley was then retrieved with gaff booms. The *Huntington* retained the installation until October 1917, when it was dismantled at Brooklyn. Other refits on the *Huntington* were those that the whole class underwent.

The California

All the class-wide modifications were made in the *California*, but certain problems peculiar to the ship were attended to. The plumbing system, reported her medical officer, Surgeon E. W. Dunbar, was detrimental to the health of the crew.

> The excessive heat of the flushing water, caused by its first circulating through the distillers, renders the shower baths, in which only salt water is used, almost useless, and constitutes a nuisance in the water-closets on account of the odor-laden steam arising from them. To remedy this it will be necessary to have a new pump. As it is now, the crew, especially the engineer's force, coming off a hot watch below, are deprived of the invigorating cool shower which lessens the liability to contract colds.[32]

The Colorado

In addition to class-wide modifications, the *Colorado* had her Niclausse boilers altered, but unlike the *Pennsylvania* she retained her composite forward boilers. The vessel was the first to receive the new Mark 6 8-inch battery.

The Maryland

Barring the major retrofitting of outboard-turning engines, the *Maryland*'s refits followed the general pattern. The ship was equipped with paravanes and minesweeping gear sometime around 1909, along with the *California* and *West Virginia*. No other information on minesweeping gear is available. Following many months of service in Mexican waters, the *Maryland* put into Mare Island on 10 September 1915 for standard repairs. It was found during the material inspection that a persistent "jink" in the train of the fore turret was caused by the sagging roller path, but this defect was never repaired. In addition to retubing the boilers, repairing searchlights, and fitting new elevating gear on the 6-inch guns, the yard was ordered to "fit prophylactic station, crew's washroom presently used as such, but not suitable."[33]

When patrolling waters off the northeast coast of South America in

Side cleaning the *Maryland* in the new floating dry dock, *Dewey*, at Olongapo, c. 1906.

early January 1918, the ship, which had been renamed the *Frederick*, on 9 November 1916, ran aground and suffered considerable damage. The double bottom and most of the underwater plane on the port side were stove-in; the starboard propeller was bent. Following temporary repairs at Balboa, the *Frederick* steamed to Norfolk, where the Board of Inspection and Survey found her fit for further service.

The South Dakota

Modifications in the *South Dakota* were standard. But during a general machinery overhaul at Mare Island in July 1914, her captain recommended to the board that she receive a new canteen. Her canteen was in the berth deck passage, where accessibility was poor, and there was not enough space for it. "While in Mexico," her captain wrote, "it was completely emptied twice on each pay day. This lack of space is accentuated by the recent prohibition of bum boats."[34] At Bremerton in 1916 the ship was fitted with two "minesweeping reels." There is no other information about the installation of new machinery and equipment.

Careers

The West Virginia

The *West Virginia* (ACR 5) was laid down at Newport News Shipbuilding and Drydock on 16 September 1901, launched 18 April 1903, and commissioned at the builder's yard by Captain Conway H. Arnold on 23 February 1905. She was completely fitted-out by early April, and the next three months were spent on a shake-down cruise along the New England coast. On 7 October she joined the *Pennsylvania* and *Colorado* at Newport and hoisted the flag of commander, Fourth Division, Atlantic Fleet, Rear Admiral Willard H. Brownson. Following a period of coaling and general drills, the division steamed south, anchoring off Key West, where President Theodore Roosevelt visited the flagship to observe the efficiency of the *West Virginia*–type vessels. The ships upped anchor and spent the next eight days cruising the Gulf of Mexico, then went back up the East Coast, arriving at Wolf Trap Light, Chesapeake Bay, on 31 October. President Roosevelt was piped over the side, and the *Maryland* joined the force, completing the division.

After a reception for the British Second Cruiser Squadron under Rear Admiral Prince Louis of Battenberg (father of Admiral of the Fleet Lord Louis Mountbatten), the division engaged in squadron exercises for the remainder of 1905. On 6 January 1906, along with the Third Division and with the floating dry dock *Dewey*, then in passage to Olongapo, it participated in the first use of wireless communication in squadron-sized exercises. The winter and spring of 1906 were taken up with division, squadron, and fleet evolutions, including a fleet-wide search problem conducted entirely by wireless. On 26 April the division anchored in North River, New York, to await dock and berth space at the Brooklyn Navy Yard.

Docking and repair completed, the *West Virginia* embarked the New York naval militia on 21 July for a cruise in Long Island Sound. The vessels reformed on 28 August off Tompkinsville, Staten Island, and proceeded to President Roosevelt's summer residence at Oyster Bay for an Atlantic Fleet review. At its conclusion the Fourth Division was ordered to Newport for a full supply of coal, ammunition, and stores. The ships sailed on 23 September for the Asiatic station.

Steaming via Gibraltar, Port Said, Bombay, and Singapore, the force arrived at Cavite on 18 November, where Admiral Brownson "fleeted up" to commander in chief, Asiatic Squadron. The force spent the next four months in Philippine waters conducting general drills.

On 4 March 1907 the *West Virginia* and her consorts shaped course for Woosung and dropped anchor in the Yangtze estuary four days later. Ostensibly a courtesy visit to a foreign port, the arrival of the four armored cruisers had a serious diplomatic purpose.

In the spring of 1906 a high-ranking delegation of Chinese bankers and merchants from the southern provinces had landed in San Francisco in the interests of furthering trade. The local immigration authorities treated them as undocumented coolies and detained them in a filthy facility to await the "contemptuous deliberations" of local officials. It finally took an appeal from the Chinese foreign ministry to Washington to obtain their release. As a result of this incident, a general boycott of all American goods was established in south coastal China, an area of 85 million people. In a very short time it reached serious proportions.

In their first attempt at lifting the boycott, the State and Navy Departments ordered Rear Admiral Charles Train and his flagship, the battleship *Ohio* (BB 12), up the Yangtze to Nanking to take up the matter with the viceroy, Tuan Tung. A self-made mandarin and nobody's fool, Tuan had secured his position by ruthlessly suppressing piracy and smuggling along the lower river. When the *Ohio* anchored off Nanking Admiral Train was met by one minor official and a motley collection of rickshas for the trip through the city to Tuan's estate. Alongside the conveyances, runners carried banners reading, "Make way for the tribute bearers to His Excellency."[35] Needless to say, the boycott continued.

A stronger message was needed, and over Tuan's vehement protests Rear Admiral Brownson led the *West Virginia*, *Pennsylvania*, *Colorado*, and *Maryland* up river, dropping anchor at Nanking on 13 March.

Admiral Brownson assembled the captains and senior officers of his ships until he had a "staff" of forty-five men, resplendent in full dress with cocked hats and swords. They were met at the landing by a more suitable party than had greeted the previous mission, and there were no bannermen this time. At the meeting in Tuan's *yamen*, the viceroy asked how long Admiral Brownson intended to remain in Chinese waters. The admiral replied that the squadron's stay was indefinite. Hardly encouraged, Tuan probed further, asking how long the ships would remain anchored off Nanking. Admiral Brownson, superb diplomat that he was and saving face all around, informed the viceroy that his force would remain until he had the honor of receiving the viceroy on board his flagship. Tuan and his entourage arrived at the fleet landing the next morning and were received on board with all

The *Maryland* in dock at Bremerton, April 1908. The aperture visible on her underwater hull, just above the yard punt, is the starboard torpedo tube.

honors, the crews manning the rail and giving three cheers. The viceroy had a complete tour of the *West Virginia*, including a loading drill in the 8-inch turrets. On 17 March the four ships steamed back down the Yangtze to Woosung, and the boycott was lifted shortly thereafter.

A fleet-wide reorganization of the Pacific commands went into effect on 17 April 1907. The old Asiatic Squadron and Pacific Fleet, the latter based on the West Coast of the United States, united as the Pacific Fleet, the *West Virginia* serving as flagship under Rear Admiral James H. Dayton. In the new organization the four vessels, now popularly called the Armored Cruiser Squadron, were designated the First Division, First Squadron, Pacific Fleet.

In mid-summer 1907, at the conclusion of battle practice at the Chefoo range, the squadron returned to the United States via Yokohama, Cavite, and Honolulu and anchored in San Francisco Bay on 27 September. For the remainder of the year and for the first six months of 1908, the vessels cruised off the West Coast of the United States and Mexico conducting general drills, including a fleet review by the secretary of the navy at San Francisco on 17 May. On 15 June the division proceeded to navy yards for repairs: the *West Virginia* and *Maryland* went to Mare Island, the *Pennsylvania* and *Colorado* to Bremerton.

With the exeption of the *Colorado*, which was having her 8-inch guns replaced, the entire First Squadron assembled at San Francisco on 19 August 1908 for a cruise to Samoa. The *West Virginia* flew the flag of the new Pacific Fleet commander, Rear Admiral William T. Swinburne. Rear Admiral Uriel Sebree commanded the Second Division, composed of his flagship, the *Tennessee*, plus the *California, South Dakota*, and *Washington*. These seven vessels, forming the most powerful naval aggregate ever assembled on the Pacific coast, were augmented by seven destroyers and the hospital ship *Solace* (AH 2). The squadron, with each armored cruiser towing a destroyer, as was then necessary given the limited bunkerage of the early types, steamed out of San Francisco Bay on 24 August and headed for the South Pacific.

The force reached its destination on 20 September without mishap to the destroyers and with only one towline parting. The First Division anchored in Pago Pago, American Samoa, and the Second Division in Apia Harbor, German Samoa. The return passage via Honolulu, where the *Colorado* rejoined the flag, terminated at Magdalena Bay on 2 November.

Immediately the vessels cleared for record target practice, but owing to conditions in Central and South America, the shooting was discontinued on 1 December. Between 8 December 1908 and 18 March 1909 the *West Virginia* led the squadron to show the flag in Panamanian, Guatemalan, Salvadoran, Honduran, and Chilean ports and protect American interests in those areas. On 24 March the squadron recommenced its target practice at Magdalena Bay. It returned to San Francisco on 17 April.

The remainder of the spring and summer of 1909 were spent along the California and Washington coasts. A reception was held for the Japanese training squadron at San Francisco on 27 May, the fourth anniversary of Japan's great victory over the Russians at Tsushima. In June and July the armored cruisers went into dock for repairs, reassembling at San Francisco on 2 September.

The eight vessels of the squadron raised anchor on 5 September, the *West Virginia* flying the flag of the new fleet commander, Rear Admiral Uriel Sebree. Once more they steamed to the Asiatic station, arriving at Honolulu on the tenth. On 5 October the *West Virginia* led the First Division on a cruise to the Admiralty Islands in the Bismarck

Scraping barnacles off the *Maryland* at a West Coast yard, c. 1911. Note the absence of safety features and precautions; the side cleaners in soft hats balance on swaying scaffolding.

Archipelago. The squadron reformed at Cavite on 17 October and operated in Philippine waters until mid-December. The force visited Hong Kong, Yokohama, and Nagasaki during the Christmas holidays. It departed from the station for the United States on 20 January 1910. On 14 February the ships dropped anchor in San Francisco.

General drills, including target practice, mining, and minesweeping, were carried out along the California coast through early April, at which time the *West Virginia* put into Mare Island for docking and repairs. She remained out of service until October.

To test fleet preparedness and the efficiency of ship organization in the navy yards, a general mobilization of the Atlantic and Pacific Fleets was ordered for 2 October. All the armored cruisers, with the exception of the *Pennsylvania*, en route from Valparaiso, participated in the exercise, which lasted to the end of the month, culminating in a fleet review at San Diego on 1 November.

On 16 January 1911 Rear Admiral Chauncey Thomas, who had recently assumed command, hauled down his flag from the *West Virginia* and transferred the Pacific Fleet operations to the *California*. The *West Virginia* remained a private ship until 8 March, when she was assigned to the Second Division, consisting of herself and the *South Dakota*, and embarked the new division commander, Rear Admiral W. H. H. Southerland.

The fleet remained on the West Coast throughout the year, performing exercises to increase its efficiency. Much time was devoted to torpedo exercises with the Pacific Torpedo Fleet under conditions simulating war. In addition to this and other fleet evolutions, the *West Virginia* participated with the *Maryland* in a three-month series of tests to determine the suitability of Pacific coast coal for the navy's ships. Between the thirteenth and twenty-ninth of March the ship had on board Company D, First Provisional Marine Regiment, for landing force training. At the conclusion of the landing exercise, the two heavy divisions of the fleet were combined in one division of four armored cruisers. The *West Virginia* was detached and placed in reserve because of a shortage of personnel.

She steamed to Bremerton to take her place in the Pacific Reserve Fleet and remained in that capacity for just over two years, relieving the *Colorado* as reserve fleet flagship in February 1914.

In the spring of 1914 the Vera Cruz crisis erupted in Mexico, and the *West Virginia* was ordered to the west coast of that country. Recommissioned into the Pacific Fleet at Bremerton on 23 April, she embarked the Fourth Marine Regiment at Mare Island and with the collier *Jupiter**

*The *Jupiter* was converted in 1920–22 to the navy's first aircraft carrier and renamed the *Langley* (CV 1).

(AC 3) shaped course for Mazatlan. She arrived off the Mexican coast the first week of May and cruised in the area until 3 July, returning to San Diego to off-load her troops.

The *West Virginia* remained in reserve status at Bremerton until 20 September 1916, when she was recommissioned for further service in Mexican waters. On 11 November her name was changed to *Huntington*, the name *West Virginia* being given to the hull of BB 48. Following five months of service protecting American interests on the west coast of Mexico, the ship was ordered north to Mare Island for refitting.

Here the yard riggers installed the second aircraft catapult fitted in a U.S. Navy vessel plus the equipment to operate four floatplanes and manned kite balloons. On 11 May 1917 the *Huntington* was detached from the Pacific Fleet and ordered to the naval aeronautical station in Pensacola, Florida, to take up her new duties as an experimental station ship.

She anchored at the base on 28 May and took on her air department, consisting of seven pilots, one boatswain's mate, one quartermaster, one turret captain, four machinist's mates, one carpenter's mate, two masters-at-arms, thirteen electrician's mates, one shipfitter, a seaman, and one coast guard wheelsman. Reporting on board to command the air group was Lieutenant (j.g.) Marc Mitscher. On 7 June the *Huntington* received her complement of four Thomas-Morse pontoon biplanes plus manned kite balloons for antisubmarine work. Operations in earnest began.

Her first catapult tests were conducted on 8 June, using a timber dead load that weighed the same as a Thomas-Morse scout aircraft. The *Huntington*'s captain, Samuel Robeson, a classic "sundowner" of the Old Navy, proved a capricious enthusiast. He suggested to Lieutenant Mitscher that he attempt a takeoff while attached to a derrick purchase with the ship under way. A suggestion from the captain was tantamount to an order, so with obvious misgivings Mitscher assented. He climbed into the control position, the derrick was rigged, and the Thomas Morse was lowered into the sea. The experiment was a miserable failure. When the *Huntington* was under way she dragged the aircraft astern until it smashed into the ship's side, nearly killing Mitscher.[36]

The early summer of 1917 was spent in the operation of aircraft and kite balloons, but without much cooperation from Captain Robeson. When an aircraft crashed alongside or a balloon snapped its mooring cable, the occurrence was noted in the deck log, but the ship was never used in recovery; that service was relegated to the station's boats. In late July one of the floatplanes caught fire on the catapult and was "put out without damage to the ship," whereupon the installation—aircraft and all—was ordered cast over the side to drift back to Pensacola on the tide.[37]

With the United States now embroiled in a world war, the *Huntington* was ordered north to take her place in the First Division of the newly formed Cruiser and Transport Force under Rear Admiral Albert Gleaves. This was the beginning of many months of arduous duty as a convoy escort.* She tied up at the Brooklyn Navy Yard on 6 August 1917 and formed with her consorts. The First Division consisted of the flagship *Seattle* (ex-*Washington*), *North Carolina, Montana,* and *Huntington;* the Second Division, the *San Diego* (ex-*California*), *Frederick* (ex-*Maryland*), *Pueblo* (ex-*Colorado*), and *South Dakota.*

Upon his arrival at Brooklyn, Mitscher penned in a letter to his wife, "We transferred ten wrecks to the yard and repaired two. The other day Donohue smashed one of the remaining two and we worked night and day to get it ready for admiral's inspection. Stone fired off with it today and smashed it again. So now we have to repair it again."[38]

On 8 September the *Huntington* was under way as flagship of Convoy Group 7. The aircraft were all stowed as there was no method of deck recovery and the ship could not stop her engines for a sea recovery in submarine-infested waters. Instead, the kite balloons were streamed from the fantail.

In the relatively calm waters off Pensacola, manning the basket was a hazardous duty at best; in the north Atlantic it was deadly. The balloon was continually jerked by the pitching of the ship, making any U-boat observation impossible and the hapless observer sick. During this first voyage, the *Huntington* began to pitch violently as sea and wind forces mounted, sending the balloon into a series of downward spirals that knocked the observer unconscious. As the balloon was about to pitch into the sea, Captain Robeson ordered the mooring cable cut away; the order was disobeyed by Lieutenant Mitscher. Order and counterorder followed, with Mitscher steadfastly refusing to cast adrift the balloon, which was now being dragged in the *Huntington*'s wake. Captain Robeson finally ordered all engines stopped, and Shipfitter Patrick McGunigal secured a lifeline around his body and jumped into the Atlantic. By the time he reached the balloon, the basket was submerged with its unconscious observer. McGunigal pulled him free from the wreckage and both were hauled aboard. The observer soon regained his senses. For this heroic action Shipfitter McGunigal was recommended for the first Medal of Honor awarded in the war.

---

*Admiral Gleaves was appointed commander of convoy operations in the Atlantic, the command being a wartime amalgam of the Cruiser Force of the Atlantic Fleet and the immediately formed Transport Service. At war's end they were separated, the Transport Service being demobilized on 31 October 1919.

The *South Dakota* on the stocks ready for launching at Union Iron Works, San Francisco, 21 July 1904.

The *Huntington* turned her charges over to U.S. destroyers in midocean and steamed back to Hampton Roads, tying up on 30 September. On 5 October she put into the Brooklyn Navy Yard for removal of the catapult and aircraft and was again at sea on the twenty-seventh, bound for Halifax, Nova Scotia. Here the vessel embarked a high-level delegation consisting of presidential counselor "Colonel" Edward House, Chief of Naval Operations Admiral William Benson, and General Tasker Bliss. The *Huntington* raised anchor and set course for

Devonport, England, depositing her passengers without incident on 7 November.

The *Huntington* returned to New York on 27 November and commenced convoy operations, completing nine turnaround passages between 19 February and 13 November 1918. On 17 November she docked at Brooklyn for conversion to a troop transport. The ship was formally assigned to the Transport Service on 14 December 1918 and began her new duties helping bring back the American Expeditionary Force on New Year's Day 1919. Until 30 June she served in this somewhat unglamorous role, as did nearly all of the U.S. armored cruisers and predreadnought battleships, making six turnarounds and carrying a total of 11,913 troops. In all, she spent 63 days in port and 118 days at sea. The *Huntington* was detached from the transport service on 8 July 1919.

The *Huntington*'s final navy service was as flagship of the First Cruiser Squadron, Cruiser Force, and in this guise she led the old Steel Navy gunboats *Wheeling* (PG 14), *Castine*, and *Topeka* (ex-German *Diogenes*) until 1 September 1920. On that date the *Huntington* tied up at the Portsmouth Navy Yard and decommissioned the same day. On 12 March 1930 the *Huntington* was struck from the navy list and sold for scrap.

The *Pennsylvania*

The keel of the *Pennsylvania* (ACR 4) was laid down at William Cramp and Sons on 7 August 1901 and launched on 22 August 1903. The wine bottle was smashed over the prow by Miss Coral Quay, daughter of Senator Matthew S. Quay of Pennsylvania. The vessel was commissioned on 9 March 1905 at League Island, with Captain Thomas McLean commanding. Her shakedown cruise lasted until 30 June and included Caribbean as well as East Coast steaming. Between the nineteenth and thirtieth of June the ship assisted in the speed trials of the protected cruiser *Charleston* (C 22).

The *Pennsylvania* formed at Tompkinsville with the Fourth Division of the Atlantic Fleet for the presidential review on 27 August and sailed with the division on 8 September for the Asiatic station. During the stay in Manila in February 1907 a severe epidemic of typhoid broke out on board. Fleet Surgeon H. E. Ames reported, "In my inspection of the *Pennsylvania* I found that they were in the habit of keeping the fresh water supplied to the gun divisions for cleaning the guns in half barrels; after [the water was soiled] it was returned to the barrels and used by the crew to wash their dirty clothes or hands indiscriminately. The other source . . . was from swimming. The fecal matter from the head . . . empties directly into the bay."[39]

The *South Dakota* on the stocks at Union Iron Works. A temporary clamp has been attached to the rudder to keep it in place during the launch. The armored belt has not yet been bolted into place, and its groove just above the depth markings is visible.

Until April 1910 the *Pennsylvania* served with the First Squadron, Pacific Fleet, and saw service identical to that of the *West Virginia*. The *Pennsylvania* cleared Bremerton following a four month overhaul on 9 August 1910 and, in company with the *California*, steamed to Valparaiso, Chile, to take part in that country's centennial celebration. She returned to San Francisco on 16 October and held a reception for the Japanese training squadron during the week of 21 November. On 4 January 1911 the *Pennsylvania* docked at Mare Island for the erection of the experimental landing deck.

Naval aviation had begun just two months earlier, on 14 November 1910, when Eugene Ely took off from an inclined platform over the forecastle of the scout cruiser *Birmingham* off the Virginia capes. Secretary George Meyer, suitably impressed, had recommended to Congress that $25,000 be authorized for the advancement of naval aviation experiments. In the service, the cause was taken up by Captain Washington Irving Chambers, former captain of the *Louisiana* (BB 19). Assigned to the Office of the Aid for Material to the Secretary of the Navy, Chambers was the initiator of the *Birmingham* flight and somehow managed to secure permission from the navigation and construction and repair bureaus to fit the *Pennsylvania* for use as an experimental aviation ship.

On the morning of 18 January 1911 Ely, in a Curtiss pusher biplane equipped with specially installed arresting hooks on its axle, took off from Selfridge Field and headed for San Francisco Bay. The *Pennsylvania*'s captain, Charles F. Pond, had suggested that the operation be carried out at sea with the ship's head to wind and at any desired speed from 10 to 20 knots. But Ely opted for a vessel at anchor, and the fleet conformed with his wishes.

In the bay the *Pennsylvania* rode to the flood tide, light breezes of 10 to 15 mph on her starboard quarter, the most disadvantageous point. She was jammed with crew and spectators. Five hundred yards to port lay the *West Virginia* and *Maryland*. Ely was sighted one-half mile from the *Pennsylvania*'s bridge at an altitude of 1,500 feet, cruising at 60 mph. The airplane dipped, passed directly over the *Maryland* at 400 feet and, still dropping, flew over the *West Virginia*'s bow at only 100 feet of altitude. Five hundred yards from the *Pennsylvania*'s starboard quarter Ely headed straight for the ship, cut his engine when he was only 75 feet from the fantail, and allowed the wind to blow the aircraft directly onto the landing deck. At a speed of 40 mph Ely landed on the centerline. The first eleven arresting lines were passed, but the second eleven caught, and Ely stopped 30 feet from the deck's edge. As Captain Pond recorded, "Nothing [was] damaged, and not a bolt or brace started, and Ely [was] the coolest man on board." Ely himself stated, "If anything, I was brought to a stop a little too short, and it probably would have been better to have a little less weight in the sand bags."[40] One hour after landing Ely revved up his engine and trundled down the deck. After dipping ten feet from the sea, he rose to 2,000 feet and headed back to Selfridge Field.

Six days later the *Pennsylvania* was in the Santa Barbara Channel, where Lieutenant John Rodgers had the dubious distinction of being the first man in the modern U.S. Navy to go aloft in a manned kite balloon.* Further aviation history was made on 17 February. The ship was again anchored in the Santa Barbara Channel. From out of the sky came a biplane, fitted with floats and piloted by Glenn Curtiss himself. He alighted alongside the *Pennsylvania* and requested permission to come aboard with his aircraft, which Captain Pond readily granted. The floatplane was hoisted aboard with a boat derrick and shortly thereafter lowered back into the sea. Curtiss took off without mishap. The incident marked the first time an aircraft had landed alongside a vessel at sea, been hoisted on board, and commenced takeoff from the water. The evolution of the amphibious patrol bomber, "mothered" by a seaplane tender, had begun.

On 1 July 1911, because of the fleet-wide personnel shortages, the *Pennsylvania* was placed in ordinary with the Pacific Reserve Fleet at Bremerton. With only a maintenance-level crew, the ship remained virtually out of commission until 30 May 1913. On 27 August 1912 her name was changed to the *Pittsburgh*, the new hull of BB 38 receiving the original designation. On 30 May 1913 the ship's status was raised to reduced reserve commission, and in this guise she trained West Coast state naval militias.

The situation in Mexico soon prompted the *Pittsburgh*'s recommissioning, and in early January 1914 she hoisted the flag of Rear Admiral Walter Cowles, commanding the Pacific Fleet. However, the condition of her boilers curbed her effectiveness, and she was relieved as flagship by the *California* in the first week of February and ordered to Bremerton. Following target practice off San Diego, the *Pittsburgh* tied up at the yard and was decommissioned.

She remained in this status until 4 February 1916, when she was placed in reserve commission. In July 1916 the *Pittsburgh*, in full commission since the spring, broke out the flag of Admiral William Caperton, the new commander in chief of the Pacific Fleet.

U.S. entry into World War I saw the *Pittsburgh* reassigned to the Scouting Force, Atlantic Fleet. The ship operated chiefly off the northeast coast of South America, hunting for German surface raiders, keeping watch on interned German merchantmen, and training drafts for the battle squadrons and destroyer divisions of the Atlantic Fleet. In October and November of 1918, during the great influenza epidemic that struck a war-ravaged world, the *Pittsburgh* lay at anchor in Buenos Aires. The ship's surgeon reported to the Bureau of Medicine and

---

*This feat was performed in 1861, when Aeronaut Thaddeus Low ascended from the planked deck of a former coal barge, renamed U.S. Balloon Boat *George Washington Parke Custis*.

The *South Dakota* in her original guise, c. 1908.

Surgery that in the city "the dead were allowed to remain in their houses and even in the streets for days. It was necessary to detail working parties from the USS *Pittsburgh* to bury the dead, as the cemetary authorities were helpless."[41]

After undergoing repairs at the Portsmouth Navy Yard, the *Pittsburgh* left home waters on 19 June 1919 and steamed for the eastern Mediterranean to assume her new duties as flagship of Rear Admiral Mark Bristol, commander in chief of U.S. naval forces in the Adriatic and U.S. high commissioner to Turkey. The vessel cruised the Adriatic, Aegean, Black, and eastern Mediterranean seas for the next ten months, during which she was home ported at Spalato, Yugoslavia. She aided in the evacuation of refugees, supplied food and medical relief to war-ravaged populations, and kept the peace between Turks, Greeks, Italians, and Yugoslavs.

In April 1920 the *Pittsburgh* was relieved of her duties in the Mediterranean by the *Olympia* and steamed north to hoist the flag of Vice Admiral Albert Niblack, commanding U.S. naval forces in Europe. She cruised the Baltic, North Sea, and North Atlantic, then was ordered back to the United States in August 1921. The *Pittsburgh* entered League Island on 18 August 1921 and immediately underwent a material inspection. On 15 October 1921 the *Pittsburgh* was taken out of commission.

Her inactive status was short-lived, and the ship was recommissioned on 2 October 1921 as flagship of U.S. naval forces in Europe. In this capacity she served until July 1926, and with her charges—the four destroyers of Destroyer Division 26 and later 27—was a familiar sight along the European and North African coasts. Relieved by the light cruiser *Memphis* (CL 13), the *Pittsburgh* returned to the Brooklyn Navy Yard on 17 July 1926 for a complete overhaul.

The *Pittsburgh*'s career was still far from over. On 1 October she cleared New York for her new assignment as flagship of the Asiatic Fleet, Admiral Mark Bristol commanding. Steaming via the Panama Canal and Pearl Harbor, where she picked up and escorted the submarine *S-33* to Cavite, the *Pittsburgh* anchored off Chefoo on 23 December, relieving the *Huron*.

Active service began almost immediately as the *Pittsburgh* landed her marines at Shanghai on New Year's Day 1927 to safeguard American and foreign nationals from the vicissitudes of the Chinese civil war. The ship lay hove to in Shanghai through the spring of that year, aiding in the evacuation of foreign nationals in the Yangtze valley. She was part of the massive concentration of naval might on the station, which consisted of U.S., British, Japanese, French, Italian, Spanish, Portuguese, and Dutch warships. The U.S. force of four cruisers, four destroyers, one oiler, one transport, a minesweeper, and a gunboat was by far the largest contingent on the station, and its four-star admiral was the senior of the eight admirals in the combined fleets. Kemp Tolley notes in his book, *Yangtze Patrol*, "At that time, unless one had pressing business topside, he carefully avoided being trapped in the open at 0800. Proper observance of the ceremony of morning colors meant standing at attention and saluting for 20 minutes while the *Pittsburgh*'s band raced through the national anthems of nine nations."[42]

The *Pittsburgh* operated in northern Chinese waters until October 1928, then returned to the Philippines. On 2 December 1928 she tied up at Yokohama to represent the navy at the coronation of Emperor Hirohito. Standard patrolling on the station took up all of 1929, with the old ship now definitely showing her age. On 24 December 1929, owing to the poor condition of her main condensers, Admiral Bristol restricted her to 15 knots, and she steamed at this speed for the remainder of her career.

By late 1929 the navy had decided the *Pittsburgh* was no longer fit for service. On 9 September 1929 Admiral Bristol was relieved by Admiral Charles McVay. The *Pittsburgh* remained on the China station through February 1930, returned to Cavite for one month, and then went back to China for the remainder of the year. Her final service included hosting the governor-general of the Philippines, Dwight Davis, on a tour of southeast Asian ports.

On 27 February 1931 the *Pittsburgh* was relieved as Asiatic Fleet flagship at Shanghai by the new heavy cruiser *Houston* (CA 30).

She returned to the United States via the Mediterranean and secured to her berth at Norfolk. In the material inspection that followed it was noted that the ship had received a great deal of care, her turrets being specially commended for their good condition. The inspection report said, however, that she was of limited military value.

The *Pittsburgh* was decommissioned on 10 July 1931, then, on 5 October 1931, towed into the Chesapeake Bay to serve as a bombing target for the new Norden Mark 5 bombsight. Dummy armor-piercing bombs were dropped to determine penetration, and static explosives were set off in the hull at the point of penetration to gauge the blast effects.

On 21 December 1931 the *Pittsburgh* was stricken from the navy list and sold for scrapping to Union Shipbuilding of Baltimore.

The California

The *California* (ACR 6) was laid down at Union Iron Works, San Francisco, on 7 May 1902 and launched on 28 April 1904. The vessel was placed in commission at Mare Island on 1 August 1907 by Captain Thomas Phelps. On 12 October Phelps died and was replaced by the executive officer, Lieutenant Commander Newton A. McCully, who had been the U.S. Navy's official observer with the Russian forces in the Far East during the Russo-Japanese War. McCully, later commander of the Control Force, Atlantic Fleet, then of U.S. naval forces in Europe, remained in temporary command of the *California* until 18 November, when he was relieved by Captain Vicendon L. Cottman.

The *California*'s shakedown cruise along the Pacific Coast took the ship from Victoria, British Columbia, to Magdalena Bay. The cruise was completed on 5 January 1908 at San Diego, where she participated in the unveiling ceremonies of the *Bennington* memorial.* On 16 March she joined the Second Division, Pacific Fleet at San Pedro. Through the end of June 1908 the *California*, with the *South Dakota*, the *Washington*, and the flagship *Tennessee*, steamed along the Pacific coast, putting into various ports and participating in civic exhibitions and festivals. The division anchored in San Francisco Bay on 4 May and was present at the Pacific Fleet review on 17 May.

The *California* formed with the division at San Diego on 3 July and engaged in squadron exercises towing destroyers. She departed with

---

*On 21 July 1905 a boiler exploded on board the gunboat *Bennington* (PG 4) while she was getting under way at San Diego. Sixty men were killed and forty wounded.

The *South Dakota* entering dry dock no. 2, Mare Island, March 1910.

the fleet on 24 August for its voyage to Samoa and cruised with the flag until 7 June 1909 (see information on the *West Virginia*, above). On 10 June 1909 she entered Mare Island for repair and overhaul, remaining in dockyard hands through 14 August, when she rejoined the Pacific Fleet.

In a change-of-command ceremony on 3 September Captain Cottman was relieved by Captain Henry T. Mayo, who would later command the Atlantic Fleet during the war. Two days later the *California* departed with the fleet for its Asiatic deployment and accompanied the flag until 7 April 1910. She was detached on that date and ordered to Mare Island for docking and repair, where she remained until 9 August.

The *California* formed with the First Division on 11 August 1910 and sailed with it for Valparaiso and the Chilean centennial. She returned with the force to San Francisco on 16 October and cruised off the West Coast through the end of the year. On 16 January 1911 she was designated Pacific Fleet flagship and hoisted the flag of Rear Admiral Chauncey Thomas. The winter and spring of 1911 were spent in squadron and fleet evolutions with the torpedo flotillas, which included submarines. On 30 June the ship was ordered to Mare Island for an overhaul.

Refitting completed, the squadron was ordered to the Asiatic station. With the *California* leading, it cleared San Francisco on 21 November. On 16 December 1911 the squadron rounded Diamond Head. The *California* was the first large ship to enter Pearl Harbor through the newly dredged 35-foot channel.

The squadron was ordered back to the West Coast in late July 1912, when a revolution in Nicaragua began to destabilize the Central American region. With Rear Admiral W. H. H. Southerland, commander of the Pacific Fleet, on board, the *California* arrived off Corinto, Nicaragua, on 28 August and began landing a marine regiment plus her own landing force, both under the command of Colonel Joseph Pendleton, USMC. The contingent of twenty-seven hundred men bombarded the capital, Managua, with their 3-inch field guns and captured the rebel army under General Mena. They captured two rebel gunboats, the *Victoria* and *93*, at Grenada. The most noteworthy event of the campaign, the storming of the rebel stronghold at Coyotepe, ended the rebellion and brought temporary peace to the country.

The year 1913 was spent on the west coasts of Mexico and the United States, where the *California* performed general duties until relieved as fleet flagship by the *Pittsburgh*. She was ordered to Mare Island for repairs and overhaul in the fall, and left San Diego for Mazatlan on 24 February 1914, when she again assumed the mantle of fleet flagship. The ship remained on the station through the spring of 1915. On 1 September 1914 she was renamed *San Diego*, the name *California* being transferred to the hull of BB 44.

A boiler explosion placed the ship at Mare Island in reduced commission through the summer of 1915. In September 1915 the vessel assumed her role as flagship of the Pacific Fleet and hoisted the flag of Admiral Cameron Winslow. Conditions in Mexico again prompted a response, and she sailed with two companies of marines on 28 November to Mexican waters. The force was not landed, and the ship returned to the United States in February 1916, continuing in service as flagship for the remainder of the year.

The *South Dakota* moored alongside the battleship *Oregon* (BB 3), Mare Island, c. 1913. Though both vessels are classic representatives of the New Navy, there was a vast jump in technology and operational theory in the decade between the dates they were authorized. The hull of the *Oregon* is that of a low-freeboard monitor, justifying her designation as a "coastline battleship," whereas the *South Dakota* has a high-freeboard, good-seakeeping hull. Note the *Oregon*'s obsolete cylindrical turrets. Lattice masts have been fitted to both ships (mainmast in the *Oregon*, foremast in the *South Dakota*).

On 12 February 1917 the *San Diego* was reduced to reserve status until the U.S. entry into the war. Placed in full commission on 7 April 1917, she served as flagship for the commander, Patrol Force, Pacific Fleet. Orders detaching the ship arrived on 18 July, and she was assigned to the Second Division, Cruiser and Transport Force, Atlantic Fleet. The *San Diego* arrived at Hampton Roads on 4 August and broke out the flag of Rear Admiral Albert Gleaves, which she flew until 19 September, when she was relieved by the *Seattle*.

Based at Tompkinsville and Halifax, the *San Diego* performed the dangerous and grueling duty of convoy escort. Steaming to a midocean meeting point, she turned her charges over to American and British destroyers and picked up a convoy steaming in ballast for the return voyage to the East Coast. On 19 July 1918 the *San Diego* met her end in this role, the only major U.S. warship to be sunk in the First World War.

At 1105 during the forenoon watch of 19 July, the *San Diego*, under Captain Harley Christy, was zigzagging at 15 knots on her way from Portsmouth, New Hampshire, to Brooklyn to pick up a convoy. Some of her crew had already shifted into their liberty uniforms, and many of those off watch were crowding the upper decks for a first look at the New York skyline. Just northeast of the Fire Island lightship, sixty miles from her destination, the ship struck a mine recently laid by *U-156*. An explosion occurred between the port engine room and the no. 8 fire-room at frame 78. The engine room and adjacent compartments were immediately flooded, and the ship rapidly assumed a 17.5-degree list.

Captain Christy, who had been conning the ship from atop the wheelhouse and thought the *San Diego* had been torpedoed, sounded submarine defense quarters and ordered the guns to fire at anything resembling a periscope. Both engines were rung full ahead, and the helm was put hard over in an attempt to beach. But the ship was flooding and listing fast, and she soon lost power and headway. The sea entered through the port of the no. 10 6-inch gun—which had been removed but not plated over—quickly flooding the gun deck and accelerating the heel. Ten minutes from the time of the explosion Captain Christy ordered the abandon ship alarm sounded. Due to a loss of electric power, the boat cranes were inoperable and the larger cutters and whaleboats could not be hoisted out; the crew took to the water in Carley floats, dinghies, and smaller hand-hoisted boats.

However, Admiral Gleaves recorded that the gun crews "were directed to stand by their guns until they could no longer fire, and this order was carried out to the letter. Thirty or forty rounds were fired from the broadside battery at possible periscopes and wakes before the port guns were awash and the starboard guns pointed up into the air by the listing of the ship. The gun crews were then ordered to take to the water."[43] The ship was abandoned in an orderly fashion, the captain being the last to leave her. The *San Diego* floated bottom up for one minute, then slowly began to sink, twenty minutes after the explosion.

Lieutenant C. J. Bright was ordered to proceed in a dinghy to the Long Island shore to send wireless messages to ships at sea and to the force command at Brooklyn. This he ably accomplished, and in short order the steamers *Malden*, *Bussan*, and *E. P. Jones* arrived on the scene to rescue the survivors. The disaster claimed the lives of but six men.

The Colorado

The keel of the *Colorado* (ACR 7) was laid at William Cramp and Sons on 25 April 1901, and the hull slid down the ways into the Delaware River on 25 April 1903. The ship was commissioned into the navy on 19 January 1905 at League Island, with Captain Duncan Kennedy in command. The vessel's shakedown cruise along the East Coast and in the Caribbean lasted until September, during which the floating dry dock *Dewey* was tested to ascertain whether it could take evenly distributed weights of the greatest proportions.

After running her final acceptance trials on the Cape Ann course, the *Colorado* joined the Fourth Division, Atlantic Fleet, at Provincetown, Massachusetts, on 11 October 1905. The *Colorado* steamed with the division for the next two and a half years, participating in various receptions, reviews, evolutions, and extended Asiatic deployments (see the *West Virginia*, above). On 12 April 1906, at the target range off Cape Cruz, Cuba, Captain Kennedy took ill and died. He was temporarily replaced by the executive officer, Lieutenant Commander Joseph L. Jayne. On 16 July, during repairs at Brooklyn, Captain Sydney A. Staunton reported on board to take command.

The *Colorado* returned with the division from its Asiatic deployment on 27 September 1907 and spent the remainder of the year and the first half of 1908 with the flag on the East Coast. On 14 June 1908 she was detached and ordered to Bremerton for repairs. The *Colorado* cleared the yard on 15 August but ran aground on Lip Lip Point, Puget Sound. She returned to Bremerton for repairs, then left San Francisco on 7 October and rejoined the flag at Honolulu on the sixteenth. She steamed with the division through the rest of 1908 and the first half of 1909 (see the *West Virginia*, above), when she was again ordered to Bremerton for overhaul.

The division reformed at San Francisco on 2 September for its Asiatic deployment, the *Colorado* steaming with the flag through April 1910. She reentered the yard at Bremerton for an annual overhaul, staying in dockyard hands until 9 August. The vessel performed general duties on the West Coast and attended the Chilean centennial with the First Division and fleet. In November 1911 she was detached and sailed for the Asiatic station.

The *Colorado* served on that station until July 1912, when she returned to the West Coast and duty with the Pacific Fleet in Mexican and Central American waters. In company with the flagship *California* and other fleet units she supported landing force operations in Nicaragua. On 17 May 1913 the *Colorado* was placed in reduced commission as flagship of the Pacific Reserve Fleet at Bremerton.

Placed in full commission on 9 February 1915, though still flagship of the reserve fleet, the *Colorado* continued her patrolling in Mexican waters. She embarked three companies of the Second Battalion, Fourth Marine Regiment, on 17 June at San Diego. They arrived at Guaymas, Mexico, but the troops were not put ashore, and the ship returned to reduced commission at Bremerton in mid-August 1915.

On 9 November 1916 the ship was renamed *Pueblo* and her original name given to the projected hull of BB 45. While still in reduced commission, the *Pueblo* kept station in Mexican waters observing interned German merchant vessels. Upon the United States' entry into World War I, the *Pueblo* was placed in full commission as Scouting Force flagship, Atlantic Fleet. For the remainder of 1917 the vessel patrolled the South Atlantic searching for German surface raiders and blockading interned enemy merchant vessels at Bahia, Brazil.

The vessel, ordered to the Second Division, Cruiser and Transport Force, reported to Norfolk on 18 January 1918 for convoy escort duty. She made seven turnaround Atlantic passages until 16 October. On 18 January 1919 the *Pueblo* was ordered to the Transport Service for repatriation of the American Expeditionary Force. In this duty she spent 116 days at sea, 65 days in port, and in six voyages from Hoboken, New Jersey, to Brest, France, returned 10,136 troops. She was detached from the force on 15 July 1919, placed in reduced commission at League Island on 8 August, and decommissioned on 22 September.

On 2 April 1921 the *Pueblo* was recommissioned for her final service as receiving ship for the Third Naval District, Brooklyn Navy Yard. She served in this capacity until 28 September 1927. On 2 October 1930 the *Pueblo* was stricken from the navy list and sold for scrap.

The Maryland

The *Maryland* (ACR 8) was laid down at Newport News Shipbuilding and Drydock on 7 October 1901, launched on 12 November 1903, and placed in commission at the building yard on 18 April 1905 by Captain Royal R. Ingersoll, father of Admiral Royal E. Ingersoll, commander in chief of the Atlantic Fleet from 1942 to 1944. The vessel's shakedown cruise took place off the New England coast and included testing the new dry dock at the Boston Navy Yard. She was the first ship to use the facility. Completing her shakedown and standardization runs on 29 August, she formed with the Fourth Division, Atlantic Fleet, at Wolf Trap Light on 31 October 1905. Until 31 December 1907 the *Maryland* cruised with the flag and saw service identical to that of the *West Virginia*.

Burdened with extra coal, stores, and drafts, the *South Dakota*, riding very low, transits the Panama Canal en route to the Asiatic station, 1919.

On 6 April 1908 Lieutenant Commander William A. Moffett reported aboard as executive officer and transformed the ship into the crack unit of the Pacific Fleet. Moffett belonged to the second generation of naval reformers that came of age after the war with Spain. An early, ardent—some might say fanatical—proponent of naval aviation, he was appointed the first chief of the Bureau of Aeronautics in 1921, a post he held until his death in 1933, when he perished in the crash of the airship *Akron* (ZRS 4). Under Moffett's tutelage, the *Maryland* claimed the Pacific Fleet battle efficiency trophy. The ship's junior engineering officer, Ensign W. L. Calhoun (later vice admiral) recalled, ''The men excelled in gunnery and engineering, and had the reputation of being among the finest and happiest on any cruiser in the Navy. The 'Mary' became the scourge of the battleships, and of her sister cruisers. . . . The good old ship held every trophy of both gunnery and engineering that was offered.''[44] Moffett had developed a searchlight control for target identification, and with the system the targets were rapidly spotted and ripped to shreds by the *Maryland*'s 6- and 3-inch guns, setting another record.

After undergoing repairs at Mare Island, the *Maryland* cleared the yard on 17 August 1908 to join the fleet on its voyage to Samoa and returned via Honolulu for target practice at Magdalena Bay. Through the latter part of March 1909 the *Maryland* lay anchored at Ampala, Honduras, protecting American interests. On 10 June she was back at Mare Island for an annual overhaul. From that time until March 1911 the ship's service paralleled that of the *West Virginia*.

During this period the *Maryland* claimed another first, though not in gunnery, engineering, or athletics. In April 1909 Commander Moffett, suffering a blood circulation disorder, reported to the ship's surgeon, Ammen Farenholt, for treatment. A medical pioneer, Farenholt had rigged the first X-ray machine ever taken to sea in the *Maryland*'s sick bay. With help from the apparatus, which was served by the auxiliary wireless dynamo, Moffett's illness was diagnosed as fistula. He was the navy's first radiology patient.

Aside from her general duties with the fleet, the *Maryland* conducted a series of steaming tests between 1911 and 1914 using West Coast coal from various fields. Ships coal had been transported by collier from East Coast navy yards to the Pacific Fleet's bases in California and Washington at great cost to the government, but new sources had recently been found. The initial testing, in company with the *West Virginia*, took place between January and March 1911, using six representative coals from Washington and three from British Columbia. It is not known whether the testing was successful, and it probably was not, as the *Maryland* was employed in further experiments with Alaskan coal from the Bering and Matanuska fields in late 1913 and early summer 1914.

In September 1912 the *Maryland* carried Secretary of State Philander Knox to Yokohama for the funeral of the Emperor Meiji. During the Mexican crisis in late 1913 and early 1914 the ship cruised off Mazatlan.

Following repairs she cleared the Mare Island yard on 1 May, then arrived at her station off Manzanillo and remained intermittently in Mexican and Central American waters through the spring of 1915.

On 25 March 1915 the navy lost its first submarine. The *F-4* (ex-*Skate*) sank with twenty-one men during maneuvers off Honolulu in 51 fathoms. At Mare Island the *Maryland* was ordered to transport the salvage party and serve as tender for the operation. Her gear proved insufficient, and the ship returned to the navy yard to load specially constructed pontoons to bring the *F-4* to the surface. The *Maryland* arrived at Honolulu on 12 August and recommenced salvage operations. The navy divers showed great courage and tenacity as they descended to attach cables to the sunken submarine. The pontoons were attached to the hull and the vessel was refloated on 29 August.

The *Maryland* remained on the Pacific coast until April 1917, conducting naval militia training cruises to Hawaii and Samoa. On 9 November 1916 her name was changed to *Frederick*, the hull of BB 46 receiving her original designation.

When the United States entered the war, the *Frederick* was ordered to the Scouting Force, Atlantic Fleet, and maintained patrols in Brazilian waters through January 1918. Detached from South Atlantic duty, the vessel reported to the Second Division, Cruiser and Transport Force, for convoy escort duty. The *Frederick* shepherded her charges to the thirty-seventh meridian, in the mid-Atlantic, then returned to the East Coast with a convoy in ballast.

Following the armistice, the *Frederick* was attached to the Transport Service on 2 January 1919. She completed six turnaround voyages between Hampton Roads and Brest, spending 124 days at sea and returning 9,659 members of the American Expeditionary Force. On 14 July 1919 she was relieved of this duty and ordered to League Island in reduced commission.

She was placed in full commission in July 1920 for naval reserve and Naval Academy practice cruising. With only a skeleton crew on board, the ship coaled at Hampton Roads and embarked fifty reserve officers and seven hundred enlisted reservists. She then steamed to Newport to pick up the midshipmen and the U.S. Olympic team and take them to the 1920 games at Antwerp.

In December 1920 the *Frederick* returned to the Pacific as flagship of the Pacific Fleet train and remained on the West Coast until her decommissioning on 14 February 1922. She reported to the reserve fleet at Bremerton, where she tied up until struck from the navy list on 13 November 1929. The *Frederick* was sold to ship-breakers for scrapping on 11 February, 1930.

The South Dakota

The keel of the *South Dakota* (ACR 9) was laid down at Union Iron Works on 30 September 1902. The hull was launched on 21 July 1904, and the vessel was placed in commission at Mare Island on 27 January 1908, with Captain Charles Fox in command.

Her shakedown cruise in Mexican and California waters was completed on 9 April, and she joined the Second Division, Pacific Fleet, at San Francisco on 16 May 1908. On 24 August she secured a towline to a destroyer and steamed with the force on its voyage to Samoa. Upon the fleet's return the ship participated in target practice at Magdalena Bay. She then sailed to Nicaraguan and Honduran ports to protect U.S. nationals and interests.

On 19 June 1909 the *South Dakota* was ordered to Mare Island for repairs, and she remained in dockyard hands until 14 August. Duty at the Seattle exposition followed, and she rejoined the division at San Francisco on 5 September. The *South Dakota*'s service through 8 March 1910 was with the fleet as it made its forward deployment to the Asiatic station in the fall and winter of 1909 (see *West Virginia*, above). Returning to the West Coast, the ship was detached, along with the *Tennessee*, to form a special service squadron for duty in connection with the Argentine centennial. The vessels formed off the Farallon Islands on 31 March 1910 and arrived at their destination, Puerto Militar, Argentina, on 15 May.

When festivities concluded on 5 June the ships departed. Following visits to Valparaiso, Chile, and Callao, Peru, the *South Dakota* put into San Francisco and rejoined the fleet on 19 July. For the remainder of 1910 and until 30 June 1911 the *South Dakota* cruised with the Second Division and the whole Pacific Fleet in exercises on the West Coast. The Japanese training squadron was received and entertained at San Francisco in November 1910, and fleet torpedo defense drills took up most of January and February 1911. Steaming and battle practice evolutions were held in the spring. On 29 June the ship received orders for docking at Mare Island.

On 21 November 1911 the Armored Cruiser Squadron assembled in San Francisco Bay under the fleet commander, Rear Admiral W. H. H. Southerland, for an Asiatic station deployment. The four vessels, the *California* (flag), *Colorado*, *Maryland*, and *South Dakota*, spent three months in Hawaiian waters before clearing for Cavite on 18 March 1912. Operating with Olongapo as a base, the force exercised in the Far East until being recalled to the United States in late July for operations in Nicaragua (see *California*, above).

For the remainder of 1912 and until December 1913 the *South Dakota* served on the West Coast with the fleet. On 30 December 1913

The USS *Huron* as flagship of the Asiatic Fleet, 1926. Her gun deck had no armament, and the lack of air ports in the embrasures made life on board the *Huron* uncomfortable in tropical waters.

she was ordered into reduced commission with the Pacific Reserve Fleet at Bremerton.

Recommissioned on 17 April 1914 for the Vera Cruz crisis, the *South Dakota* led the protected cruiser *Raleigh* and the gunboat *Annapolis* (PG 10) to Acapulco, where fighting had broken out between federalist and constitutionalist factions.

At the conclusion of a Hawaiian voyage in August, the *South Dakota* reverted to reserve status at Bremerton on 28 September. She was flagship of the Pacific Reserve Fleet from 21 January 1915 until she was relieved by the *Milwaukee* (C 21) on 5 February 1916, but remained in reduced commission at the yard until 5 April 1917, when she was reactivated.

Transferred to the Atlantic Fleet, the *South Dakota* stood out from Bremerton on 12 April, and after transiting the Panama Canal she joined the *Pittsburgh*, *Pueblo*, and *Frederick* at Colon, Panama, on 29 May. She served on the old South Atlantic station until October 1918, when she was detached to the Cruiser and Transport Force. On 13 October she hoisted the flag of the commander, Second Division, Cruiser and Transport Force, and commenced convoy escort operations out of New York. On her first convoy the *South Dakota*, augmenting the transports, embarked 2,422 troops, many of whom had already contracted influenza. Eighty-eight men were afflicted during the passage, and four died en route.

Assigned to repatriation duty on 21 December 1918, the *South Dakota* completed two turnaround voyages and returned 3,463 troops before being detached on 20 July 1919. Following an overhaul in Brooklyn, which included replacement of one of her propeller shafts, the *South Dakota* began new service as flagship for Admiral Albert Gleaves, who had just been awarded his fourth star and command of the Asiatic Fleet.

The *South Dakota* sailed from New York on 5 September 1919 in conditions that reflected the parsimonious policies of the navy following a major war. In addition to her crew, at this time about five hundred men, the ship carried fourteen hundred raw drafts for the Asiatic Fleet. Five hundred were still in civilian clothes, and the Bureau of Medicine and Surgery reported that

> they had not been protected with cowpox or typhoid vaccination. They knew nothing of caring for themselves or their effects aboard ship. It is believed that only the hand of a kind Providence kept us free from some epidemic disease in the 50-odd days between New York and Manila. . . . Many of these men were much below the standard physically and looked to be below the minimum age. . . . At Colon it was necessary to take aboard 700 tons of coal in excess, which was stowed about the main and gun decks, thereby increasing the crowded conditions. . . . [Men had to sleep] in all sorts of out-of-the-way places. The galley, baking and bathing facilities were crowded to . . . excess.[45]

The *South Dakota* finally arrived at Cavite on 27 October 1919 to begin her seven-year career as flagship. As a first order of business, Admiral Gleaves transited the station and took the ship to the southern Philippines, Tahiti, Samoa, and Japanese and Chinese ports. In January 1920 the *South Dakota* and the old protected cruiser *Albany* were ordered to help keep order at Vladivostok during the withdrawal of U.S. and allied forces. During the vessel's stay, through February 1920, the temperature ranged from 1°F to −20°F, resulting in sixty-seven cases of influenza.

The troops were withdrawn by mid-February, when the *South Dakota* and her consorts, the *Albany, New Orleans*, and Destroyer Division 13, retired to Chefoo for short-range battle practice. On 7 June 1920 the *South Dakota* was renamed *Huron*, her original name going to the never-to-be-completed hull of BB 49.

This period of the *Huron*'s service on the Asiatic station was one of continual strife in China. The most active of the U.S. forces on the station, the Yangtze Patrol, was constantly escorting river traffic, suppressing bandits and piracy, evacuating refugees, and opening fire on whichever faction happened to be disturbing the orderly flow of commerce. As fighting erupted between the capital and Tientsin, threatening to sever the railroad, the *Huron* embarked the Asiatic Fleet Provisional Marine Battalion at Cavite on 25 April 1922 for China service. On 25 May she anchored off Taku and offloaded the landing force, which went into barracks at Tientsin.

In September 1922 the *Huron* led the northern elements of the fleet to Yokohama to aid the Japanese following the devastating Kanto earthquake. The ship's distillery and evaporating systems provided at times the only potable water for the city's hospitals. Field hospitals were established by fleet medical officers, and food and medical supplies were delivered.

The *Huron*'s career was now coming to a close. The sparce funds allocated by Congress were barely enough to keep modern vessels in repair and commission, and unless the *Huron* was provided with new boilers, she could not remain in service beyond 1926. She was relieved at Chefoo by the *Pittsburgh* on 23 December 1926 and ordered to Bremerton. She steamed from Cavite on New Year's Eve and tied up at Bremerton on 3 March 1927. Decommissioned on 17 June, the *Huron* was struck from the navy list and sold for scrap on 11 February 1930.

Pennsylvania-Class Characteristics

Dimensions

Pennsylvania and *Colorado*, 504' ½" oa x 69' 6½" max beam; *West Virginia* and *Maryland*, 503' 10¼" oa x 69' 6¼" max beam; *California* and *South Dakota*, 503' 11" oa x 69' 10½" max beam x 24' 1" mean draft, all

Displacement

Pennsylvania, 13,680 tons normal, full supply ammunition & stores, normal coal 15,138 tons full load
Tons-per-square-inch immersion at normal draft: *Pennsylvania*, 57.80
Metacentric height: 2.66' normal draft.

Armament

Original: four 8-in 40-cal Mk 5; fourteen 6-in 50-cal Mk 8 RF; sixteen 3-in 50-cal Mk 3 RF; two 6-pdr.; eight 1-pdr.; TT, two 18-in Whitehead; two 3-in field guns.
1910: four 8-in 45-cal Mk 6 replace originals, remainder as original
1918: four 8-in 45-cal Mk 6; four 6-in 50-cal Mk 8 RF; ten 3-in 50-cal Mk 3 RF; two 3-in Mk 2–3 AA

Protection

Belt: 6" KNC amidships, 5" KNC upper strake; 3½" Harvey ends
Transverse armored bulkheads: 4" Harvey
Barbettes: 6" KNC

Turrets: 6½" KNC front; 6" KNC sides; 1½" NS roof
Conning tower: 9" KNC circumference; 1½" NS roof
Conning tower tube: 5" KNC
Signal tower: 5" KNC circumference; 1½" NS roof
Main deck casemate: 2" NS
8-inch ammunition tubes: 3" Harvey
Armored deck flats: 1½" NS
Armored deck slopes: 4" NS
Cofferdam: cornpith cellulose

Machinery

Engines, original: *Pennsylvania, Colorado, California, South Dakota,* two
  sets 4-cyl VTE, outboard-turning; *West Virginia* and *Maryland,* two
  sets 4-cyl VTE, inboard-turning
1905: *West Virginia* and *Maryland,* two sets 4-cyl VTE, outboard-turning
Boilers, original: *Pennsylvania* and *Colorado,* thirty-two Niclausse WT;
  West Virginia, Maryland, California, South Dakota, sixteen Babcock &
  Wilcox WT
1911: *Pennsylvania* and *Colorado,* twenty-four Niclausse WT, eight composite Niclausse drums with Babcock & Wilcox headers and tubes
1914: *Pittsburgh* and *Colorado,* twelve Babcock & Wilcox WT, eight composite
1926: *Pittsburgh,* twelve Babcock & Wilcox WT
Indicated horsepower: 23,000
IHP generated on trials: *Pennsylvania,* 28,600; *West Virginia,* 25,726;
  California, 29,658; *Colorado,* 26,154; *Maryland,* 27,571; *South Dakota,*
  28,158
Trial speed: *Pennsylvania,* 22.43 kts; *West Virginia,* 22.14 kts; *California,*
  22.2 kts; *Colorado,* 22.22 kts; *Maryland,* 22.4 kts; *South Dakota,* 22.24
  kts
Coal capacity: *California,* 900 tons normal; 2,025 tons maximum
Steaming radius: *South Dakota,* 6,840 miles at 10 kts
Propellers: twin shaft, three-bladed

Complement

41 officers, 791 men (as commissioned)

Contract price (hull and machinery)

Pennsylvania, $3,890,000; *West Virginia,* $3,885,000; *California,*
  $3,800,000; *Colorado,* $3,780,000; *Maryland,* $3,775,000; *South Da-*
  kota, $3,750,000

Total cost

Pennsylvania, $5,707,579; *West Virginia*, $5,729,057; *California*, $5,580,450; *Colorado*, $5,692,142; *Maryland*, $5,682,894; *South Dakota*, $5,637,982

Pennsylvania-*Class Engineering Characteristics*

No. of engines	2, *West Virginia* and *Maryland*, inboard-turning
No. of cylinders, each engine	4 (2 low-pressure)
Diameter of high-pressure cylinders	38.5″
Diameter of intermediate-pressure cylinders	63.5″
Diameter of low-pressure cylinders	74″
Stroke of all pistons	48″
No. of main steam condensers	2
Combined cooling surface	28,718 sq. ft., *Pennsylvania*

Boilers, *Pennsylvania* and *Colorado*

No. of watertube boilers	32 Niclausse
Heating surface per boiler, 13 element	2,062 sq. ft.
Heating surface per boiler, 14 element	2,221 sq. ft.
Total heating surface, all boilers	68,537 sq. ft.
Grate surface per boiler, 13 element	48 sq. ft.
Grate surface per boiler, 14 element	52 sq. ft.
Total grate surface, all boilers	1,600 sq. ft.
Ratio heating to grate surface	42.83:1
Working pressure, all boilers	250 psi

Boilers, *West Virginia, California, Maryland, South Dakota*

No. of watertube boilers	16 Babcock & Wilcox
Heating surface per boiler	4,434 sq. ft.
Total heating surface, all boilers	70, 944 sq. ft.
Grate surface per boiler	100 sq. ft.
Total grate surface, all boilers	1,600 sq. ft.
Ratio heating to grate surface	44.34:1
Working pressure, all boilers	265 psi

5

The *Tennessee* Class

Introduction

The *Tennessee* (ACR 10) and *Washington* (ACR 11) were authorized by a congressional act of 1 July 1902 calling for "two first-class armored cruisers of not more than fourteen thousand and five hundred tons trial displacement, carrying the heaviest armor and most powerful armament for vessels of their class, and [having] the highest practical speed and great radius of action, and to cost, exclusive of armor and armament, not exceeding four million six hundred and fifty-nine thousand dollars each."[1] The second two vessels in the class, the *North Carolina* (ACR 12) and *Montana* (ACR 13), were authorized in the act of 27 April 1904 at a cost of not more than $4,400,000 per vessel.

Cramp received the builder's contract for the *Tennessee* at a contract price of $4,035,000. The parties signed on 9 February 1903 and arranged for a delivery date to the government forty-two months later. The New York Shipbuilding Company of Camden, New Jersey, was given the *Washington*, the first naval vessel to be built by that firm; she was to cost and take as much time to complete as the *Tennessee*. Newport News Shipbuilding and Drydock received the contracts for both the *North Carolina* and *Montana*, the costs for each being $3,575,000. The documents were signed on 3 January 1905 and 3 June 1905, respectively, and forty-two months were given for completion. Owing to various delays for which Newport News was not held responsible, the dates were extended to 27 April 1908 and 10 July 1908.

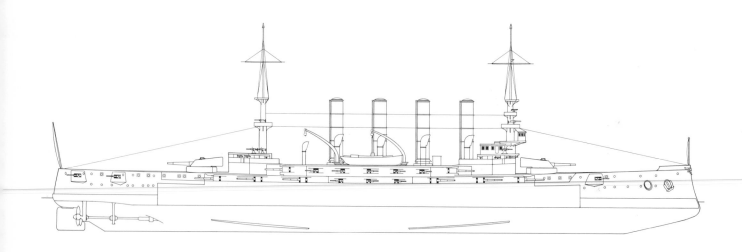

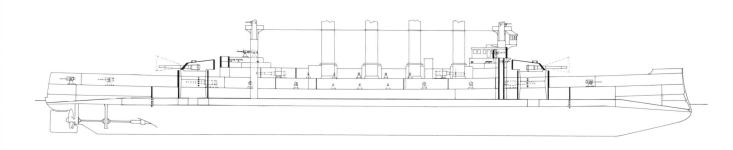

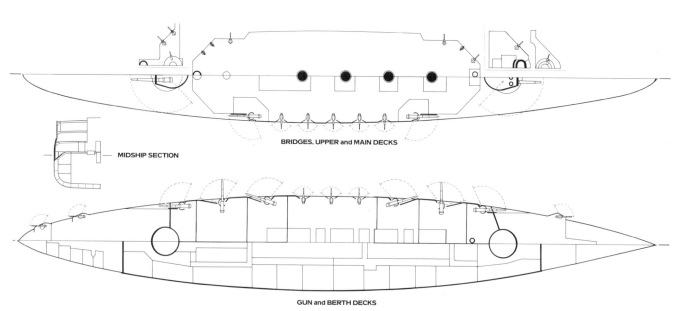

MIDSHIP SECTION

BRIDGES, UPPER and MAIN DECKS

GUN and BERTH DECKS

The USS *Tennessee* (ACR 10)

All contracts stipulated a trial speed averaging 22 knots, with a penalty clause of $50,000 for each quarter knot below the designed figure.

All vessels were to be fitted as flagships capable of carrying at least 816 men, including 60 marines.

The *Tennessee*s were essentially improvements of the *Pennsylvania*s, with an enhanced 10-inch main battery and a protection scheme that eliminated many of the glaring faults of the previous class. These were to be the most powerful cruisers built by the U.S. Navy until the mid-1930s. When they were designed they surpassed any armored cruiser in battery power and protection and rivaled most battleships.

Hull

With some important modifications, the hull design was the same as that of the *Pennsylvania* class. Overall length was increased to 504 feet 6 inches, the beam to 72 feet 10.5 inches, for a ratio of 6.91 to 1 (the *Pennsylvania*'s ratio was 7.2 to 1). The underwater hull form was built to finer lines and, coupled with the beamy waterline plane, produced a

The *Tennessee*, c. 1907. The vessel to starboard is probably the *Washington*.

remarkably steady class of vessels able to steam at 22 knots without an increase in horsepower specifications. Pitchers rather than rollers, they had a metacentric height of 3.30 feet and were very satisfactory seakeepers. Designed draft, which was limited by the depth of U.S. harbors, was 25 feet at normal load and 27 feet at full. Forward, the freeboard rose 24 feet at normal, 18 feet amidships, and 21.5 feet aft, which had the advantage of providing "commodious quarters for all officers and men above the waterline."[2]

For the first time the hulls were composed wholly of plates and shapes of commercial measure, all patterns previously used for naval vessels only being discarded. This resulted in not only cheaper construction costs but prompt delivery of steel, which was not the case when special shapes of relatively small quantities were ordered.

The hull was constructed on 123 frames, spaced four feet apart, with the forefoot cut away at frame 14 and the deadwood at frame 115. Bilge keels extended from frame 37 aft to frame 87. A balanced rudder with an area of 274 square feet was fitted. The double bottom spanned the inner hull from frame 19 forward to frame 105 aft and was subdivided into thirty-five watertight compartments. Underwater protection was increased when the subdivision was carried up the entire side of the subsurface hull to the lower edge of the armored deck slopes.

Beneath the armored deck, watertight integrity was maintained by twenty-eight electrically operated Long-Arm watertight doors and five armored hatches.

According to contemporary practice, full bridges were fitted forward and aft, and a flying bridge was installed forward. On the fore bridge there was a spacious bronze pilothouse with a steering wheel, engine telegraphs, indicators, voice tubes, telephones, and other fittings. Theoretically, the telephone was a great technological advance over the voice tube in interior communications. It was first used afloat in 1890, when Bradley Fiske's system was introduced in the *Baltimore*. But the trials board of the *Washington* reported the arrangement unsatisfactory: It was practically impossible to get through an intelligible and reliable message from any of the ammunition passages, handling rooms, steering engine room, or [anywhere that] machinery . . . makes much noise. . . . The same difficulty occurs on the bridge. If possible, the telephones and voice tubes on the bridge should be put inside the mast."[3]

The arrangement of masts followed the *Pennsylvania* pattern. The foremast carried upper and lower tops, plus a crow's nest above the signal yard; the mainmast carried a lower top only. Both masts were fitted to carry wireless antennae.

The *Tennessee* anchored in the Hudson River during the naval mobilizations and review, October 1912. The ship, having just undergone a major refit, has a grim, warlike appearance, in contrast to that of the white, buff, and bow-scrolled New Navy ships. Note the rangefinder atop the foremast and the absence of an after bridge.

Woodwork was kept to a minimum, but unlike woodwork in the *Pennsylvania*, it was not fireproofed. The exposed portions of the main deck, the boat and bridge decks, and the pilothouse roof were all planked in yellow pine with teak margins.

The usual large number of boats was shipped: three steam cutters, four 36-foot sailing cutters, two 36-foot sailing launches, five 30-foot whaleboats, one 30-foot whaleboat gig, one 30-foot admiral's barge, three dinghies, two balsas, and two Carley floats. Four large cranes, sited on either side of the number three and four funnels, plus eight sets of main deck davits, handled the complement.

At a time when British armored cruisers carried a minimum of top-hamper and fittings, U.S. naval vessels by comparison were over-burdened. The trials board criticized the "great weight taken up by such peacetime appurtenances as the flying bridge, the after bridge, heavy signal tower, the large pilot house, large ventilators and boat cranes, and heavy masts with fighting tops. . . . The Board can find no reason for loading these ships with great top weights of no military value."[4]

Armament

Commander William Hovgaard termed them "cruiser destroyers," and with their four 10-inch and sixteen 6-inch batteries, that is just what they were. If one discounts the original ACR 1 designation of the old *Maine*, the *Tennessee*s mounted the heaviest-caliber ordnance of any U.S. cruisers until the commissioning of the *Alaska* and *Guam* in 1944. When compared with the *Pennsylvania* class, they represented a 29.7 percent increase in ordnance weights and a huge 47.5 percent jump in weight of broadside. With very few exceptions, the class outgunned every foreign armored cruiser afloat or building. Their British contemporaries of the *Duke of Edinburgh*, *Warrior*, and *Minotaur* classes mounted a substantial portion of their armament on low-freeboard main decks, athwart sweeping forecastles, making them very wet and often useless in any sort of running sea. By comparison, the 10-inch guns of the *Tennessee*s were 30 feet above the waterline, and the quartet of main deck 6-inch guns were 25 feet above. Hovgaard considered the main battery, when comparing it with the broadside-mounted 9.2-inch guns of the *Duke of Edinburgh* and *Warrior*, "beyond question, the best gun position in a ship. The arc of fire is more than twice that which can be obtained on the broadside, the field of view is entirely free, and a combination of longitudinal and broadside fire on both sides is obtained, which is alone possible in the end positions."[5]

In terms of broadside weight, the *Tennessee*s slightly outmatched the four vessels of the Italian *Pisa* and *San Giorgio* classes. Designed by Vittorio Cuniberti, they mounted batteries of four 10-inch and eight 7.5-inch guns, the whole housed in six twin turrets, an advance over the broadside-mounted 6-inch guns of the *Tennessee*s. They were good ships that could make 22.5 to 23 knots, but they had low coal endurance, being designed primarily for Mediterranean service.

The major challenge to the *Tennessee* class came from the Japanese, when they completed the proto-battle cruisers *Tsukuba* and *Ikoma* in 1907–8. On a normal displacement of 13,750 tons, nearly identical to that of the *Pennsylvania*, the Japanese mounted the extreme armament of four 12-inch and twelve 6-inch guns (the 6-inch in broadside), making them in effect light, moderately fast, second-class battleships. These were the first large ships completely designed and built by the Japanese, and their two-and-a-half to three-year construction period reflected creditably on the shore establishment of the Imperial Navy. Two near sisters, the *Kurama* and *Ibuki*, were laid down at the Yokosuka and Kure yards in 1906 and 1907. Mounting a four-gun, 12-inch main battery and a heavily augmented intermediate battery of eight 8-inch guns in twin turrets on a 14,600-ton displacement, these two vessels blurred the distinction between the armored cruiser and the battle cruiser. Impressive as they were, these four Japanese vessels were too slow to perform the classic functions of a cruiser and too lightly protected to steam in the battle line. With the commissioning of HMS *Invincible* in 1908, all these ships became obsolescent.

The ordnance scheme for the *Tennessee* and *Washington*, completed in 1902, was four 10-inch 40-caliber guns, mounted in two balanced elliptical turrets; sixteen 6-inch 50-caliber RF guns, sited in four sponsons and twelve embrasured ports on the broadside; and a light battery of twenty-two 3-inch 50-caliber RF guns, two 1-pdr. RF guns, eight 30-caliber Colt machine guns, and two 3-inch field pieces for the marine detachment. No torpedo armament was initially planned. When the designs for the *North Carolina* and *Montana* were prepared in 1904, the General Board, in an inexplicably retrograde mood, advocated in lieu of the 10-inch battery the retention and mounting of eight 8-inch guns in four twin turrets, disposed in a lozenge formation as in the *Brooklyn*. This arrangement would have reduced the number of 6-inch guns to fourteen or even twelve had it been adopted. The exchanges concerning this decision that passed between the board and the Bureaus of Ordnance and Construction and Repair were acrimonious. The General Board finally conceded to the original 10-inch layout, as the plans for the vessels were almost complete and any radical design changes would have delayed construction.

The 6-inch Mark 8 guns were the same as those mounted in the *Pennsylvania* class. Four were installed in independent casemates at the corners of the main deck superstructure, 25 feet above the waterline, and sited for axial fire. The remaining guns were behind embrasured ports on the gun deck, the forward and after pairs placed so they could deliver axial fire and the entire battery training through an arc of 115 degrees. The 6-inch guns were so arranged that the barrels trained inboard of the line of the armored belt, thus facilitating the vessels coming alongside colliers.

Of the twenty-two 3-inch guns, twelve were mounted on the gun deck—six in small, flat-sided sponsons forward and aft and six in broadside mounts—and the rest were fitted in broadside mounts in the main deck superstructure. The 3-inch guns and mounts could be quickly removed from their stations and secured on board if the need arose.

Magazines and shellrooms were located fore and aft so that one half of the total ammunition supply could be stored at either end of the ship. A central longitudinal passage running the length of the hull facilitated handling. Magazine bulkheads adjacent to firerooms, engine rooms, bunkers, and generator compartments were fitted with dead air spaces as a heat-retarding measure. Four electric turret hoists delivered charge and shell from the magazine and shellroom into the turret

The *Tennessee* with visitors on board, New York, 1914. (Navy Department)

chamber; to aid the movement of the heavy 10-inch ammunition, the handling rooms were equipped with a track and trolley mechanism. Ammunition for the 6-inch and smaller guns was delivered directly from the magazines and shellrooms to the gun stations; there were sixteen electric hoists for the 6-inch guns and fourteen for the 3-inch and minor-caliber guns. The 10-inch guns were served with two rounds per minute for each gun, and each 6-inch gun was designed to receive six to seven rounds per minute. Ammunition allowances were sixty rounds for each 10-inch, two hundred for each 6-inch, and three hundred for each 3-inch gun. Improvements in the internal division of the *North Carolina* and *Montana* provided for a 20 percent increase in 10-inch and 6-inch ammunition in time of war.

During the final trials of the *Tennessee*, it was found that the baskets on the 10-inch hoists were too short to carry a full four-bag charge of 207 pounds. Additionally, the "toes" of the 6-inch continuous-chain hoists were spaced too far apart to allow the six/seven rounds per minute stipulated in the plans; in practice they served only three to four rounds per minute to each gun.

The torpedo armament of four submerged tubes, firing the 21-inch model 1905 Bliss-Leavitt torpedo, was the result of a protracted and often bitter controversy begun in 1899, with the General Board and the reactionary Bureau of Navigation on one side and the Bureaus of Ordnance and Construction and Repair on the other. The General Board had had its way in the installation of torpedo tubes in the *Virginia* and *Pennsylvania* classes. But the employment of tubes in armored vessels was no longer favored, and the Board on Construction, with Francis Bowles as president, omitted the outfit in the original plans for the *Tennessee* and *Washington*, reserving the space for added bunkerage. These plans were accepted by the General Board and approved by Secretary William Moody. But to the surprise of the constructors, on 20 December 1903, barely three weeks before the awarding of the builders contracts, the General Board questioned the lack of torpedoes in the design. Writing for the Board on Construction, the chief of the Bureau of Ordnance, Rear Admiral Charles O'Neill, questioned whether "any important feature on a battleship or armored cruiser [should be sacrificed] for the installation of a secondary weapon of remote value, . . . which requires tactics differing entirely from those best adapted to the gun, the primary weapon of such vessels."*[6] The contracts were awarded on schedule, but the question remained unresolved.

In the summer of 1903 Rear Admiral Henry C. Taylor, newly appointed chief of the Bureau of Navigation and actually a leading progressive, wrote to the General Board,

> The range, speed, and accuracy of torpedoes have so greatly increased within the past year or two that at the present time the torpedo may be considered a weapon of offense to be seriously reckoned with up to 3,000 yards, and even more. Since gun fire, in order to result in a decisive action, must be delivered at a range not greatly exceeding 3,000 yards, it follows that the tactics of fleet actions will hereafter be influenced by the presence or absence of torpedoes.[7]

The Bliss-Leavitt torpedo did indeed surpass its Whitehead predecessor. Packing a 300-lb. warhead, it had an extreme range of 4,000 yards and, depending on range, a speed of 27 to 36 knots. When compared with the 2,000-yard, 22-knot Whitehead, its use seemed to justify Admiral Taylor's position. But battle ranges were soon to multi-

---

*The battleships referred to were the *Connecticut* (BB 18) and *Louisiana* (BB 19), both laid down in 1903.

ply, making a 4,000-yard torpedo useless in large armored ships. For example, at the Battle of the Yellow Sea the Russian battleships *Tsarevitch* and *Retvizan* opened fire with their 12-inch guns at a range of 19,000 yards and dropped shot over 200 yards beyond the Japanese battleships *Mikasa* and *Asahi*.

In November 1903 Chief Constructor Bowles was relieved by Rear Admiral Washington L. Capps, whose first order of business was, as he put it, "the to be or not to be of the torpedo tube on armored vessels."[8] The Board on Construction reached its final decision in January 1904. Capps noted to Secretary Paul Morton, "After full consideration of the condition of the work on the battleships and armored cruisers in the course of construction, and . . . the very radical change in 'service sentiment' with respect to torpedoes, . . . the Board on Construction recommends that as many tubes be installed [as is possible] without serious interference to essential features."[9] Four subsurface tubes were subsequently fitted on the forward and after platform decks, at frames 37 and 101. In his recommendation for the change, Capps was careful to note that it would decrease bunker capacity and stowage space.

When the *Tennessee* and *Washington* entered service, the "seagoing element," as Capps described the Bureau of Navigation and its allies, astounded the Board on Construction with its criticism of the lack of bunkerage and concomitant decrease in steaming radius; the board advocated the removal of the tubes. Even Bradley Fiske, then commanding the *Tennessee* and an avid proponent of retaining the torpedo in armored vessels, reported to the General Board that the submerged torpedo tubes should be removed. In his final response to the matter, Capps noted to Secretary Victor Metcalf that the matter was yet "another instance in which *changes in the original design* have been subsequently discredited by those of the same branch of the naval service originally responsible for the changes in question."[10]

Protection

The *Tennessee* class presented the heaviest and most comprehensive protection of any U.S. cruisers to date and were not to be matched in this respect until the commissioning of the *Alaska* class in 1944. As greatly improved *Pennsylvania*s, the vessels carried 282 additional tons of Krupp and Harvey armor for a total of 2,190 tons and a 30 percent increase in total protection weight. The armor contracts for the *Tennessee* and *Washington* were signed on 28 February 1903, Carnegie and Bethlehem, respectively, receiving the order. The contracts for the *North Carolina* and *Montana* were signed on 1, 3, and 5 April 1905, the above firms receiving the award for 1,921 tons per ship and the Midvale Steel

The *Memphis*, 29 August 1916, thrown on the rocks by a seismic tidal wave and abandoned by her crew.

Company for the remaining 269 tons per vessel. It should be noted that the Midvale contract resulted in a saving to the navy of fifty-five dollars per ton. In its distribution, all armor six inches and thicker was Krupp armor and all five inches or thinner was Harveyized or untreated nickel steel.

The major improvements in the protection plan gave greater strength to the guns and ammunition supply and, most importantly, substantially increased the area of side armor. In the *Tennessee* and *Washington* the belt covered the length of the hull, being 18 feet high abreast the boiler and machinery spaces between frames 23 and 105 and descended from the gun deck port sills to five feet below the normal-load waterline of 25 feet. This area maintained a constant thickness of five inches of Krupp steel. Forward of frame 23 and aft of frame 105, the belt narrowed to seven feet in height and carried three inches of Harvey armor to stem and stern.

The upper strake of the belt, 5 inches thick and 320 feet long, extended from frames 30 to 95 and reached upward from the gun deck port sills to the main deck. This armor was carried up to the boat deck level at the corners of the superstructure to form bastions for the 6-inch guns on the main deck. The center of the upper strake, between frames 55 and 71, from the 3-inch gun deck sills to the boat deck, was sheathed in 2 inches of nickel steel.

A double set of armored transverse bulkheads of 5-inch thickness closed the belt, creating a twin citadel within the hull. The lower pair extended up from the armored to the gun deck at frames 23 and 105 and were complete athwartship enclosures. The upper pair from gun to main deck, at frames 30 and 95, came inboard only to the forward and after barbettes, to which their ends were secured.

In the *North Carolina* and *Montana* hull protection was modified. At its maximum width, the belt was reduced to 17 feet 3 inches with a consequent reduction to 4 feet 9 inches below the waterline. To compensate, the thickness of the armored transverse bulkheads was increased to 6 inches.

For the first time in U.S. cruiser design proper barbettes were constructed. At a height of five feet above the main deck and extending down fully to the armored deck, they completely enclosed the 10-inch ammunition tubes and thus rectified a glaring weakness of the *Pennsylvania* class. In the *Tennessee* and *Washington* the front and sides of the barbettes were sheathed in seven inches of Krupp armor from gun deck level to crown. On their unexposed upper rear surfaces and where they ran between the armored and gun decks, the barbettes were protected by four inches of Harvey steel. This protection was enhanced in the *North Carolina* and *Montana* by sheathing the front and side surfaces of the barbettes from the main deck to the crowns in eight inches and from the gun deck to the main deck in six inches. The area from the armored deck to the gun deck and the rear surfaces above the main deck were protected as in the *Tennessee* and *Washington*.

Surmounting the barbettes was a pair of balanced elliptical turrets housing the 10-inch guns. Unlike the diminutive turrets of the *Pennsylvanias*, which appeared incongruous with the ships' 502-foot length, the turrets mounted in the *Tennessee* class made for an imposing profile. Their faces were covered in nine inches of Krupp, their sides in seven, and their rear plates in five. The roof and sighting hoods were two and a half inches of nickel steel.

The trials board, however, noted a flaw in design during the *Washington*'s gunnery trials. "Attention is called to the lack of clearance between the sloping front of the turret and the gun mechanism," reported the board, "and a comparatively slight deformation of the front by a projectile is apt to wreck or deform the gun lugs."[11]

Complete athwartship splinter screens of one-and-a-half-inch nickel steel isolated the gun deck battery, protection augmented by a two-inch nickel steel longitudinal bulkhead running the length of the deck. One-and-a-half-inch nickel steel screens separated the 3-inch battery in the superstructure. The gun deck 3-inch sponsons were also covered with two inches of nickel steel.

Forward, a huge nine-inch-thick conning tower, located one deck higher than in the previous class, was fitted to all four vessels. There was also a five-inch signal tower at the after end of the superstructure. In the *Tennessee* and *Washington* the conning tower was provided with a nine-inch curved shield immediately abaft the structure. In the *North Carolina* and *Montana* the shield was not fitted, the saved weight being employed on the barbettes. Access to the conning tower was provided by a six-inch armored hatch. The conning tower tube was sheathed in five inches of Krupp and extended downward from the tower base to the central station on the armored deck.

Following the trials of the *Tennessee*, the conning tower came in for severe criticism from the trials board. It reported that the

> design and interior arrangement of the conning tower are entirely unsatisfactory. The sight holes in the armor are so small and the space so encumbered by battle order and other fittings for interior communication, that it is impossible to handle the ship safely . . . . The steering wheel, helm indicator, and engine telegraph should constitute the only equipment of the conning tower. The slots should be greatly enlarged to give a clear view, with as great an arc as possible, leaving only sufficient metal to support the top of the tower.[12]

Bradley Fiske also advocated the removal of most of the tower fixtures. But regarding the design, he deviated completely from the trials board recommendations. "I had become most impressed," he later wrote in his autobiography, "as most naval officers had, with the extreme vulnerability of the conning tower, and also with the liability of the captains and others in the tower to be disabled by smoke and fragments of all kinds through the slits . . . . My remedy was to abolish the slits altogether, and to have the people in the conning tower use periscopes, projecting upward through the top of the tower."[13]

These opinions suggest that there was disagreement over the

lessons drawn from the recently concluded Russo-Japanese War. Fiske's design most likely reflected a reaction to the disaster in the Russian flagship *Tsarevitch* at the Battle of the Yellow Sea on 10 August 1904. Leading the battle line and inflicting heavy punishment on the Japanese ships, she was struck square in a sight port of her conning tower by a 12-inch high-explosive shell. The entire complement of the structure, including the vice admiral commanding and the ship's captain, were killed instantly. The helmsman fell across the wheel, and the *Tsarevitch* sheered out of the line. The Russian battleships, in line astern of the flagship, followed the stricken vessel, thinking her movement a tactical maneuver. The fleet was thrown into disorder and the battle degenerated into a melee during which the Russian ships took flight.

The signal tower at the after end of the *Tennessee's* superstructure, which was covered with five-inch plates, also came in for criticism from the trials board. With its small size and obstructed view, it was not made for handling a division or squadron. The trials board advocated flagships fitted with armored shelters for flag officers, having an unobstructed view fore and aft, and able to communicate easily with the conning tower.

As was the case with several other elements of the protection scheme, the armored deck differed from one vessel of the class to another. In the *Tennessee* and *Washington*, the flats throughout the length of the deck were one-and-a-half-inch nickel steel. The slopes amidships, covering the boilers, machinery spaces, and magazines, were built up to four inches of nickel steel, tapering to three inches at the ends of the hull. The *North Carolina* and *Montana*, in order to accommodate the decreased area of the belt below the waterline, maintained two inches of nickel steel on the flats over the critical spaces amidships, tapering to one inch at the ends. The slopes were four inches amidships, thinning to three inches at the extremities.

The cellulose cofferdams used for the last time in the *Tennessee* and *Washington*, was omitted in the *North Carolina* and *Montana*.

Machinery

With the exception of appendage modifications, the propulsion machinery of the class was a near duplicate of the generally successful arrangement in the *California* and *South Dakota*. Twin outboard-turning engines, generating 22 knots with 23,000 IHP and fired by sixteen Babcock & Wilcox boilers, were installed. There was some criticism that the 22-knot contract speed placed the class at a disadvantage; the four British *Drake*-class armored cruisers (1902–3) were officially one knot faster.

A view of the *Washington* in her original guise, Puget Sound, 1908.

The original recommendations of the General Board had stipulated an inboard-turning plant for the *Tennessee* and *Washington* of 25,000 IHP and 23 knots, which would have given them the most powerful triple-expansion engines in the New Navy. However, it was soon noted that this was a dubious advantage, as the additional machinery weights would severely affect the armament and protection weight. To prove the point, Chief Constructor Francis Bowles placed before the board the trials report of the *Drake*-class cruiser, *Good Hope*. This ship, while easily reaching 22 knots with 22,500 IHP, needed to generate 31,000 IHP with forty-three notoriously inefficient Belleville boilers to stretch out the extra knot. The *Drake*s, and the *Good Hope* in particular, paid dearly for this "asset," since the machinery weights meant that the main battery could not exceed two 9.2-inch guns. This factor contributed to the loss of the *Good Hope* at Coronel.

Convinced by the chief constructor's arguments, the General Board reconsidered and in 1902 ordered the *California/South Dakota* design. Commander Hovgaard, among others, considered this a wise decision which made the *Tennessee* and *Washington* far better fighting ships.

As in the *Pennsylvania*s, the engines were placed in separate water-tight compartments on either side of a longitudinal bulkhead. They were the standard: vertical, inverted cylinder, direct acting, four cylinder, triple expansion, outboard turning. The cylinders were arranged, forward to aft, in the following order: low pressure, high pressure, intermediate pressure, low pressure.

In a successful experiment, the New York Shipbuilding Company fitted the *Washington*'s engines with the "improved Lovekin-Thom assistant cylinder."* The function of this device was to assist the valves in providing additional steam to the main cylinders at critical moments of expansion and contraction, thus permitting the forces of gravity and inertia to continue their motion and force at the point of greatest downward thrust by the engine pistons. The steam was forced through the valve chest into the main cylinders at the lowest point of expansion, and the inertial force continued into the upward compression stroke. The major advantage of the assistant cylinder was that it evened unequal weights on the crankshaft and bearings, reducing friction on the major elements and the need for water service on the shaft bearings. Consequently, less maintenance and fewer overhauls of critical propulsion elements were required.

In tests comparing the *Washington*'s plant with that of the *Tennessee*, it was found that the "unbalanced" load on the *Washington*'s crank shaft was 5,000 pounds and that on the *Tennessee*, without the assistant cylinder, 13,080 pounds. Had the steam in the *Washington* been properly regulated, the results would have been more impressive still.

Engines were generally lubricated as they were in the *Pennsylvania* class, with oil reservoir tanks holding 3,000 gallons and located at the after ends of the engine rooms. Pumps bolted to the centerline bulkhead drew oil from the tanks and discharged it into smaller distribution tanks, where gravity fed it into the boxes on the engines.

The ships were fired by sixteen Babcock & Wilcox boilers. The boilers were sited, two together, in eight watertight firerooms.

Forced draft was achieved as in the previous class: two Sturtevant 60-inch fan blowers were bolted to the underside of the armored deck over each fireroom, and suction was provided from the fireroom ventilators.

Coal capacity was 900 tons normal and 2,000 tons maximum for the *Tennessee* and *Washington*, though this was exceeded by 20 tons in the former vessel and 160 tons in the latter. There were thirty bunkers, twenty below the armored deck and ten above it. Coal endurance at ten knots was 7,300 miles, and the class outdistanced the *Pennsylvania* and *Colorado* by three hundred to five hundred miles. In the modified designs of the *North Carolina* and *Montana*, 200 tons of additional capacity were provided by relocating all firemen's and machinists' washrooms above the waterline to the berth deck; coal was to be fed from the upper tier of bunkers directly into the firerooms, without having to be

---

*This cylinder was also fitted to two other ships, the battleships *Kansas* (BB 21) and *Nebraska* (BB 14), but only after they had been installed and tested in the *Washington*.

The *Washington* shortly after commissioning. The vessel partially visible on her port quarter is the *Brooklyn*.

trimmed through the lower tiers. But the trials board still found the supply wanting and, following the *Montana*'s speed trials, reported that the coal supply was inadequate: "The capacity is 1,939 tons—by very careful stowage and by filling the bunkers 2,040 tons have been stored. The only feasible way [to store additional coal] seems to be by utilizing the forward torpedo room as a coal bunker; also by filling the coffer-dams in the bunkers with briquettes." By this means an additional 540 tons could be shipped, and the after torpedo tubes could still be employed for "defense, offense, and moral effect."[14]

Eight ash-hoisting engines were fitted in the funnel hatches adjacent to the fireroom ventilating shafts. Each engine lifted 300 pounds in five seconds to the chutes on the main deck. Dumping ashes from the main deck was considered far more conducive to the crew's health than dumping ashes from the berth deck, and it had the added benefit of not disrupting their sleep. After many classes of ships had been built in the New Navy, the department finally noticed that ships were unable to hoist ashes while running under forced draft. The trials board reported in the case of the *North Carolina* that "when the ship is under forced draft, ashes cannot be hoisted without impairing the forced draft. Steps should be taken to correct this condition by installing ash ejectors, or a suitable device."[15]

The boiler feed tanks, placed on the outboard after end of each engine room, had a combined capacity of 12,020 gallons. The tanks, with the exception of the heating system, were fed by the drains from all steam lines as well as by the evaporators and distillers. As in the

Pennsylvania class, the pumping system fed through a hot well to the suction of the main feed pumps.

The majestic quartet of funnels rose 100 feet above the grates and, in the *Tennessee* and *Washington,* were fully encased. In the *North Carolina* and *Montana* the outer casing ended 18 feet short of the caps, giving these vessels a distinctive if slightly unsatisfactory appearance.

Each main condenser was, as usual, located in an engine room, and each consisted of 6,292 seamless-drawn cooling tubes for a total cooling surface of 28,822 square feet.

The electrical plant, just forward of the engine rooms, beneath the armored deck, was divided by the central ammunition passage. Each vessel was equipped with six General Electric 100kw generators, three in each dynamo room. Transverse switching was provided by duplicate panels in each compartment. There were two turning motors for each turret, and separate elevating motors were fitted for each 10-inch gun. With the exception of the power for the steering engine, anchor windlass, ash hoists, forced-draft blowers, and evaporating/distilling plant, all power was electrical. The vessels were lighted by 1,325 incandescent lamps (with minor variations), including one arc light in each fireroom and two in each engine room. Refinements in the *North Carolina* and *Montana* included "a dish-washing machine . . . driven by an electric motor" and "a kneading machine."[16] There were six searchlight projectors, of 30-inch diameter in the *Tennessee* and *Washington.* In the *North Carolina* and *Montana* the outfit comprised two 60-inch and four 30-inch lights. All were hand operated and manufactured by General Electric. The 60-inch lights were on platforms atop each mast, and of the remainder there were two on the fore bridge and two on a small platform fitted to the mainmast immediately above the after bridge. Search lights were similarly placed in the *Tennessee* and *Washington,* albeit with 30-inch projectors in each station. The trials board thought the position of the stations on the fore bridge was awkward and recommended they be placed on platforms built out from the wings, as in the *Rhode Island.*

All main compartments below the gun deck, except the coal bunkers, which were provided with exhausts, had forced-air ventilation. Twenty-six fan blowers with a combined capacity of 110,000 cubic feet per minute were fitted. Paying heed to lessons of previous classes, the designers gave special attention to spaces subject to habitually high temperatures, such as engine, fire, and dynamo rooms. Crew habitability, on the other hand, was found wanting. During the *Washington*'s shakedown cruise to the Caribbean, quarters for both officers and crew on the berth and gun deck levels were decidedly uncomfortable when the outside temperature reached 80°F; and as the ship's executive officer reported, "when the wind is ahead and temperature is 80 or above, [the after wardroom] becomes uninhabitable for sleeping, as the blowers cannot be run, unless the compartments are filled with smoke and gasses."[17]

The evaporating and distilling apparatus operated on the berth deck just forward of the engine room hatch. With four evaporators and four distillers, there was a combined capacity of 46,000 gallons of fresh water every twenty-four hours.

Shafting and propellers were the same size as those in the *Pennsylvania*s. Designs called for twin shafts 48 feet 5.6 inches long and 19.25 inches in diameter. They were constructed of nickel steel forgings, oil tempered and annealed. The three-bladed propellers were made of manganese bronze, 18 feet in diameter and pitched to 23.5 feet. During construction the *Washington*'s propellers were incorrectly machined to 18 feet 6 inches, an error that undetected would have resulted in uneven wear on the entire shafting system. This situation was rectified prior to preliminary acceptance trials by grinding three inches off the tip of each blade.

Trials

The Tennessee

The *Tennessee* underwent dock trials on 24 August 1905 and steamed from the Delaware on 1 February 1906 for government trials at Rock-

Foreshadowing a new age, the *Seattle* carries her complement of Curtiss hydroplanes as flagship, Destroyer Force, Atlantic Fleet, in early 1917. Note the boat crane extensions for handling aircraft.

land, Maine. Builder's trials were considered unnecessary, final adjustments being performed while the ship was under way to Boston for scraping and painting. The original date for standardization runs had been set for 8 February, but delays in coal delivery and heavy weather kept her in Boston for two days.

The first of the fourteen standardization runs over the measured mile began at 0700 on 11 February. It was calculated that 126.2 propeller rpm was necessary to obtain her 22-knot contract speed. Certain problems, however, arose. Although sufficient steam was provided by the boilers, the safety valves remained closed, and there was almost no reserve in the steam jackets. According to a trials synopsis, "The firemen were worked hard, and the [forced-draft] blower engines made about 600 rpm."[18] It was noted that the fires, which were carried to a thickness of six to eight inches, had burned through the grate bars in places, admitting a large excess of air and reducing the effective heat of the firebox. The mediocre quality of the coal, a mixture of Pocahontas and New River, demanded a thicker fire of 12 to 14 inches to maintain adequate reserves of steam.

Observations were also made of firing procedures. Firing signals were given in one-minute intervals for each of the six fireboxes in each boiler. Upon hearing the signal, the firemen opened the door, raked the fires, then immediately coaled them, keeping the door open for approximately one minute. With this system the fireman had to open the firebox door, rake the fire, pick up his shovel, and coal the fires, all the while keeping the firebox open. Thus at any given time sixteen fireboxes in the plant were open, admitting rushing air and adversely affecting fuel consumption. This problem was partially rectified during the *Tennessee*'s speed trials, where the two leading firemen on boilers O and Q opened and closed the doors for the firemen working the fires, thus reducing the time the doors were open to 34 and 38 seconds, respectively.

Four-hour speed trials were conducted the next day; the weather was overcast and cold, and gentle breezes blew from the west. The ship's draft was measured at a mean of 25 feet 2 inches on a displacement of 14,639 tons. Coal was run-of-the-mine Pocahontas. Steam pressure was set at 250 psi at the high-pressure receivers, and the fires were increased to 12 to 14 inches.

The *Tennessee* crossed the starting line at 0843 hours and rapidly worked up to speed. At 0958 it was reported to Cramp's officials on the bridge that the low-pressure crank pin brasses on the starboard forward engine were overheating and sheering the dowel pins, and unless the engines were immediately stopped major damage would result. The request was made of the trials board, and the *Tennessee* lay at anchor having repairs made until 1600.

The ship recommenced her trials, but after one and a half hours the starboard feedwater heater broke down, reducing the temperature from 220°F to 65°F. By lowering the rpm of the forced-draft blowers, enough steam was provided to maintain 127.4 rpm on the main engines, and the *Tennessee* continued without pause. With a combined main engine horsepower of 26,534, speed averaged 22.44 knots, and except for the malfunctioning of the crank pins, the trials board deemed the machinery performance satisfactory. The board also called attention to the "filthy and disorganized condition of this vessel at the time of the preliminary trial."[19]

Maneuvering exercises were held on the run back to Boston. Thirty seconds were required to answer the helm from amidships to hard aport, 20 seconds to hard astarboard; to swing through 360 degrees it took a full 4 minutes 47 seconds. The trials board noted that it required more than one man to steer the ship properly, and that her steering gear was unsatisfactory because of the time it took to put the helm over.

On 11 July 1906 the *Tennessee* was accepted on a preliminary basis and delivered to the commandant of the Philadelphia Navy Yard at League Island.

The Washington

Dock trials were held in the *Washington* during December 1905, and because of their success builder's trials were dispensed with. On 29 March 1906 the *Washington* left her berth at Camden, New Jersey, for docking at Newport News. Scraping and painting completed, the ship cleared for Rockland, Maine, on 7 April, accomplishing the 645-mile voyage in thirty-four hours and averaging 19 knots under natural draft.

Standardization runs were scheduled for the tenth, but as the weather was stormy they were postponed one day. Average speed over the measured mile was tabulated at 22.54 knots at 124.9 rpm. The four-hour trials were held on the twelfth. The *Washington* displaced 14,600 tons on a mean draft of 25 feet 2 inches. Coal was excellent hand-picked Pocahontas.

The ship left her anchorage off Rockland at 1015 hours and steered a straight southeast course to sea. After two hours were spent working up to full power, the signal was given at 1215 to begin the trial. Steam pressure at the gauges was measured at 274.2 psi, and due to the good-quality coal, the fires were built to an eight- to ten-inch thickness. Conditions in the firerooms were optimum, with one watertender, four firemen, two coal passers, and one apprentice boy in each compart-

Flying a four-star admiral's flag, the *Seattle* is serving as administrative flagship of the commander in chief, U.S. Fleet, c. 1922.

ment. One firebox was fired every 72 seconds. Boiler space temperatures were abnormally low, generally hovering at 80°F, with hot pockets reaching only 95°F.

The speed trials concluded successfully at 1615. Combined, the main engines generated 26,862 hp and a mean speed of 22.27 knots. The Lovekin-Thom assistant cylinders were praised for running smoothly.

Maneuvering evolutions following the speed trials were also completely successful. The helm answered in ten seconds from rudder amidships to both hard astarboard and hard aport, with a respective maximum heel of seven and four degrees. Tactical diameter was measured at 600 yards.

In its summation, the trials board praised the *Washington* for being clean and orderly, expressed satisfaction with the inspections, and commended the work of the contractors. On 30 July 1906 the *Washington* was accepted on a preliminary basis and delivered to the commandant of the yard at League Island.

The North Carolina

Documentation concerning dock and builder's trials is no longer extant for the *North Carolina*. The first recorded trial standardization runs were held off the Rockland course on 6 January 1908; with 118.64 rpm 22 knots was achieved.

The speed trials were conducted the next day in overcast weather and moderate seas. Displacement was 14,613 tons on a mean draft of 25 feet 1.75 inches. Coal was hand-picked New River. The *North Carolina* steered a course south by southwest, worked up to speed, and in four hours obtained a maximum speed of 22.19 knots but a calculated mean of only 21.91 knots. At the request of the contractors, and with the approval of the secretary of the navy, a second speed trial was scheduled for 9 January, when the vessel would be on her twenty-four-hour endurance run.

On the second trial, the *North Carolina* displaced 14,623 tons on a mean draft of 25 feet. Coal was run-of-the-mine New River. The trial began at 0814 hours off Cape Cod. At 1400 the contractors appeared on the bridge and requested that the doors into the fireroom bulkheads be opened, as there were not enough qualified men to supervise the firing. These doors, 30 by 21 inches, were a temporary feature in both the *North Carolina* and *Montana*, meant as a quick means of escape in the event of a steam rupture and for communication between fireroom personnel. Prior to the standardization runs, the Bureau of Steam Engineering agreed to the temporary cutting of the bulkheads, but it wanted the doors sealed during the trials and used not as a means for ordinary communications but for emergencies only. The president of the trials board, Rear Admiral Richardson Clover, informed the contractors that he could not grant permission for their request, and if they wished to open the doors it was their own responsibility. At 1414 the seals were broken and the doors opened. The *North Carolina*'s mean speed, however, calculated at 21.60 knots, was still not satisfactory.

A third trial, held on 18 January off Fortress Monroe, Virginia, was also unsuccessful. After one hour and 15 minutes the port high-pressure, starboard intermediate-pressure, and after low-pressure crank pin brasses overheated, requiring heavy use of the water service. The trial was discontinued.

A fourth and final trial was held on 15 February, and had the *North Carolina* not obtained her contract speed, the penalty clause of $50,000 per quarter knot below 22 knots would have been applied to Newport News Shipbuilding and Drydock. The vessel displaced 14,847 tons on a mean draft of 25 feet .05 inches. Coal was excellent hand-picked Nuttelberg, and steam pressure at the high-pressure cylinders was raised from 250 to 260 psi. The combined horsepower of the main engines reached 29,225; speed was averaged at 22.481 knots.

The Montana

As with the *North Carolina*, records of the *Montana*'s dock and builder's trials, if there ever were any, no longer exist. She arrived off Rockland on 1 April 1908 for standardization, and during the runs was barely able to maintain her contract requirement, speed averaging 22.03 knots. The contractors requested that the valve settings be reset, as in the fourth trial of the *North Carolina*, to permit a higher steam pressure. After deliberation the trials board unanimously agreed and wired its decision to Secretary Metcalf. But to the consternation of all, especially since the adjustments had already been made, he denied the request. Urgent communications now passed between Newport News and the secretary as the contractors pleaded with him to rescind his decision, which he did.

The speed trials were conducted on 4 April off Monhegan Island, twenty-eight miles east of Cape Cod. Displacement was 14,531 tons on a mean draft of 25 feet 0.43 inches. Coal was excellent hand-picked Nuttelberg. The weather was clear and cold; there were fresh breezes from the northeast at the outset, increasing to a strong gale at the trial's conclusion, during which the ship was worked heavily and had a maximum windward roll of 11.5 degrees and a leeward roll of 18 degrees.

Pressure in the boilers reached 272 psi, and the engines generated 27,489 hp for a maximum speed of 22.43 knots and a mean of 22.26 knots. The trials board considered the machinery, with the exception of faulty throttle valves and leaky tubes in boilers N and Q, satisfactory, and the *Montana* was accepted on a preliminary basis on 10 July 1908.

Modifications and Refits

For several reasons the *Tennessee*s did not undergo as much refitting as the *Pennsylvania*s that preceded them. First, their major propulsion components were built to general specifications, with common Babcock & Wilcox boilering and outboard-turning engines. Second, as designed improvements of the *Pennsylvania* class, they were constructed with ordnance features such as automatic ammunition-hoist shutters, longitudinal turret bulkheads, and turret officer booths, which obviated the need for retrofitting. Third, as they were commissioned as much as three years after the first units of the *Pennsylvania* class, the *Tennessee*s reached the point of obsolescence earlier in their careers.

Major class-wide modifications, which were begun in 1911, included fitting lattice foremasts with modern bridges and removing, in 1918–19, the entire gun-deck battery of twelve 6-inch and twelve 3-inch guns.

The Tennessee

Early in her career, while escorting President Roosevelt in the *Louisiana*, the *Tennessee* suffered a major engine breakdown en route to Colon, Panama. Temporary repairs were made on board, but the ship had to

The *North Carolina* during her unsuccessful speed trial of 7 January 1908.

dock at League Island from 18 December 1906 to 12 April 1907. The Board of Inspection and Survey attributed the breakdown to the inferior grade of lube oil used on the engines.

Until 1912 the *Tennessee*'s modifications were comparatively minor. Turret sights were fitted in 1907, and improved fire control apparatus was installed at Bremerton in 1908 and early 1909. A general overhaul was conducted at Portsmouth in September and October 1910, which included the installation of modernized hydraulic elevating gear for the 10-inch guns.

The *Tennessee* went into reserve at Portsmouth on 15 June 1911 and underwent further refits, including the replacement of her foremast and bridge with a lattice mast and modern control stations. Again at Portsmouth in September 1915, the 10-inch guns were unshipped and replaced with new barrels. This was the *Tennessee*'s last major refit before she met her fate at Santo Domingo on 29 August 1916.

The Washington

Like the *Tennessee*, the *Washington* suffered an engine breakdown due to faulty lube oil, and from 11 December 1906 to 11 April 1907 she was at League Island overhauling her plant. Following a year of operations on the West Coast, the *Washington* entered Bremerton on 15 July 1908 for a month's docking and repair. The ammunition cars and loading trays for the 10-inch guns were reworked to accept a full charge, and turret sights were fitted, as were bore-sighting scopes for the 6-inch battery.

In September 1910 the *Washington* returned to the Atlantic Fleet to begin a decade of hard, active service. On 14 May 1912 she underwent a material inspection at Portsmouth, which resulted in the removal of her foremast. She received a new lattice foremast and adopted the hybrid appearance of the great majority of New Navy battleships and armored cruisers as they quickly entered the age of director firing.* To the new mast were fitted a modern chart house, emergency cabin, and "standard" compass platform.

A period of relative inactivity followed, the *Washington* alternating between an Atlantic Fleet reserve ship and receiving ship at Brooklyn. On 23 April 1914 she was recommissioned for Caribbean service. From mid-December 1914 to mid-January 1915 the *Washington* underwent another overhaul at Portsmouth. A new interior communications system was installed as well as a new wireless outfit. A battle radio station was added on the forward platform deck, and the topmasts were lengthened for the new antennae. Two 36-inch searchlights were fitted to the foremast, replacing two of the original six 30-inch lamps. Minor items included the conversion into a dental station of the office formerly occupied by the first sergeant of the marine detachment.

The *Washington* quit the yard on 11 January 1915 and assumed her duties as flagship, Cruiser Squadron, Atlantic Fleet, under Rear Admiral William Caperton. She steamed once again for the Caribbean, unable to exceed 16 knots because her condensers were in extremely poor condition. The vessel was to remain on the station for nearly one year before she could be spared for a period in dock.

On 29 February 1916 she tied up at Portsmouth for a complete boiler and machinery overhaul. The topside torpedo defense station was moved from the boat deck, where it was "practically useless," to the after searchlight platform on the mainmast.

One major alteration reflected how rapidly technology had progressed since the inception of the armored cruiser; the *Washington* was the third vessel, along with the *Huntington* and *North Carolina*, to be equipped with an aircraft catapult, which was built over her stern.

On 31 March the ship passed into reserve at the yard, and on 9 November she was renamed *Seattle*, her original name being transferred to the hull of BB 47, the never-to-be-completed third unit of the new

*Of all the New Navy battleships and armored cruisers still in commission in 1911, only the *Texas*, *New York*, and *Brooklyn* would complete their service with their near-original masting.

The *North Carolina* lies moored to a Camden, New Jersey, pier during Philadelphia Founders' Week, October 1908.

Colorado-class battleships.* On the same day she was recommissioned as flagship, Destroyer Force, Atlantic Fleet, under Rear Admiral Albert Gleaves.

Within five months the United States was at war with Germany, and the *Seattle* tied up at Brooklyn on 3 June 1917 to have her catapult removed and two 3-inch AA guns installed on her after bridge deck. There she was refitted for her new assignment as flagship of the Atlantic Fleet's Cruiser Force. The *Seattle*'s service was almost continuous during the war, and immediately following its conclusion she was refitted at Brooklyn for troop transport duties. As with the other armored cruisers employed in this role, the 6-inch and 3-inch gun deck batteries and ammunition hoists were entirely unshipped, as were a pair of main deck 3-inchers.

On 17 July 1919 the *Seattle* underwent a material inspection at Norfolk. The engineering plant needed an overhaul, even though her machinery, as the Board of Inspections and Survey noted, had been

*BB 47 was the third unit of the class; the hull numbers of the completed units did not run sequentially: *Colorado* (BB 45), *Maryland* (BB 46), and *West Virginia* (BB 48).

well cared for. A forced lubrication system replaced the gravity feed on the engines, the inner stack casings were replaced, and the forward torpedo flat was converted into bunkerage. There were also plans to remount the twelve 6-inch guns removed from the gun deck, but the board considered this unwise because experience had shown the difficulty of using them in that position. The blank ports were not plated over but were fitted with air ports to increase ventilation and habitability on the gun deck. The *Seattle*'s captain also requested that the 3-inch gun deck sponsons be plated over and made flush with the hull, as they "offered much resistance in any seaway, and both forward and aft they are apt to cause damage" when alongside another ship, but this was not done.[20]

Both active and reserve duty with the Pacific Fleet followed, and on 26 June 1922 the *Seattle* received a complete machinery overhaul at Bremerton. This time, however, the Board of Inspection and Survey noted that from the looks of the machinery it appeared that the ship had been "hastily been placed out of commission and neglected during [her] inactive period."[21]

In late 1923, as administrative flagship for the commander in chief, U.S. Fleet, the *Seattle*'s boilers almost completely broke down, and an emergency material inspection had to be conducted at Brooklyn on 1 December. The boiler headers were so corroded that safety was compromised. Because neither material, time, nor funds were available for a thorough repair, the board recommended that the Bureau of Engineering* issue a new, safe working pressure for the boilers that would enable the ship to steam at a maximum of 15 knots.

In August 1927 the *Seattle* tied up at Brooklyn to assume her last service, as station ship for the yard. The fore and after fire control stations were housed over, and a new pilothouse was fitted to the navigation bridge. All guns, except the main battery and the four 6-inch guns at the corners of the superstructure, were unshipped and placed in store. Two 3-inch saluting guns were mounted alongside on the pier for ceremonial duties.

The North Carolina

The *North Carolina* received essentially minor refits during the early years of her service. In 1908 hand-loading trays were supplied to the 6-inch guns, and in 1910 she, along with the *Montana* and scout cruiser *Chester* (CS 1), were equipped with experimental portable wireless sets. Intended for use in battle, they needed only a wire hoisted to the signal yard as an antenna. With a maximum range of twenty miles, it was

---

*This designation replaced the earlier one, Bureau of Steam Engineering, in 1919.

expected that these wireless sets would serve well for short distances and could be modified for use with landing parties.

From November 1910 to January 1911 the vessel had her machinery overhauled at Portsmouth. She received a new set of propellers, designed to provide more efficient service at cruising speeds. Following Caribbean duty, the ship again entered the yard at Portsmouth for ordnance and topside refits. New electric motors were fitted to the 10-inch-battery elevating gear, a new fire control system was installed, and a torpedo defense station was put in abaft the mainmast. The foremast was unshipped and replaced with a lattice mast that had a new chart house and sea cabin at its base.

In the summer of 1915 the *North Carolina* was station ship at the new naval air center at Pensacola, Florida, and under the direction of Lieutenant Commander Henry Mustin, station commander, the first shipboard catapult ever installed was bolted to her quarterdeck. This device was completely experimental and far more rudimentary than those later shipped aboard the *Huntington* and *Washington*. It consisted of a narrow-gauge track, 50 feet long, rising 4 feet above the deck, and reached from the after barbette to the ship's stern. The catapult was powered by compressed air from the ship's torpedo air service at 300 psi, which hurtled the trolley down the track at 50mph. The *North Carolina*'s boat cranes proved unsuitable for hoisting aircraft, so a jury rig was improvised by wrapping a boat boom in canvas and inserting it down the barrel of the portside after 10-inch gun; the contraption was stabilized by an upright spar secured to the rear of the turret, a cumbersome, unsatisfactory arrangement.

In June 1916 an improved catapult was installed, of the same general type that was put in the *Huntington*. It extended just over 103 feet and was raised 12 feet 10 inches from the quarterdeck, passing over the roof of the after turret. Special 40-foot extensions were rigged on the boat cranes to enable them to handle aircraft. When the catapults were unshipped from the three vessels, these extensions remained. It is not known exactly when the *North Carolina*'s catapult was unshipped. Photographs of the ship in her world war dazzle camouflage show no launching device, so it was probably removed in late 1917 or early 1918.

In 1918 the gun deck battery was taken off and the ports permanently plated over; although it was considered advisable to fit air ports in the embrasures, this was never carried out. Additionally, two 3-inch (low-angle) guns were installed under the fore bridge.

The Montana

The *Montana* underwent the alterations common to the class. In 1908 the 10-inch-battery ammunition hoists were refitted to receive a full charge, and new hand-loading trays were provided for the 6-inch guns. On 26 July 1914 the *Montana* docked at Portsmouth for a major overhaul, which included the fitting of a lattice foremast with its accompanying bridges and appurtenances. Again at Portsmouth in 1913, the vessel, fitted to serve as the fleet torpedo school, received installations of 21-inch and 18-inch torpedo tubes on the main deck.

There were plans to install an aircraft catapult on the *Montana* in May 1916, and though preliminary outfitting was begun, the catapult was never shipped. During World War I the vessel was assigned to the Cruiser and Transport Force and was converted in late 1918 for transport duty. The gun deck batteries were unshipped, the ports permanently blanked. As with the *North Carolina*, the Board of Inspection and Survey proposed that air ports be fitted in the embrasures, but this was not done.

Following hard service in the Atlantic, the *Montana* arrived at Bremerton on 16 August 1919. The combination of continuous North Atlantic steaming under wartime conditions and the very rapid demobilization of crews following the armistice had taken its toll. The Board of Inspection and Survey reported, "The ordnance, ordnance material, and magazines of this vessel are in good condition, [but] the personnel is so reduced that all guns, range finders, range keepers, and the director scope have . . . working parts [that are] white-leaded instead of . . . bright and clean."[22] A new set of funnels was placed on board, the originals being "so thin above the umbrellas that the hand can be pushed through in places."[23] The ship's last refit occurred in June 1922, when the catapult base was unshipped and the after fire control system reinstalled.

Careers

The Tennessee

The *Tennessee* (ACR 10) was laid down at William Cramp and Sons on 20 June 1903 and launched on 3 December 1904 by Miss Annie K. Frazier, the daughter of the governor of Tennessee and subsequent founder of the Society of Sponsors of the United States Navy. The ship was placed in commission at League Island on 16 July 1906, with Captain Albert G. Berry commanding.

The *Tennessee* was fitted out at the navy yard until 1 November, when she departed for Hampton Roads to form part of the escort for President Roosevelt, then taking passage in the *Louisiana* to inspect the Panama Canal site. Following stops in Panama and Puerto Rico, the vessels returned to Hampton Roads on 26 November. On 18 December the *Tennessee* docked at League Island for repairs to her engines and

Lieutenant Commander Henry Mustin prepares to take off on the first ship-board catapult launch, 5 November 1915. The contraptions used to handle the aircraft are clearly visible about the after turret. Note the boom thrust down the barrel.

remained through 12 April 1907. A shakedown cruise along the East Coast took up the greater part of the spring, and then the vessel was ordered, along with the *Washington*, to form a special service squadron for a goodwill visit to France. The ships departed from Newport on 14 June and arrived at Royan, France, on the twenty-third. After cruising the French Atlantic coast for one month, the squadron cleared Brest on 25 July and anchored off Tompkinsville one week later.

Until mid-October the *Tennessee* steamed along the East Coast, conducting final speed trials and general drills. On 12 October, as flagship of a special service squadron, the *Tennessee* left Hampton Roads with the *Washington* and steamed via Rio de Janeiro, Montevideo, and Punta Arenas to the Pacific. Exercises were held at Magdalena Bay from 29 December to 15 February 1908. On 20 February the ships arrived at San Francisco.

For the next four months the *Tennessee*, at times in company with the *Washington* and *California*, cruised the West Coast of the United States. On 6 May the *South Dakota* joined the force for squadron evolutions in San Francisco Bay. Off Mare Island Light on 15 June Rear Admiral Uriel Sebree hoisted his flag in the *Tennessee*, and the four vessels were designated Second Division, First Squadron, Pacific Fleet.*

Beginning 1 July, preparatory to the fleet's voyage to Samoa, the *Tennessee* operated out of San Francisco conducting exercises in towing destroyers, first the *Preble* (DD 13), then the *Farragut* (TB 11). On 7 July Captain Bradley Fiske reported to take command.

Fiske, often exasperated by the reactionary sundowner element that held positions of power, especially in the Bureaus of Navigation and Ordnance, had allied himself with such forward-looking progressives as Stephen B. Luce, Caspar Goodrich, Henry Clay Taylor, and William S. Sims. A minor example of Fiske's frustration with the Navy Department is illustrated in the rudder indicator he invented while commanding the *Tennessee*. A mechanical device that fit over a ship's stern to indicate, both by day and by night, the exact position of the rudder to the vessel steaming astern, it proved a great boon in regulating movements during squadron evolutions. Admirals Sebree and Swinburne, Fiske's new division and fleet commanders, respectively, wrote enthusiastic letters of support. The department, however, ordered him to remove the indicator from the *Tennessee*'s stern immediately.

During Fiske's command of the *Tennessee*, his insistence on the use of rangefinders was regarded as an eccentricity and laughed at in the wardroom. Following a target practice at Magdalena Bay in November 1908, Admiral Sebree's flag secretary, Lieutenant Holmes, and the *Tennessee*'s surgeon, Dr. Kaufman, composed a poem:

With the organization of the Second Division, the Pacific Fleet became an extremely powerful force which bore no relation to the motley collection of vessels that carried the title when the *New York* sailed to join it five years before. Under Rear Admiral James H. Dayton, the First Squadron consisted of four *Pennsylvania*-class cruisers in the First Division and the vessels noted above in the Second Division. The Second Squadron, under Rear Admiral W. T. Swinburne, comprised the Third and Fourth Divisions, made up of the three *St. Louis*–class protected cruisers plus the *Albany* and the gunboat *Yorktown*. Four "peace cruisers" of the *Denver* class and seven gunboats of varying age and utility constituted the Third Squadron. (This squadron was formerly the Asiatic Squadron, an independent command from 1865 to 1908, when it was formed into the Pacific Fleet. In 1910 it became an independent force, the Asiatic Fleet, and was maintained as such until its demise in 1942.) Four torpedo boats formed the First Torpedo Flotilla, and the ancient monitors *Monadnock* and *Monterey* made up the Coast Defense Squadron. Also in the Pacific, but not attached to the Pacific Fleet, were three flotillas consisting of thirteen boats of the Pacific Torpedo Fleet. The union of the two heavy divisions was a clear signal to Japan and Britain of the United States' determination to play a dominant role in the Pacific.

Gig ready in case of accident, Curtiss AB-2 ("F" type) shoots down the track.

The air was full of whizzing shell,
From the enemy on the lee;
In fact, the atmosphere felt like hell
On the bridge of the *Tennessee*.
And the cruiser captain's brow was hot,
And he used words loud and strange,
As he called aloft to the fighting top
To find out the latest range.
Then the cruiser captain's right-hand man,
The cruiser's rangefinder lad,
Said he had the range when the fight began,
But the fog made his readings bad.
And the cruiser's captain thought awhile,
And he sent for his glass and a log,
And he divided a pint by a cubic mile,
and measured the range through the fog.[24]

Towing the *Whipple* (DD 15), the *Tennessee* led the Second Division
out of San Francisco on 24 August 1908 to begin the Pacific Fleet's cruise

to the South Pacific. "We had the idea in the fleet at that time," Fiske would later write, "that the real purpose of the trip was to get a considerable fighting force into the neighborhood of Japan."[25] Halfway to Honolulu the fleet was struck by a violent gale, comparatively rare in central Pacific waters.

After an eight-day stay in Honolulu, the fleet departed on 10 September for Samoa. The force arrived at Apia, on the twentieth, the Second Division shifting anchorage to Pago Pago on the twenty-third. On 7 October the fleet steamed from southern latitudes to Honolulu, remained for one week, and put into Magdalena Bay on 2 November for a month's target practice.

During one night shoot, a horrendous collision between the *Tennessee* and the fleet flagship *West Virginia* was only just avoided. According to Fiske, the *Tennessee* was beginning a high-speed run, "going 19 knots and trembling all over. The wind was making a great deal of noise, and the foam was being dashed up by our bow. I could see nothing in the darkness ahead except the lights of the *West Virginia*, which was anchored somewhere on our port bow." As was customary during gunnery drills in the *Tennessee*, Fiske's "rangefinder lad," Midshipman Frank Russell, was up in the foretop calling down the range by megaphone. "Finally the target became visible under the rays of the searchlight. Our men were at the guns; everything was ready; everything was at tension," Fiske wrote. As the range came down, he suddenly realized that if the *Tennessee* continued on course to the firing point, she would head directly for the flagship with no hope of averting disaster; orders were immediately given for the ship to come about. Fiske continued, "The ship's bow began to come about slowly to the left in the darkness toward the lights of the *West Virginia*, which I saw were closer than I supposed." Helm was changed from starboard to port, and the starboard engine backed full emergency.

> But our bow continued to swing farther and farther to the left, closer and closer to the direction of the *West Virginia*, while we tore through the water with unabated speed. I did not know exactly how far away she was, but I saw that if she were as close as she might be, nothing could prevent the *Tennessee* from striking her fair on the starboard side, and cutting her literally in two. Finally the *Tennessee* stopped swinging to the left, and began to swing right, and I knew the danger was past. . . . In half a minute I had the satisfaction of leaving behind our port beam the lights of a ship carrying nearly a thousand men, some of whom I could hear singing and talking about the decks.[26]

Exercises were concluded on 1 December, and the *Tennessee* led the Second Division on fleet visits to Central and South American ports

Mustin makes history, 5 November 1915.

through early March 1909. While with the division at Coquimbo, Chile, on 20 January, a large hotel fire broke out in the city. Fiske volunteered to take command ashore of the ship's fire-fighting parties and the division's marines to contain the blaze and prevent looting.

During this cruise in Latin American waters, Admiral Swinburne took the opportunity to exercise the fleet. According to Fiske, the *Tennessee*, as flagship of the Second Division, had the most difficult part in the evolutions. He and the ship, however, must have performed splendidly, as a wireless message from Swinburne to Admiral Sebree read, "Congratulations on your flagship's good work. When we all get up to her standing, we can make drills shorter."[27] The *Tennessee* returned with the fleet to Magdalena Bay on 17 March for another month of gunnery drills before steaming to the United States in mid-April. For the first part of June the ship visited West Coast ports and participated in the receptions for the Japanese training squadron at Tacoma and Seattle. On 10 June she went into dock at Bremerton for general and fire control repairs.

On 18 August 1909 the *Tennessee* once again formed at the head of the Second Division and shaped course with the fleet for deployment to the Asiatic station. As Fiske recorded during the leg to Honolulu, "The fleet made the trip at the highest speed they could, which averaged nearly 18 knots. This was the record up to that time, for so long a journey made by so many ships."[28]

The fleet operated in Philippine waters, conducting target practice from mid-November to mid-December. As could be expected, "The *Tennessee* did better than any other ship in the fleet, and there was a long period before the results of the target practice had been fully worked out in the Navy Department when the *Tennessee* was supposed to have done better than any ship in the navy."[29] The official results, when they finally came in, were only slightly less favorable. The Atlantic Fleet's *Vermont* (BB 20) came in first, *Tennessee* second, and the *Maryland* third.

The fleet cleared Manila Bay on 10 December and steamed for China and Japan. Anchoring at Woosung before moving up river to Shanghai, the fleet remained on the Chinese coast until the end of the month. On New Year's Day in 1910 the Pacific Fleet anchored in the Sea of Japan to culminate its cruise with a goodwill visit. Following a flag and captain's audience with the emperor, the fleet upped anchor and sailed for Honolulu. On 12 February, as a result of the Argentine government's request for a U.S. naval force to be present at its independence centennial, the *Tennessee* and *Washington* were detached to form a special service squadron for duty in the Atlantic.

While the rest of the fleet steamed to San Francisco, the *Tennessee* and *Washington* made for Bremerton. During the passage, a smallpox epidemic broke out in the *Washington*, and the *South Dakota* was substituted for her. At Bremerton on 19 March the *Tennessee* slipped her lines, threaded the Juan de Fuca Strait and shaped course south. On the twenty-first the *South Dakota* was sighted off the Farallon Islands, and Fiske, as acting commodore, ordered her to take station 2,000 yards off the *Tennessee*'s starboard beam. Fiske wrote, "In an hour or so, she had corrected her compass and her speed of engines so as to go at exactly the same speed and in the same direction as the *Tennessee*, and after that we were able to keep together without any signaling whatever all the way to Maldonado."[30]

Punta Arenas and the Straits of Magellan were passed on 1 May. The ships sighted Maldonado, Uruguay, on the fifth, finding the rest of the special service squadron—the *North Carolina*, flying the flag of Rear Admiral Sidney Staunton, the *Montana*, and the scout cruiser *Chester*—already at anchor. Although the major centennial events were held at Buenos Aires, the cruisers' deep draft precluded their presence at the capitol, and they moored at the naval base of Puerto Militar from 15 May until the first week of June. Following visits to Uruguayan and Brazilian ports, the squadron anchored at Hampton Roads on 22 July, where it was disbanded. On the twenty-seventh the *Tennessee* hoisted the flag of Rear Admiral Staunton, commander, Fifth Division, Atlantic Fleet.

For most of July and August the *Tennessee* operated off the coast of Maine with the *North Carolina* and *Montana* before docking at Portsmouth for two months of general overhaul. She quit the yard on 31 October and steamed south for Hampton Roads, there to take on coal and provisions in preparation for the embarkation of President Taft, who was to inspect progress on the Panama Canal. The president came on board at Charleston, South Carolina, on 10 November. Cristobal was reached on the fourteenth, and after three days on the site the *Tennessee* steamed via Guantanamo back to Hampton Roads, where the president disembarked.

Until mid-February 1911 the *Tennessee* led the Fifth Division. Joined by the *Washington*, it was up to full strength and arguably the most powerful armored cruiser squadron afloat. But the ships of the squadron had become strategically obsolescent. Britain had in commission four brand-new battle cruisers, the three *Invincibles* (1908) and the *Indefatigable* (1911), and although their structure and protection were weak, they mounted eight 12-inch guns on a 26-knot 17,000- to 18,000 + -ton hull. If Japan, Germany, and Great Britain could be considered potential enemies of the United States in 1911, only in a fleet action with the Japanese navy would our armored cruisers stand a reasonable chance of success. The lessons of the world war proved that it was death to commit the type to the van of the battle fleet or to engage it with battle cruisers.

The *Tennessee* lay off New Orleans in late February as the navy's goodwill representative during Mardi Gras. On 13 March she rejoined the division at Guantanamo and engaged in fleet scouting problems through the rest of spring. For five days off Nantucket Shoals Lightship the *Tennessee* tested experimental submarine signaling devices. She tied up at Portsmouth on the fifteenth to begin an extensive overhaul before going into reserve on 26 June.

During this period in reserve, the *Tennessee* took her place with the rest of the division in the great naval mobilization and review held on 14 October 1912 on New York's Hudson River. Reviewed by President Taft, the Atlantic Fleet comprised thirty-one battleships, seven of which were modern dreadnoughts; the four *Tennessee*-class armored cruisers; the three *Chester*-class scouts; the old *Baltimore*; twenty-four destroyers; and ten submarines. Putting into League Island at the conclusion, the *Tennessee* and *Montana* were ordered, while in reserve, to form a special service squadron for duty in the Levant during the Balkan Wars. Secretary Meyer noted in his annual report, "As an example of the preparedness of the Reserve Fleets, the *Tennessee* and *Montana* were ready to sail on November 11, 1912, on the voyage from Philadelphia to the Mediterranean about 72 hours after receiving orders."[31] The credit for their preparedness was largely due to Rear Admiral Austin Knight, commander of the Atlantic Reserve Fleet.

The squadron steamed through the eastern Mediterranean for the next five months, using its presence to protect American interests, though there was no occasion for military action. Smyrna was cleared on 3 May 1913, and the squadron anchored in Hampton Roads the twenty-third. After operating off the East Coast through the summer and fall, the *Tennessee* again went into reserve at League Island, this time for six months. Then she steamed the short journey north to Brooklyn, tying up on 2 May 1914 to act as receiving ship.

With the war in Europe just begun, the *Tennessee* was recommissioned on 4 August and, along with the *North Carolina* and collier *Jason* (AC 1), ordered across the Atlantic to support the American Relief Expedition in its efforts to aid the thousands of U.S. citizens caught in the war zone. There followed nearly a year of steaming in European and Mediterranean waters, transporting neutrals from hostile ports to places of safety. In early August 1915 the *Tennessee* returned to League Island for extended Caribbean service.

The United States had just begun its intervention in Haiti, and on 10 August, in response to Rear Admiral William Caperton's request for additional troops, the *Tennessee* embarked seven companies of the First Marine Regiment, a signal company, and the First Marine Provisional Brigade headquarters, and shaped course for Port au Prince. The *Tennessee* landed her troops on 15 August, returning immediately to League Island to await further orders; they were not long in coming. On 20 August Admiral Caperton telegraphed to Secretary Daniels, "Some disturbance Port Au Prince last night, many rifles still in hands of populace." The next day Brigadier General Commandant William Biddle ordered the marine artillery battalion at Annapolis to "embark fully armed and equipped both as artillery and infantry, on board the *Tennessee* for passage to Port au Prince."[32] The ship landed the battalion headquarters plus the First and Ninth Companies at Port au Prince on 31 August, shifting to Cape Haitien to land the Thirteenth Company. Returning to the East Coast, the *Tennessee* tied up at Portsmouth on 18 September, there to remain through 1 January 1916.

The *Tennessee* arrived on station at Port au Prince on 26 January 1916. Five days later she hoisted Admiral Caperton's flag, temporarily shifted from the *Washington*, and served as flagship for the commander, Cruiser Force, Atlantic Fleet, for a month. In early March the *Tennessee* was withdrawn for two months to convey a party of government officials to Uruguay.

Dead-load tests with the improved catapult installed in June 1916. Note the view of the after 3-inch gun and sponson.

The ship was back at League Island in late May for more important tasks. On the twenty-first she took on the marine detachment of the laid-up battleships *New Jersey* (BB 16), *Rhode Island* (BB 17), and *Louisiana* and with the scout *Salem* (CS 3) steamed for Santo Domingo.

The Dominican situation had begun the month before when a combination of revolution and national bankruptcy moved Woodrow Wilson to send a marine force to the republic. The first units of what was to become a full military occupation by the marine corps went ashore from the *Tennessee*, *Salem*, and gunboat *Sacramento* (PG 19) on 1 June at Santo Domingo.

During her voyage from League Island, the *Tennessee*'s name was changed to *Memphis*, her original designation going to the hull of BB 43.

For the remaining three months of her life, the *Memphis* operated between Port au Prince and Santo Domingo, and she was at the latter when disaster struck on 29 August 1916.

The *Memphis* was at anchor in the harbor and liberty parties were ashore. The sea was smooth, there was no wind, and no storm warning of any sort had been received. Suddenly the sea rose and swells as large as tidal waves began rolling into the harbor. One by one they lifted the *Memphis* and in less than an hour deposited her on the rocky bottom, in 12 feet of water, 40 feet from the shoreline. Three men washed overboard and seven members of the black gang died of injuries received from bursting pipes. Thirty other men drowned in the ship's boats as they attempted to return to the vessel from the beach.

The *Memphis*'s navigator, Lieutenant Commander Thomas Withers (later rear admiral commanding Submarines, Pacific Fleet, 1940–42) left an excellent account of this disaster. The anchorage, he noted, was not entirely safe, being on a narrow ten-fathom shelf and somewhat open to the weather. As it was hurricane season, an emergency steaming watch was continually set and boilers were primed. In any given situation, the *Memphis* could put to sea and get up power within forty-five minutes. At 1600 hours Withers, on the bridge, "noticed ahead, to the eastward, an immense wave or swell approaching. As this swell got close to the ship, its face became very steep, but the ship rode over it." The gunboat *Castine*, also in the harbor, immediately attempted to head to sea. The enormous wave, however, batted the little 1,770-ton craft about like a toy boat. With her rudder jammed hard left, she was thrown bows-on toward the beach. Backing full emergency, the *Castine* drifted toward the stricken *Memphis*, seemingly out of control and doomed to smash against the cruiser's armored sides. "At no time," recalled Withers, "was the *Castine* more than 1,000 yards from the *Memphis*, and yet from the bridge, 45 feet above the water, the *Castine* disappeared time and time again. Even her mastheads disappeared! To see the *Castine* fighting for her life was a terrifying sight."[33] With luck the gunboat was able to close the *Memphis*, which was acting as a breakwater, and regain control. She turned under the cruiser's stern and clawed her way to sea.

Aboard the *Memphis* the waves were coming at thirty- to forty-second intervals. They were so large and steep, Withers wrote, that they "simply flowed over the ship. They flowed over our bridge many feet deep. They flowed over our stacks and flooded our fires." Fifteen minutes after the first wave hit, the *Memphis* touched bottom. Several attempts to let go the second bower were not successful, and at 1620 hours she began to drag her bottom 200 feet with each successive wave. As the boilers had already been doused, all hope of saving the ship vanished, and Captain Edward Beach's sole thought was to get the crew ashore.*

---

*Edward Beach was the father of Captain Edward L. Beach, USN, who commanded the *Triton* (SSRN 586) on the first submerged circumnavigation of the globe in 1960.

The *North Carolina* with her improved catapult and aircraft handling extensions fitted to her boat cranes, c. 1916.

Five minutes after the *Memphis* had begun to drag her hull, a wave dashed her on the bottom with such force that everyone in her was thrown to the deck. Mess tables were torn from their brackets, ready shells for the 6-inch and 3-inch guns burst from their racks, and the spaces below decks became a death trap. Captain Beach ordered lifelines rigged, and the men, divided into groups by officers and petty officers, huddled in the lee of the stacks and bridges. No one panicked, and excellent order and discipline prevailed.

Below decks all power had ceased, but the black gang stuck to their posts until ordered up. Two boilers, crushed by a coral pinnacle that had rammed the ship's bottom, smashed against the armored deck, horribly scalding seven men in the fireroom. The chief engineer, Lieutenant C. A. Jones, went on deck to see his men away and, thinking the engines were still turning, returned to the throttle. The engines were not turning, however—they were breaking up because of the pounding from below. "On deck, it was difficult to keep the engineer's force from going below in a body when they heard that Lieutenant Jones was hurt and couldn't be gotten out," Withers wrote.[34]

At 1650 hours, the *Memphis* lay in her final position, 40 feet from the beach cliffs. Attempts to get lines ashore were thwarted by offshore breezes, until finally the ship's quartermaster heaved a leadline from the port bridge wing, to which lines and hawsers were bent. On the beach the lines were not secured, as the ship's motion would have snapped them. Instead they were manhandled by the *Memphis*'s marines and many citizens of the city. In three and a half hours 750 men were lifted to safety. As the numbers on deck thinned, the lines were cast off until only one remained for the final party of twenty-two officers, two chiefs, and Captain Beach, who was the last to leave the ship. Withers continued:

> Three times during the wreck the crew cheered, once when the *Castine* got to sea; again when the first line reached the shore; and again, when Captain Beach landed safely. . . . I beg to state that never have I been more proud of being an officer in our navy than I was during the wreck of the *Memphis*, when every man stuck to his duty, helped his shipmates and proved himself worthy of the best traditions of the service.[35]

The wreck was carefully examined by both naval and civilian salvage experts. They reported that salvage, while possible, would be expensive, and delivery to a repair port a difficult and dangerous undertaking. Further, the cost of salvage would approach the book value of the vessel, a type no longer built by any naval power. Repair work would take up to three years, leaving the ship with little or no active service life. The Navy Department decided to strip the wreck of all ordnance and valuable fittings and consign the hulk to scrapping.

The *Memphis* lay on her deathbed, a sad tourist attraction for more than five years. On 17 December 1917 her name was struck from the navy list, and she was sold for scrapping on 17 January 1922 to the A. H. Radetsky Iron and Metal Company.

The Washington

The *Washington* (ACR 11) was laid down on 23 September 1903 by the New York Shipbuilding Company, launched 18 March 1905, and placed in commission at League Island on 7 August 1906 with Captain James D. Adams in command. Following a short, final fitting out, the vessel reported to Newport News on 2 November for escort duty in connection with President Roosevelt's trip to the Panama Canal site. On 11 December the *Washington* put into League Island for repairs to her engines, which had suffered damage owing to faulty lube oil, and she remained in dockyard hands until 11 April 1907. East Coast cruising, including two goodwill visits to the Jamestown exhibition, took up most of the spring, until she was ordered, along with the *Tennessee*, to form a special service squadron for a cruise to France. On 13 June the squadron steamed from Newport. It arrived at Royan ten days later.

For much of the year and into the next, the *Washington*'s service closely mirrored that of the *Tennessee*. From 24 August to 1 October the ship underwent repairs at Brooklyn, then left the East Coast for duty in the Pacific. Off Hampton Roads on 2 October, the *Washington*, under her new captain, Austin Knight, joined the *Tennessee* for the voyage to Punta Arenas and the Pacific. The ships reached that port on 23 November, and four days of coaling and provisioning commenced. During a month's easy steaming up the West Coast of South America, the ships visited Magdalena Bay and conducted preliminary target practice. On New Year's Eve, 1907, Rear Admiral James Dayton led the Pacific Fleet into the bay, incorporating the *Washington* and *Tennessee* as the nucleus of the Second Division.

Through August 1908 the *Washington* steamed with the fleet. From 6 to 17 May she was at San Francisco for the review of the Pacific Fleet by the secretary of the navy, and on 29 June she went into dry dock at Hunter's Point.

At San Francisco on 24 August the *Washington*, towing the destroyer *Perry* (DD 11), set sail with the Pacific Fleet for its voyage to Samoa. Honolulu was reached on 2 September, Pago Pago on the twentieth. The fleet departed on 4 October and arrived off Magdalena Bay on 2 November for a month's target practice.

While at Coquimbo, Chile, with the division on 20 January 1909, the *Washington* sent out her fire brigade, which was the first to reach the blazing hotel mentioned earlier in connection with the *Tennessee*.

For the next five months the *Washington* steamed with the fleet, mainly in Central American waters. From 27 May to 7 June she was tied up at Seattle in connection with civic exhibitions and the reception of the Japanese training squadron. On 10 June she entered Bremerton for a two-month repair.

The *Washington* remained in dockyard hands until 18 August and on 5 September left San Francisco with the armored cruisers of the Pacific Fleet for Asiatic service. Following stops at Honolulu and Nares Harbor in the Admiralty Islands, the fleet arrived at Manila on 30 October. The *Washington* accompanied the fleet on its visits to Chinese and Japanese ports before clearing Honolulu on 8 February 1910. Although she had originally been slated to form a special service squadron with the *Tennessee* for Atlantic duty, a smallpox epidemic broke out and she was quarantined at Port Discovery, Washington, from 15 to 26 February. On 21 March she went into dock at Bremerton for extended repairs.

Four months later the *Washington* quit the yard and steamed to waters off San Francisco for a period of subcaliber target practice. On 8 August she took on coal at San Francisco and cruised with the First Division, Pacific Fleet, on its visit to Valparaiso for the Chilean centennial. At Talcahuano, Chile, on 27 September, the *Washington* was detached and ordered to the Atlantic.

An excellent view of the *North Carolina*'s improved catapult. Note the trolley on the portside track, c. 1916.

She passed Punta Arenas on 4 October, took on coal at Rio de Janeiro, and following stops in the West Indies, where she conducted further target practice at Culebra, arrived at Hampton Roads on 14 November. The next day the *Washington* was ordered to dock at Norfolk. On the twenty-third she formed with the Fifth Division, Atlantic Fleet. For the remainder of the year, and through 17 January 1911, the *Washington* conducted battle practice with the division and engaged in fleet scouting exercises along the East Coast. On 20 January she entered the yard at Portsmouth for an overhaul that lasted until 13 March.

Following her refit, the *Washington*, loaded with stores and drafts for the Fifth Division, headed south. She arrived at Guantanamo on 20

March and remained in the Caribbean through the spring. The summer of 1911, spent operating off the East Coast, included a naval militia cruise. She was in the Chesapeake Bay when the target ship *San Marcos*, formerly the old *Texas*, was sunk by gunfire. On 1 July the reorganization of the Atlantic Fleet placed the *Washington* at the head of the Fifth Division, and she hoisted Rear Admiral Staunton's flag.

On 2 October Secretary Meyer ordered the mobilization of the Atlantic and Pacific Fleets for one month hence. Ten days prior to the exercise Rear Admiral Bradley Fiske relieved Sidney Staunton as division commander and broke out his flag in the *Washington*. The review in New York, which culminated the mobilization, stretched nine miles along the Hudson River. After the fleet was inspected by President Taft, the *Connecticut*, with the fleet commander, Rear Admiral Hugo Osterhaus, on board, led the divisions in line-ahead formation out of the harbor and north to Newport for scouting exercises.

Temporarily detached on 18 November, the *Washington* and *North Carolina* were ordered to Santo Domingo to investigate the alleged murder of the Dominican president. Arriving on the twenty-sixth, Fiske ascertained that no murder had taken place, but the situation there was nonetheless volatile. Rumor had it that a prominent rebel, Vasquez by name, currently in exile at St. Thomas in the Danish West Indies, was about to return to his homeland and rally his followers. Undertaking a diplomatic mission on his own initiative, Fiske in the *Washington* steamed to St. Thomas and received assurances from the Danish authorities that Vasquez would not leave the island. To further cool the situation, Vasquez, at Fiske's behest, sent a cable to the American ambassador at Santo Domingo saying that he favored a peaceful solution. Dominican affairs once again judged tranquil, the *Washington* and *North Carolina* were relieved by the gunboats *Wheeling* and *Machias*.

Following a short period at Norfolk, the *Washington* led the division out of Hampton Roads on 3 January 1912 for fleet scouting exercises. The next day, during very heavy weather and a northwesterly gale, the "enemy" battleship *Rhode Island* was sighted from the masthead. Due to the *Washington*'s superior speed and, Fiske wrote, "the fact that her comparatively sharp bow enabled her to behave better in the heavy seas than did the *Rhode Island*'s bluff bow, I was able to cut her off from the rest of her force, none of which was then in sight."[36]

As a result of the heavy weather, the maneuvers were cancelled and the *Washington* and *North Carolina* were ordered to Key West to partake in civic ceremonies marking the completion of the railway bridge to the mainland. Up to that time no large ships had ever anchored in the inner harbor, and during the Spanish-American War all deep-draft vessels had anchored in the outer roads, coaling and provisioning by lighter. Fiske decided to take the big ships in. Checking first at the Navy Hydrographic Office, he examined all available charts, which convinced him the channel was deep enough to take vessels drawing 28 feet. The hydrographer, nonetheless, urged him not to make the attempt. At daybreak on 21 January the ships hove into view off Key West. They were soon met by a pilot in a yard tug, who upon learning the admiral's intentions informed him that no vessel drawing more than 25 feet had ever entered the inner harbor. But Fiske was still determined to maneuver his ship in, and leaving the *North Carolina* in the roads, the *Washington* took station astern of the tug. Fiske's reasoning was simple: He concluded that while no ship equaling his armored cruisers in draft had indeed ever anchored in the harbor, the channel was so short and so much used that any hazard would have already been discovered. As a prudent measure, men were stationed at all watertight doors. Fiske, as he recollected, was "perfectly calm, although if any undiscovered coral lump was touched, our bottom would be broken in, and I would be immediately relieved of my command and disgraced." The *Washington* threaded the channel and anchored in perfect safety. The *North Carolina* soon followed, and the scout *Birmingham* arrived the next day.

The stay at Key West was brief, and the *Washington* with her consorts was ordered to Hampton Roads to embark Secretary of State Philander Knox for a cruise to Panama and the Caribbean. The secretary and his party boarded the *Washington* at the Washington Navy Yard on 23 February 1912, and following stops at Colon, Santo Domingo, and Guantanamo, they quit the ship at Piney Point, Maryland, on 16 April.

On 19 April the *Washington* tied up League Island and, as temporary flagship of the Atlantic Fleet, hoisted Rear Admiral Osterhaus's flag. Unrest in Cuba culminating in a stillborn revolution prompted orders to the *Washington* to proceed to Hampton Roads, where along with eight battleships she embarked a marine provisional brigade for "temporary foreign tropical service ashore." President Taft wanted to give a strong show of force for possible intervention, and on 25 May the *Washington* led the battle squadron to Key West. The vessels anchored off Havana on 10 June for "duty in connection with the Cuban rebellion," remaining in the harbor but not disembarking the landing force until 1 July.[37] The Cuban government handling the situation on its own, the fleet withdrew to its bases.

The *Washington* discharged her marines at Hampton Roads and on 9 July went into "first reserve" at Portsmouth. She lay inactive at the yard through 8 October, then steamed to New York to participate in the fleet mobilization and review. On the seventeenth she resumed her reserve status at Portsmouth, remaining at the yard for the next nine months. On 20 July 1913 the *Washington* shifted to Brooklyn, where she was assigned duty as receiving ship.

On 23 April 1914 the *Washington* went into full commission with Captain Edward W. Eberle (future chief of naval operations) commanding. Taking on drafts at Norfolk and Port Royal, she steamed from Key West on 2 May for Santo Domingo. As yet another revolution seemed imminent, the *Washington* arrived off Puerto Plata to show the flag and protect American interests.

Eberle attempted to mediate the situation and invited leaders of the various factions on board; the effort, however, came to naught. The strife still unresolved, the *Washington* was ordered to Vera Cruz and lay off that port from 10 to 24 June. Continuing her Caribbean shuttle operations, she steamed to Cape Haitien to protect American citizens during an outbreak of violence. On 9 July the *Washington* was back at Puerto Plata, as unrest continued to dog the troubled Hispaniolan states. Through the fall of 1914 the ship lay off Puerto Plata, and at one point Eberle directed the *Machias* to use her 4-inch guns to silence a government battery randomly shelling civilians. On 20 November the *Washington* left Dominican waters and sailed for League Island. Arriving on the twenty-fourth, she tied up and, as flagship of the Cruiser Squadron (later changed to Cruiser Force), Atlantic Fleet, hoisted the flag of Rear Admiral William Caperton.

After an overhaul at Portsmouth, the *Washington* cleared the yard on 11 January 1915, embarked the Twelfth Company, USMC, at Hampton Roads, and sailed once again to Haiti. Arriving at Cape Haitien on the twenty-third, the *Washington* spent the next five months observing the political situation there, where General Vilbrun Guillaume Sam had recently overthrown the existing government.

The political situation continued to decline. A new revolutionary group led by General Rosalvo Bobo rose against the Sam regime, and by late June it had reached the outskirts of Cape Haitien in its advance on the capital. From their cruiser *Descartes* the French, first to intervene, landed a force of fifty men on the cape to protect French interests. Receiving reports of an imminent crisis from the American ambassador at Port au Prince, the State Department ordered Admiral Caperton to coal and provision the *Washington* at Guantanamo, attach the armed yacht *Eagle* to his command, and return to Cape Haitien for impending active service.

The *Washington* and *Eagle* anchored off the cape on 1 July. Government forces controlled the town, but the insurgents were pressing in from the east. Caperton sent word to the faction and government leaders that fighting would not be tolerated in the town environs and

The *North Carolina* recovering aircraft, c. 1917. Note the aircraft positioned on the catapult, ready to launch.

that he was prepared to land his forces to back up the warning. On 9 July fighting reached the outskirts, and the admiral ordered a force of one officer and twenty-nine marines from the *Washington* to dig in astride the east road; the vessels shifted anchor to cover the marines with their guns. This action initiated U.S. intervention in Haiti, an operation that continued until the marines withdrew in 1934.

On 7 July Admiral Caperton learned from the U.S. ambassador at the capital that revolutionary elements had attacked the palace and overthrown the government, and that Sam and several of his followers had taken refuge at the French legation.

Leaving the *Eagle* to look after affairs at the cape, Caperton reembarked his marines and steamed for Port au Prince. In a cable to Secretary Daniels the admiral stated that he was taking the *Washington* to Port au Prince and requested a company of marines from the naval station in Guantanamo Bay to stand by and embark on the *Jason* for service in Haiti. He would use the company to reinforce the *Washington*'s "battalion" if necessary.

Arriving at Port au Prince on 28 July, Caperton learned that the French legation had been stormed and about seventy political prisoners, including General Sam and ex-president Zamor, had been taken from that refuge and summarily executed. Sam's body was then hacked to pieces and paraded about the city on long poles. Finding no governmental authority in control of the capital, Admiral Caperton realized that the "intervention of American naval forces in the affairs of Haiti was necessary; and to prevent European complications which were most probable in view of the violation of the French legation, prompt action was required."[38]

The situation was growing worse by the hour, anarchy reigned, and the danger to foreign nationals was apparent. At 1600, barely four hours after anchoring, Admiral Caperton ordered in the landing force, consisting of the *Washington*'s marine detachment, the Twelfth Company, USMC, and three companies of the *Washington*'s sailors, the whole amounting to 340 men under the command of Captain George van Orden, USMC.

The landing was made in the ship's boats, and save for some sniping no resistance was met. As at Cape Haitien, the *Washington* positioned herself as close inshore as possible to lend fire support to the troops. Additionally, two armed steam launches kept abreast of the column's left flank as it marched into the city in open order. The final advance into Port au Prince was accomplished by night march, and the objective was secured by early morning the next day, when the collier *Jason* arrived bearing the marine company embarked at Guantanamo.

For the remainder of the year the *Washington* remained in Haitian waters. On 31 January 1916 she steamed for the East Coast and entered Portsmouth for overhaul and the fitting of her aircraft catapult. On 31 March she went into reserve at the yard for seven months. On 9 November she was renamed the *Seattle*, her honored name transferred to the hull of BB 47.* Recommissioning the same day, the *Seattle* broke out the flag of Rear Admiral Albert Gleaves and became flagship of the Destroyer Force, Atlantic Fleet.

Service in Cuban waters soon followed, and according to Admiral Gleaves, the *Seattle* initiated the use of U.S. Navy aircraft at sea for military purposes, when Lieutenant Whiting made a flight over San Juan del Sur, Cuba, to observe the movement of insurgent forces. During these operations the first aircraft radio was installed aboard the *Seattle*'s hydroplanes.

On 23 May 1917 Admiral Gleaves was appointed commander of convoy operations in the Atlantic, and the *Seattle* tied up at Brooklyn on 3 June to be fitted for war service. The task Admiral Gleaves had before him dwarfed any operation undertaken by the navy to that time. A total of 2,770,000 American troops were convoyed to British, French, and Italian ports, with resources scraped and put together from virtually nothing.

---

*The new *Washington* was sunk in bombing tests according to the provisions of the 1922 Five-Power Naval Limitations Treaty signed at the Washington Conference.

The *North Carolina* catapults a Curtiss "F" type (AB-3), 10 July 1916.

Eventually, seventy-five fast merchant liners, which included seventeen splendid ex-German passenger vessels plus thirteen foreign flag ships, comprised the Transport Force. Admiral Gleaves formed the transports into two divisions. The first, based in New York, comprised twenty-nine transports and was under the admiral's direct command; the second, with twenty-six transports, operated out of Newport News under the command of Rear Admiral Hilary Jones. The escorts were also divided into two units, the First and Second Squadrons, based at New York, Newport News, or Halifax, Nova Scotia, as the situation demanded. Generally the larger and faster cruisers of the First Squadron escorted the troop transports. The Second Squadron convoyed the cargo ships.

General procedure called for the escorts, which rarely touched a European port, to turn over their charges to British, American, or French warships when almost across the Atlantic. To this end they had to pile as much coal as possible into the bunkers and in bags on deck. This deck storage, which provided for five hundred to one thousand miles of endurance steaming, was consumed before the bunker coal was tapped. Heavy North Atlantic weather ate a prodigious amount of the coal supply. The *Seattle* at one point put into Halifax with 150 tons remaining; and the all-time squeaker *St. Louis* arrived at Hampton Roads at the end of a convoy turnaround with ten tons left in her bunkers.

The first U.S. troop convoy was originally set to steam on 9 June 1917. But due to the lack of available shipping and the full moon off the French coast, Admiral Gleaves postponed the sailing until the fourteenth. The convoy comprised four groups, totaling fourteen transports; two armed merchant cruisers; the cruisers *St Louis*, *Charleston*, and *Birmingham*; thirteen destroyers; and an assortment of armed colliers and yachts. The *Seattle*, flying Admiral Gleaves's flag, led the first group and exercised overall command.

The convoy, under way at first light on 14 June, steamed uneventfully for eight days. At 2215 hours on 22 June two events occurred almost simultaneously. The *Seattle*'s rudder jammed hard astarboard, and seconds later her lookouts sighted the phosphorescent wakes of two torpedoes streaking fifty yards off the ship's starboard bow. The ship sounded her whistle to warn the convoy of her erratic behavior and to alert the transport *deKalb* of the torpedoes heading for her. Skillful maneuvering by the *deKalb*'s captain averted disaster.

The convoy steamed on without further incident and on 24 June was met by two French destroyers and an American destroyer force based at Queenstown, Ireland. Suffering no losses, the convoy arrived at St. Nazaire on 29 June. On this first passage the *Seattle* remained at St. Nazaire through 14 July, on which date she escorted seven merchantmen to New York, completing the voyage without mishap.

The *Seattle* eventually conducted nine convoy-escort missions before the armistice. During one turnaround in the Bay of Biscay, on the morning of 27 April 1918, she received a distress signal from the army freighter *K. I. Luckenbach*, wallowing with disabled engines about two hundred miles away. Using various identification codes, the *Seattle* approached quickly but cautiously, as there could have been a submarine trap. Identity confirmed, towlines were laid out but rough seas precluded their use until the next morning. Then with all lines made fast, the *Seattle* began the tow at four knots, west to the Azores. At 2130 hours the ten-inch manila hawser parted, and another was not ready until the next morning, when the tow was commenced at six knots. It was not until 3 May that two fleet tugs from the U.S. naval station in the Azores arrived to take charge of the *K. I. Luckenbach*, upon which the *Seattle* cast off her tow and proceeded to New York.

On 21 December 1918 the *Seattle* was detached from the Cruiser Force and transferred with Admiral Gleaves's flag to the Transport Service for repatriation duty. Fitted with temporary standee bunks for 1,600 returning troops, she made six turnaround voyages, carrying 9,397 members of the American Expeditionary Force. On 4 July 1919 she completed her last passage and was detached from the force two days later.

Admiral Gleaves hauled down his flag on 1 September 1919, and the *Seattle* passed into reduced commission at Bremerton. Two months later, on 1 November, she was reactivated as flagship of the Cruiser Force, Pacific Fleet. Placed again in reduced commission at Bremerton in early 1920, the ship was reclassified from her obsolete ACR designation to CA 11 on 17 July 1920.

On 1 March 1923 the *Seattle* was recommissioned as flagship of the commander in chief, U.S. Fleet, in which role she would serve four four-star admirals: Hilary Jones, Robert Coontz, Samuel Robeson, and Charles Hughes. In the four years the *Seattle* carried the flag, she operated primarily in the Pacific, taking a fleet cruise to Australia in the summer of 1925. In June 1927 she was relieved by the *Texas* (BB 35) and passed into the Atlantic. She relieved the *Pueblo* on 29 August as receiving ship at Brooklyn, in which billet the *Seattle* was to serve for the next nineteen years. On 1 July 1931 she was stripped of her CA 11 hull number and listed as unclassified, a designation changed on 17 February 1941 to IX 39. During her long tenure at Brooklyn, the *Seattle* provided crews for yard tugs and craft, served as a school ship for the Third Naval District, mustered personnel for patriotic functions, and assembled crews for ships entering commission. On 28 June 1946 she was taken out of commission and struck from the navy list on 19 July. On 3 December 1946 she was sold to Hugo Neu of New York for scrapping.

The North Carolina

The *North Carolina* (ACR 12) was laid down by the Newport News Shipbuilding and Drydock Company on 21 March 1905 and launched on 6 October 1906. On 7 May 1908 she was placed in commission at the Navy Yard, Norfolk, with Captain William Marshall commanding. Fitting out at the yard was completed by 26 May, and the ship spent a month shaking down on the East Coast and off Guantanamo. On 7 July she returned to Norfolk for completion of her ordnance plant. For the

The *North Carolina* with a full load of Curtiss N-9 hydroplanes, c. 1917.

next five months the *North Carolina* shifted between Norfolk and League Island as further refinements were made to fire-control apparatus.

The vessel's first foreign service began on 16 December, when she embarked the U.S. ambassador to Venezuela at Hampton Roads and steamed for La Guaira. On 3 January 1909 the *North Carolina* was back at Hampton Roads, where preparations were made to receive President-elect Taft for a voyage to the Panama Canal site. Mr. Taft stepped on board at Charleston on the fifth and after a four-day passage disembarked at Colon. After reembarking the president-elect on 7 February, the ship returned to the United States and saw Mr. Taft off at South Pass, Louisiana.

After taking on coal and provisions, the *North Carolina* sailed round to the East Coast, anchoring in Hampton Roads on George Washington's birthday. Rear Admiral Charles Sperry, flying his flag in the *Connecticut*, had just brought the Atlantic Fleet battleships to anchor following their great circumnavigation of the globe.

On 1 March the *North Carolina* formed temporarily with the Third Division of the Atlantic Fleet. Upping anchor with the next morning tide, she headed south for a period of target practice and squadron evolutions in the Caribbean. Six weeks later, on 5 April, she was ordered to form a special service squadron with the *Montana* for possible dispatch to the Levant, where the Turks were about to depose Sultan Abdul Hamid II and, in the Ottoman province of Cilicia, thousands of Armenians were being slaughtered by government troops. On 23 April the squadron was ordered to relieve those entitled to the protection of the United States and others suffering from the disturbance.

Passing Gibraltar on 7 May, the vessels arrived at Mersina, Turkey, to protect American interests and render assistance. At that port a medical relief party under the *North Carolina*'s surgeon, assisted by four hospital corpsmen, set out to organize relief facilities in the town of Adana. The *North Carolina* group was relieved on 30 May by a medical party from the *Montana*.

The *North Carolina* left Mersina on 30 May for flag-showing visits to Levantine ports, including Rhodes, Jaffa, Haifa, and Alexandretta, before returning to Mersina on 18 June. On 9 July the vessels upped anchor for the return voyage to the United States. At Naples from 10 to 17 July, they were met by the *New York*, and all entered Boston on 3 August.

For the remainder of 1909 the *North Carolina* steamed up and down the East and Gulf coasts, participating with the Atlantic Fleet in New York's Henry Hudson–Robert Fulton celebration from 22 September through 4 October and visiting New Orleans in late October–early November. From 7 November to 19 February 1910 the *North Carolina* was at Norfolk for a period of extended repairs. Until 17 March the ship lay at Hampton Roads, awaiting the arrival of the Brazilian ambassador. As escort to the Brazilian battleship *Minas Gerais*, the *North Carolina* steamed south, anchoring at Rio de Janeiro on 9 April. At Montevideo on 9 May she formed with a special service squadron under Sidney Staunton for the Argentine centennial. She steamed with the force for Puerto Militar, anchoring in that port from 15 May through 5 June.

In mid-July the *North Carolina*, before putting into Hampton Roads, conducted subcaliber practice off Culebra with the special service squadron. On 14 August she joined the Fifth Division of the Atlantic Fleet and steamed with it off the East Coast until September, conducting mine and torpedo exercises. Taking on coal and provisions at Boston, the ship was ordered to Guantanamo for special duty in connection with the misfortune of the gunboat *Dubuque* (PG 17), which had lost her starboard propeller and lay immobilized. The *North Carolina* put into Guantanamo Bay on 29 September; she made the 1,497-mile voyage to

Following hard North Atlantic service, the *North Carolina* arrives in New York, January 1919, carrying members of the American Expeditionary Force.

Portsmouth, with the *Dubuque* in tow, in eight days. On 1 November the cruiser went into dockyard hands at Portsmouth for a two-month repair period.

Quitting the yard on New Year's Day, 1911, the *North Carolina* spent the first six months of the year cruising with the Fifth Division between the East Coast and Guantanamo. On 23 June she departed from Hampton Roads with Secretary of War Henry Stimson on board and proceeded to La Guaira and the Venezuelan centennial. During the summer she cruised the Caribbean, then returned to Washington with the bones of the sailors killed in the old *Maine* explosion for interment in Arlington Cemetary.

As critical personnel shortages sent all available men to man the new battleships, the *North Carolina*, although only four years old, went into her first reserve at Portsmouth. With complements numbering scarcely one hundred less than the complement of the battleship *Wyoming* (BB 32), the big armored cruisers of the *Pennsylvania* and *Tennessee* classes had become economically untenable. No new light cruiser construction was available to fill the gap, and the battle fleet had to rely for scouting on either destroyers, which could not perform the mission, or a variety of multiclass small cruisers, hangovers from the heyday of the New Navy. While Britain laid down class after class of 25 + -knot light cruisers to screen and scout for their battle fleet, the General Board saw fit not to recommend any light cruiser construction between 1904 and 1916. By 1914 the gap had become too great to ignore, and under the heading "Scout Cruisers" the board noted to Secretary Daniels,

> In the struggle to build up the purely distinctive fighting ships of the Navy—battleships, destroyers and submarines—the cruising and scouting element of the fleet has been neglected in recent years, and no cruisers or scouts have been provided for since 1904, when the *North Carolina, Montana, Birmingham, Chester,* and *Salem* were authorized. This leaves the fleet particularly lacking in this element so necessary for information in a naval campaign. . . . The General Board believes that this branch of the fleet has been too long neglected and recommends that the construction of this important and necessary type be resumed.[39]

In October 1912, while still in reserve, the *North Carolina* participated with the rest of her class in the fleet mobilization and review at New York, at the conclusion of which she returned to Portsmouth. On 7 August 1914 she was recommissioned as an experimental station ship at the Naval aeronautic station in Pensacola.

This duty, which would make the *North Carolina* an aviation pioneer, came almost by accident. The original station ship, the battleship *Mississippi* (BB 23), had been called to duty at Vera Cruz, and shortly thereafter, with her sister ship, the *Idaho* (BB 24), she was sold to Greece. A replacement was needed, and the *North Carolina*, laid up in reserve without assignment, was a logical choice.

The world war, however, took precedence over aviation experiments, and the *North Carolina* was ordered, along with the *Tennessee* and the collier *Jason*, to assist Americans and other neutrals and refugees. With her air complement aboard, which included such early luminaries of naval aviation as Henry Mustin, John Towers, William Herbster, Richard Saufley, and Patrick Bellinger, the ship sailed in mid-August 1914 for Europe. The aviation personnel were to make a study of

Near the end of her career, the *North Carolina* transits the Panama Canal on her way to Bremerton and decommissioning, 31 July 1919. Note that the aircraft catapult has been unshipped, but the feeder tracks and boat crane extensions remain. Note also the absence of the gun-deck batteries.

European aeronautic development, and to this end Mustin was dispatched to Berlin, Towers to London, and Lieutenant B. L. Smith, USMC, to Paris.

By order of the Bureau of Navigation, on 9 September 1915 the *North Carolina* resumed her former duties as a training ship for personnel in aeronautics.

In 1913 the aviation facility was transferred to Pensacola, and Lieutenant Commander Henry Mustin assumed command. A new 103-foot catapult was secured to a coal barge, and a successful launching was made by Ensign Patrick N. L. Bellinger.

When the *North Carolina* returned from Europe, work on her catapult began immediately. It was shortened to 45 feet so that it could fit over the ship's stern. This position, rather than the bow, was chosen for three reasons: first, it gave a longer runway than the bow; second, if the launch were unsuccessful and the pilot was dumped, he would not be run down by the ship; and third, as the boat cranes without modification could not handle aircraft at any extremity, the temporary hoisting apparatus of a wooden boat boom, wrapped in canvas and shoved down the port after 10-inch gun, was less distasteful from the after angle.

Throughout September and October dead-load and drone runs with the controls lashed in place met with success. On 5 November the pilot, Lieutenant Commander Henry Mustin, considered everything ready for testing. The first piloted catapult launch from a ship at sea stalled at the end of the track, and the plane, with Mustin in it, tipped into the sea. Neither aircraft nor pilot was hurt. Mustin's second attempt, on Curtiss AB-2, succeeded, and naval aviation passed another milestone.

In late 1915 preparations were made in the *North Carolina* to launch aircraft while she was under way in the open sea. Lieutenant A. A. Cunningham, USMC, was selected to pilot the plane, which dipped a wing immediately after takeoff and flipped over on its back. Lieutenant Cunningham was able to swim from the wreckage and was picked up in a ship's boat. In February 1916, with Mustin again at the controls, the launch was successfully completed while the ship was under way.

Also in February 1916, by his own request, Captain Mark Bristol assumed command of the *North Carolina*. On 20 March, with five Curtiss aircraft embarked, plus Mustin, Towers, Bellinger, and a newcomer to the group, Lieutenant (j.g.) Marc Mitscher, the *North Carolina* steamed with the fleet to Guantanamo for exercises "designed to establish facts as a guide for future development of aeronautics within the Navy without regard to pre-conceived ideas."[40]

The United States entry into the world war took the *North Carolina* north for convoy duty. On 1 July 1917 she formed at New York with the flagship *Seattle*, the *Montana*, and the *Huntington* as the First Division, First Squadron, Cruiser Force, Atlantic Fleet. The ship's seventeen months of ocean escort service in the North Atlantic, while arduous, was without incident, and following the armistice she was transferred to the Transport Service to return the American Expeditionary Force.

The *Montana* in the early years of her service.

In this capacity, the *North Carolina* completed six turnaround voyages, carrying 8,962 troops. At New York on 3 July 1919 she was detached from the force and ordered to the Pacific.

The *North Carolina* transited the Panama Canal on 31 July, then went into reduced commission at Bremerton. On 7 July 1920 her name was changed to *Charlotte*, the original designation being transferred to the never-completed hull of BB 52. She was decommissioned on 18 February 1921 and for nine years lay silent and empty at the yard. On 25 July 1929 she underwent a material inspection, the Board of Inspection and Survey finding her "a vessel of an obsolete type which has very limited military value, and no commercial value" except for scrapping.[41] The *Charlotte* was struck from the navy list on 15 July 1930 and sold for scrapping on 29 December.

The Montana

The last armored cruiser authorized and commissioned for the U.S. Navy, the *Montana* (ACR 13), was laid down at Newport News on 29 April 1905, launched on 15 December 1906, and placed in commission by Captain Alfred Reynolds at Norfolk on 21 July 1908. A shakedown cruise along the East Coast, including a goodwill visit to Philadelphia for Founders' Week celebrations, took up the remainder of the year. On 24 January 1909 she joined the *North Carolina* at Charleston and participated in the voyage of President-elect Taft to Panama.

From this point until September 1911 the *Montana*'s career mirrored that of the *North Carolina*. On 30 March 1909 she joined the special service squadron at Guantanamo for service in Turkish waters and steamed in the Levant through early July before returning to Boston with the force on 3 August. She steamed the East Coast with the Atlantic Fleet, participating in the Hudson-Fulton fete at New York, and then on 7 November went into dock at Norfolk for a four-month overhaul period.

The *Montana* cleared the yard on 31 March 1910 and spent the first week of April testing submarine signaling apparatus in Hampton Roads. On 14 April she steamed with the *North Carolina* and *Chester* as part of Sidney Staunton's special service squadron to the Argentine centennial. The *Montana* returned to the United States with the force and on 14 August joined the Fifth Division, Atlantic Fleet. For the next month she cruised with the division along the East Coast, then went into dock at Portsmouth until 1 November. On 31 October she joined the *Tennessee* at Hampton Roads for the voyage to Panama with President Taft. For the remainder of 1910 and through June 1911, the *Montana*'s service paralleled that of the *Tennessee*. On 26 July 1911 the vessel was placed in first reserve at Portsmouth.

While still in reserve the *Montana* participated in the great fleet mobilization and review at New York in October 1912. The ship, manned primarily by members of various East Coast states militias, did

The *Montana*, flag at half-mast, carries home the dead from Vera Cruz, April 1914.

Fitted with a new lattice foremast, the *Montana* makes bare steerage way,
c. 1914. Note the absence of the 3-inch gun in the forward sponson.

very well, achieving a speed of 18.5 knots on half-boiler power on the trip to New York.

On 11 November the *Montana* and *Tennessee* formed a special service squadron for duty in Turkish waters. No reason arose for military intervention, and the vessels returned to the United States on 23 May 1913. On 8 September the ship went into a short period of reserve at Portsmouth and received her extra complement of torpedo gear before being assigned as a torpedo school ship.

The *Montana* went into full commission on 30 December and in January 1914 replaced the cruiser *Montgomery* as the fleet's torpedo training ship, "not only to thoroughly instruct the personnel . . . but to test all classes of torpedo tubes and torpedoes at the highest rate of speed [at] which they would be fired in battle."[42] The classes, which included very junior officers who would become most of the senior submarine commanders during World War II, consisted of about twenty students in a five-month course, of which two were held per year. One officer from each battleship of the fleet was selected to attend.

Throughout 1914, training cruises were made to the Caribbean during which the *Montana* brought the dead home from Vera Cruz. For the remaining years before the U.S. entry into the war she performed similar duties. The greater part of 1916 was spent in major overhaul at Portsmouth.

In April 1917 the *Montana* began her war service, conducting training and providing escort for East Coast traffic. Inevitably, the torpedo school was disbanded on 17 July 1917, and she was assigned to First Division, First Squadron, Cruiser Force, Atlantic Fleet. Operating out of all the major embarkation ports, the *Montana* escorted her convoys to their midocean meeting points and returned to the East Coast.

On 12 January 1919 the *Montana* was attached to the Transport Service for repatriation duty. She was hastily fitted with temporary standee bunks for 1,500 troops and eventually returned 8,800 in six turnaround passages. Donald C. Heath, of the army's Thirty-third Engineer Regiment, was one of those who boarded the ship at Brest, and he recollected with satisfaction sixty-five years later, "She was a remarkably comfortable ship, she ran remarkably steady, and I was struck by the almost complete absence of vibration from the engines. . . . She was in immaculate shape, better than almost any liner I've sailed on since. . . . The food was far superior to anything we got in the army."[43]

The *Montana*'s transport service ended at her return to New York on 30 June 1919, and on 3 July she was formally detached from the force.

Ordered to the Pacific, the *Montana* arrived at Bremerton on 16 August and immediately went into reduced commission. On 7 June 1920 her name was changed to *Missoula*, the original designation going

With an increased outfit of boats, her gun deck devoid of armament, and her hull in dazzle camouflage, the *Montana* is on convoy escort duty, 1918. Her appearance has changed radically since her earlier days.

to the uncompleted hull of BB 51, and her hull number was changed to CA 13. On 2 February 1921 she was decommissioned. The *Missoula* lay at the yard for nine years and was stricken from the navy list on 15 July 1930. On 20 September she was sold to John Irwin for scrapping.

Tennessee-Class Characteristics

Dimensions

504' 6" oa x 72' 10½" max beam x 25' mean draft

Displacement

Tennessee: 14,500 tons normal, two-thirds supply ammunition and stores, normal coal
15,712 tons full load
Tons-per-square-inch immersion at normal draft: *Tennessee*, 59.70
Metacentric height: 3.30' normal draft

Armament

Original: four 10-in 40-cal Mk 3; sixteen 6-in 50-cal Mk 8 RF; twenty-two 3-in 50-cal Mk 2 RF; two 1-pdr.; eight 30-cal mg; TT, four 21-in Bliss-Leavitt; two 3-in field guns
1918: four 10-in 40-cal Mk 3; four 6-in 50-cal Mk 8 RF; ten 3-in 50-cal Mk 2 (*North Carolina*, twelve 3-in); two 3-in 50-cal Mk 2–3 AA (none in *North Carolina*)

Protection

Belt: 5″ KNC amidships, 5″ KNC upper strake; 3″ Harvey ends

Transverse armored bulkheads: *Tennessee* and *Washington*, 5″ KNC; *North Carolina* and *Montana*, 6″ KNC

Barbettes: *Tennessee* and *Washington*, 7″ KNC front and sides, upper; 4″ Harvey rear, upper; 4″ Harvey circumference, lower; *North Carolina* and *Montana*, 8″ KNC front and sides, upper; 4″ Harvey rear, upper; 6″ KNC gun to main deck; 4″ Harvey lower

Turrets: 9″ KNC front; 7″ KNC sides; 5″ KNC rear; 2½″ NS roof

Conning tower: 9″ KNC

Conning tower tube: 5″ KNC

Conning tower shield: *Tennessee* and *Washington*, 9″ KNC

Signal tower: 5″ KNC

Main deck casemate: 2″ NS

Armored deck flats: *Tennessee* and *Washington*, 1½″ NS; *North Carolina* and *Montana*, 2″ NS amidships; 1″ NS ends

Armored deck slopes: 4″ NS amidships; 3″ NS ends

Machinery

Engines: two sets 4-cyl VTE

Boilers: sixteen Babcock & Wilcox WT

Indicated horsepower: 23,000

IHP generated on trials: *Tennessee*, 26,534; *Washington*, 26,862; *North Carolina*, 29,225; *Montana*, 27,489.

Trial Speed: *Tennessee*, 22.44 kts; *Washington*, 22.27 kts; *North Carolina*, 22.48 kts; *Montana*, 22.26 kts

Coal capacity: *Tennessee*, 900 tons normal, 2,020 maximum; *North Carolina*, 900 tons normal, 2,200 tons maximum

Steaming radius: *Tennessee*, 5,423 miles at 10 kts

Propellers: twin shaft, 3-bladed

Complement

39 officers, 777 men (as commissioned)

Contract price (hull & machinery)

Tennessee, $4,035,000; *Washington*, $4,035,000; *North Carolina*, $3,575,000; *Montana*, $3,575,000

Total cost

Tennessee, $6,164,673; *Washington*, $6,157,425; *North Carolina*, $5,901,725; *Montana*, $5,874,260

Appendixes

A

Should the Armored Cruisers Have Been Built?

A popular ditty of the late New Navy era posed the ultimate question regarding the *Pennsylvania* and *Tennessee* classes: "Why oh why did Uncle Sam, / Build these ships not worth a damn?" Were they really necessary, and did they conform to the requirements set by the standard naval practice of the era? To both questions the answer should be yes. In most of its mainstream functions the U.S. armored cruiser was directly analogous to the later heavy cruiser, especially in the decades between the world wars. The two types of cruisers had an identical scouting role, with or without aircraft, and the introduction of naval aviation on board the *Pennsylvania, Huntington, Seattle,* and *North Carolina* presaged the continuous use of cruiser scout aircraft in U.S. and most foreign heavy cruisers throughout World War II (and beyond, if one substitutes rotary for fixed-wing aircraft).

Some argue that rather than building the *Pennsylvania* and *Tennessee* classes, the navy would have done better to spend money on a number of near-equally-gunned big protected cruisers—in essence, bigger and better *Olympia*s or large numbers of scout or "light" cruisers, for which the three 24-knot and relatively unsuccessful *Chester*-class ships were the model. More ships could have been provided, at least twelve protected cruisers and probably sixteen scout cruisers. But it is questionable whether these vessels could in light of the prevailing doctrine of the time have served as a powerful and indeed survivable van for the battle fleet. The point was moot by 1908 with the commissioning of the 12-inch-gunned HMS *Invincible*. However, it should be noted that early designs for that ship recommended main and secondary batteries of 10-, 9.2-, and 7.5-inch guns in various combinations.

The fault did not lie with the ships themselves, although the *Pennsylvania* class had a relatively weak main armament, but with the fact that they were anachronistic at the time of commissioning. They entered service, at the very end of the era of coal-burning, reciprocating-engine, steam-driven ships, as appendages to the predreadnought battle fleet. With the advent in 1905 of the all-big-gun battleship and oil-fired turbine engines, they became strategically obsolescent.

During their service, the Big Ten, as some historians call the armored cruisers, provided platforms for a variety of experiments and innovations in ordnance, engineering, electronics, and aviation. In the trouble spots of the pre-1914 world they were extensively employed, their wide radius of steaming and seakeeping ability enabling them to remain on distant stations with substantial force without denuding the battle fleet. In 1907–8 the Big Ten cruisers were made the backbone of the reconstituted Pacific Fleet specifically to counter Japanese military adventurism. They would have provided an impressive addition to the Atlantic Fleet during its round-the-world cruise, being newer and far more handsome than some of the battleships. But the Navy Department wished to keep a squadron of force in continental waters should any contingency arise.

It is a futile exercise to guess that "better" vessels would have given better service than the Big Ten ships, because no such better vessels existed. The armored cruisers were called upon to perform a myriad of duties in every corner of the world and were engaged in every conceivable type of situation. In a novel experiment, the *Seattle* was employed as flagship of the commander in chief, U.S. Fleet, service comparable to that of the *Indianapolis*'s service as Admiral Spruance's Fifth Fleet flagship in World War II. If criticism is to be made, it should focus on the fact that the navy's designers confined themselves to the high technology of their era, which produced obsolescent ships. To have done otherwise, they would have had to either revive the Old Navy practice of wait and see or foretell the future.

B

Armored Cruiser Ordnance Characteristics

	10-in 40-cal Mk 3	8-in 40-cal Mk 6	8-in 40-cal Mk 5
Weight, unmounted (tons)	33.4	18.7	18.1
Barrel length (feet)	33.4	30	26.6
Weight of AP shot (lbs)	510	260	250
Weight of service charge (lbs)	207.5 smokeless	95.5 smokeless	115 smokeless
MV, service charge (fps)	2,800	2,750	2,700
Max. penetration (in) of KNC armor at 9,000 yds	6.9	4.4	4
Max. penetration (in) of KNC armor at 6,000 yds	9	6.1	5.3
Max. penetration (in) of KNC armor at 5,000 yds	11.75	—	7.25
Max. penetration (in) of KNC armor at 3,000 yds	15	6.6	7.5
Max. penetration (in) of Harvey armor at 5,000 yds	—	—	10.25
Max. penetration (in) of MS at 1,500 yds	—	—	—
Rate of fire	2/min	1/50 sec	1/50 sec

8-in 35-cal Mk 3	6-in 50-cal Mk 8 RF	5-in 40-cal Mk 2 RF	4-in 40-cal Mk 3 RF
13.1	8.6	3	1.5
23.25	25	16.66	13.33
250	105	50	33
105–15	37	28–30	—
brown powder	smokeless	brown powder	
—	2,800	2,300	2,000
—	2.3	1.4	—
—	3.2	1.4	1.2
3	—	—	—
4.75	5.2	2.75	1.7
—	—	—	—
12.33	—	—	—
1/77 sec	1/10 sec	1/4 sec	1/7 sec

Source Notes

Introduction

1. George Dewey, Memorandum to President of the United States, 15 January 1907.
2. Robert Gardiner, ed., *Conway's All the World's Fighting Ships—1860–1905* (hereafter cited as *Conway*), p. 186; Donald Mitchell, *A History of Russian and Soviet Sea Power*, p. 179.
3. Oscar Parkes, *British Battleships*, pp. 308–9.
4. Donald Mitchell, *History of the Modern American Navy*, p. 41.

Chapter 1

1. Charles Paullin, "A Half Century of Naval Administration in America, 1861–1911," part 5, United States Naval Institute Proceedings (hereafter cited as *USNIP*), p. 1244.
2. Secretary of the navy, *Annual Report of the Secretary of the Navy* (hereafter cited as *Annual Report*), 1888, p. 10.
3. Harold and Margaret Sprout, *Rise of American Naval Power, 1776–1918*, p. 173.
4. Ibid., pp. 167–68.
5. Ibid.
6. Paullin, "Naval Administration," part 3, pp. 748–49.
7. Ibid., p. 1266.
8. Ibid., pp. 752–53.
9. E. B. Underwood, "An International Incident," *USNIP*, pp. 83–86.
10. Paullin, "Naval Administration," part 5, p. 1217.
11. Ibid., p. 1218.
12. Ibid., part 3, p. 751.
13. Ibid., part 5, p. 1222.
14. Sprout, *American Naval Power*, p. 184.

15. John Spears, *The History of Our Navy from Its Origin to the End of the War with Spain*, p. 21.

16. Walter Herrick, *The American Naval Revolution*, p. 25; Spears, *History of Our Navy*, pp. 22–23.

17. Mitchell, *Modern American Navy*, p. 10.

18. *Annual Report*, 1887–88, p. 66.

Chapter 2

1. *Annual Report*, 1890, p. 290.

2. Ibid., p. 10.

3. Ibid., p. 11.

4. Augustus C. Buell, *Memoirs of Charles H. Cramp*, p. 189; "Report of the Policy Board," *USNIP*, p. 251.

5. Buell, *Charles O. Cramp*, pp. 189–90.

6. "Report of the Policy Board," p. 252.

7. *Annual Report*, 1890, pp. 10, 48.

8. Bureau of Construction and Repair, *Specifications for Building Steel Twin-Screw Armored Cruiser No. 2*," p. 8

9. Winfield S. Schley, *Forty-Five Years Under the Flag*, pp. 247–49.

10. "Report of the Policy Board," p. 251.

11. *Annual Report*, 1894–95, p. 446.

12. Buell, *Charles O. Cramp*, p. 191.

13. Robley Evans, *A Sailor's Log*, p. 369.

14. *Annual Report*, 1893–94, pp. 444–45.

15. Evans, *A Sailor's Log*, p. 375.

16. French Chadwick, *The Relations of the United States and Spain*, vol. 1, p. 142.

17. W. Millis, *The Martial Spirit*, p. 165.

18. W. Goode, *With Sampson Through the War*, p. 63.

19. Ibid., p. 201.

20. French Chadwick, "The *New York* at Santiago," *The Century Magazine*, p. 113.

21. Ibid.

22. Herbert W. Wilson, *The Downfall of Spain: Naval History of the Spanish-American War*, p. 319.

23. *Army and Navy Register*, 12 January 1900, p. 18.

24. *Annual Report*, 1903, p. 549.

Chapter 3

1. *Annual Report*, 1892, p. 12.

2. "Speed Trials of the *Brooklyn*," *USNIP*, p. 499.

3. Francis Cook, "The *Brooklyn* at Santiago," *The Century Magazine*, p. 97.

4. *Annual Report*, 1894, pp. 239–40.

5. Bradley Fiske, *From Midshipman to Rear Admiral*, p. 201.

6. Ibid., p. 202.

7. Ibid., p. 203.

8. *Annual Report*, 1894, p. 237.

9. Philip Alger, "Armor for Ships of War," *USNIP*, pp. 768–69.

10. Elting Morison, *Admiral Sims and the Modern American Navy*, p. 169.

11. George Melville, "Advantages of the 100-Foot Smoke-Pipes of Armored Cruiser No. 3," *Journal of the American Society of Naval Engineers* (hereafter cited as *ASNE*), pp. 175–77.

12. "Speed Trials of the *Brooklyn*," *USNIP*, pp. 498–99.

13. *Annual Report*, 1896, p. 481.
14. Ibid., 1898, part 1, pp. 521–22.
15. Ibid., 1901, pp. 637–38.
16. Ibid., 1906, p. 510.
17. Ibid., 1898, part 2, p. 25.
18. Schley, *Forty-five Years*, p. 290.
19. Cook, "*Brooklyn* at Santiago," pp. 95–96.
20. John Philip, "The *Texas* at Santiago," *The Century Magazine*, pp. 90–91.
21. Cook, "*Brooklyn* at Santiago," p. 99.
22. *Sampson-Schley: Official Communications to the United States Senate*, p. 98.
23. Kemp Tolley, *Yangtze Patrol*, p. 54.
24. Yates Stirling, *Sea Duty: The Memoirs of a Fighting Admiral*, p. 93.
25. *Annual Report*, 1908, p. 336.
26. George Kennan, *Russia Leaves the War*, p. 239.

Chapter 4

1. *Navy Yearbook*, 1916, pp. 147, 160–61.
2. David Taylor, "Our New Battleships and Armored Cruisers," *USNIP*, p. 595.
3. *Army and Navy Register*, 30 September 1905, p. 1.
4. *Navy Yearbook*, 1916, p. 147.
5. Trials Board, "USS *Colorado* Final Trials Report," letter to William Cramp and Sons, 2 August 1905.
6. Trials Board, "USS *Colorado* Preliminary Trials Report," 25 October 1904, p. 17.
7. *Annual Report*, 1900, p. 651.
8. Philip Hichborn, "Recent Designs of Battleships and Cruisers for the United States Navy," *Transactions of the Society of American Naval Architects and Marine Engineers* (hereafter cited as *SNAME*), p. 262.
9. Trials Board, "USS *Colorado* Preliminary Trials Report," 25 October 1904, p. 49.
10. *Annual Report*, 1907, p. 458.
11. *Annual Report*, 1901, part 2, p. 637.
12. *Annual Report*, 1901, part 2, p. 638.
13. Ibid., p. 638.
14. *Annual Report*, 1903, pp. 681–82.
15. Ibid., pp. 681–82.
16. William Hovgaard, "The Cruiser," *SNAME*, p. 111.
17. Taylor, "New Battleships and Armored Cruisers," p. 595.
18. *Annual Report*, 1901, part 2, p. 641.
19. Ibid., p. 765.
20. *Annual Report*, 1902, p. 495.
21. Francis Bowles, "Remarks on the New Designs of Naval Vessels," *SNAME*, p. 285.
22. "Maneuvering Qualities of Battleships: In-Turning vs. Out-Turning Screws," *ASNE*, pp. 433–34.
23. G. W. Danforth, "U.S.S. *California*," *ASNE*, p. 8.
24. E. H. Scribner, "United States Armored Cruiser *Colorado*," *ASNE*, pp. 1135–36.
25. Danforth, "*California*," p. 17.
26. J. J. Raby, "U.S.S. *South Dakota*," *ASNE*, p. 25.
27. *Annual Report*, 1911, p. 111.
28. U.S. Navy, Board of Inspection and Survey, "USS *Pittsburgh* Material Inspection Report," 20 September 1921, p. 3.
29. *Annual Report*, 1910, p. 487.

30. Board of Inspection and Survey, "USS *Huntington* Material Inspection Report," 14 February 1917, p. 34.

31. Ibid., pp. 13, 35, 51.

32. *Annual Report*, 1908, p. 933.

33. Ibid., p. 18.

34. Board of Inspection and Survey, "USS *South Dakota* Material Inspection Report," 15 July 1914, "Report of the Captain," no page.

35. G. E. Gelm, "The Admirals and the Viceroy," *USNIP*, p. 82.

36. Theodore Taylor, *The Magnificent Mitscher*, p. 42.

37. George van Duers, "Pete Mitscher and Armored Cruiser Aviation," *USNIP*, p. 152.

38. Taylor, *The Magnificent Mitscher*, pp. 42–43.

39. *Annual Report*, 1907, pp. 1242–43.

40. Charles Pond, "Report of the Commanding Officer, USS *Pennsylvania*," p. 191.

41. *Annual Report*, 1919, p. 2330.

42. Tolley, *Yangtze Patrol*, p. 165.

43. Albert Gleaves, *A History of the Transport Service*, p. 139.

44. Edward Arpee, *From Frigates to Flat-Tops*, p. 43.

45. *Annual Report*, 1920, p. 832.

Chapter 5

1. *Navy Yearbook*, 1910, p. 419.

2. "Professional Notes," *USNIP*, vol. 28, December 1902, pp. 979–80.

3. Trials Board, "USS *Washington* Final Trials Report," 26 January 1907, p. 3.

4. Board of Inspection and Survey, "USS *North Carolina* Final Trials Report," 26 January 1907, p. 17.

5. Francis Bowles, "Remarks on the New Designs of Naval Vessels," *SNAME*, p. 283.

6. *Annual Report*, 1907, p. 542.

7. Ibid., p. 543.

8. *Annual Report*, 1907, p. 543.

9. Ibid., pp. 542–43.

10. Ibid., p. 543.

11. Ibid., 1903, p. 783.

12. Trials Board, "USS *Tennessee* Preliminary Trials Report," 26 February 1906, p. 14.

13. Fiske, *Midshipman to Rear Admiral*, pp. 443–44.

14. Lewis Kenney, "U.S. Armored Cruiser *Tennessee*," *ASNE*, p. 427.

15. William Leavitt, "Description and Official Trials of the U.S.S. *Washington*," *ASNE*, p. 792; Kenney, "*Tennessee*," p. 414.

16. *Annual Report*, 1908, pp. 308–9.

17. William White, "U.S. Armored Cruiser *Montana*," *ASNE*, p. 879.

18. Lewis Kenney, "U.S. Armored Cruiser *Tennessee*," *ASNE*, pp. 454–55.

19. Trials Board, "USS *Tennessee* Preliminary Trials Report," 26 February 1906, pp. 10, 13.

20. Board of Inspection and Survey, "USS *Seattle* Material Inspection Report," 17 July 1919, p. 25.

21. Ibid., 26 June 1922, p. 4.

22. Board of Inspection and Survey, "USS *Montana* Material Inspection Report," 26 August 1919, p. 13.

23. Ibid., p. 32.

24. Fiske, *Midshipman to Rear Admiral*, p. 429–30.

25. *Annual Report*, 1909, p. 381; Fiske, *Midshipman to Rear Admiral*, p. 424.

26. Fiske, *Midshipman to Rear Admiral*, pp. 428–29.

27. Ibid., pp. 430–31.

28. Fiske, *Midshipman to Rear Admiral*, p. 448.

29. Ibid., p. 449.

30. Ibid., pp. 456, 458–59.

31. *Annual Report*, 1912, p. 23.

32. *Annual Report*, 1920, p. 258; *Army and Navy Register*, 9 October 1915, p. 459.

33. Thomas Withers, "The Wreck of the USS *Memphis*," *USNIP*, p. 1461.

34. Ibid., p. 1463.

35. Ibid.

36. Fiske, *Midshipman to Rear Admiral*, p. 498.

37. U.S. Navy, *Dictionary of American Naval Fighting Ships*, vol. 8, p. 127.

38. R. B. Coffey, "A Brief History of the Intervention in Haiti," *USNIP*, pp. 1326–27.

39. *Annual Report*, 1914, p. 64.

40. Taylor, *Magnificent Mitscher*, p. 39.

41. Board of Inspection and Survey, "USS *Charlotte* Material Inspection Report," 25 July 1929, p. 7.

42. *Annual Report*, 1914, pp. 160, 237.

43. Donald C. Heath, interview with the author.

Bibliography

Works frequently cited are identified by the following abbreviations:

ASNE   *Journal of the American Society of Naval Engineers*
SNAME   *Transactions of the Society of Naval Architects and Marine Engineers*
USNIP   United States Naval Institute *Proceedings*

General Reference

Gardiner, Robert, ed. *Conway's All the World's Fighting Ships, 1860–1905*. New York: Mayflower Books, 1979.

Jane's Fighting Ships. 1905, 1914, 1919. London: Sampson Low Marston, 1905, 1914, 1919.

U.S. Navy Department. *Dictionary of American Naval Fighting Ships*. 8 vols. Washington, D.C.: GPO, 1959–81.

Government Publications

U.S. Congress. Senate. *Sampson-Schley: Official Communications to the United States Senate*. 55th Cong., 3rd sess. Washington, D.C.: GPO, 1899.

U.S. Navy Department. *Annual Report to the Secretary of the Navy, 1881–1935*. Washington, D.C.: GPO, 1881–1935.

U.S. Navy Department. Bureau of Construction and Repair. *Specifications for Building Steel Twin-Screw Armored Cruiser No. 2*. Washington, D.C.: GPO, 1890.

U.S. Navy Department. Bureau of Construction and Repair. *Specifications for Building Steel Twin-Screw Armored Cruiser No. 3*. Washington, D.C.: GPO, 1892.

U.S. Navy Department. Bureau of Navigation. *Appendix to the Report of the Chief of the Bureau of Navigation.* Washington, D.C.: GPO, 1899.

U.S. Navy Department. *Navy Yearbook.* 1910, 1916. Washington, D.C.: GPO, 1910, 1916.

U.S. Navy Department. *Record of Proceedings of a Court of Inquiry in the Case of Rear Admiral Winfield S. Schley.* 2 vols. Washington, D.C.: GPO, 1902.

Wheeler, Gerald. *Admiral William Veazie Pratt, U.S. Navy.* Washington, D.C.: Department of the Navy, 1974.

Unpublished Government Documents

U.S. Navy Department. Board of Inspection and Survey. Material inspection reports: USS *Pennsylvania,* ACR 4 (*Pittsburgh*); *West Virginia,* ACR 5 (*Huntington*); *California,* ACR 6 (*San Diego*); *Colorado,* ACR 7 (*Pueblo*); *Maryland,* ACR 8 (*Frederick*); *South Dakota,* ACR 9 (*Huron*); *Tennessee,* ACR 10 (*Memphis*); *Washington,* ACR 11 (*Seattle*); *North Carolina,* ACR 12 (*Charlotte*); *Montana,* ACR 13 (*Missoula*). Record Group 38. National Archives, Washington, D.C.

U.S. Navy Department. General Board. Memorandum to the President of the United States, 15 January 1907. G.B. No. 420-2. National Archives, Washington, D.C.

U.S. Navy Department. Office of the Judge Advocate General. Various memoranda to the Board of Inspection and Survey: USS *Pennsylvania,* ACR 4 (*Pittsburgh*); *West Virginia,* ACR 5 (*Huntington*); *California,* ACR 6 (*San Diego*); *Colorado,* ACR 7 (*Pueblo*); *Maryland, ACR 8 (Frederick); South Dakota,* ACR 9 (*Huron*); *Tennessee,* ACR 10 (*Memphis*); *Washington,* ACR 11 (*Seattle*); *North Carolina,* ACR 12 (*Charlotte*); *Montana,* ACR 13 (*Missoula*). Record Group 38. National Archives, Washington D.C.

U.S. Navy Department Trials Board. Final trials reports: USS *Pennsylvania,* ACR 4; *West Virginia,* ACR 5; *California,* ACR 6; *Colorado,* ACR 7; *Maryland,* ACR 8; *South Dakota,* ACR 9; *Tennessee,* ACR 10; *Washington,* ACR 11; *North Carolina,* ACR 12; *Montana,* ACR 13. Record Group 38. National Archives, Washington, D.C.

U.S. Navy Department. Trials Board. Preliminary trials reports: USS *Pennsylvania,* ACR 4; *West Virginia,* ACR 5; *California,* ACR 6; *Colorado,* ACR 7; *Maryland,* ACR 8; *South Dakota,* ACR 9; *Tennessee,* ACR 10; *Washington,* ACR 11; *North Carolina,* ACR 12; *Montana,* ACR 13. Record Group 38. National Archives, Washington, D.C.

Books

Alden, John D. *The American Steel Navy.* Annapolis: Naval Institute Press, 1972.

Arpee, Edward. *From Frigates to Flat-Tops.* Lake Forest, Illinois: private printing, 1953.

Belknap, Reginald. *Routine Book: Including General Features of Organization, Administration, and Ordinary Station Bills.* 1910. Reprint. Annapolis: United States Naval Institute, 1918.

Bennet, Frank M. *The Steam Navy of the United States: A History of the Growth of the Steam Vessel of War in the U.S. Navy, and of the Naval Engineer Corps.* Pittsburgh: W. T. Nicholson, 1896.

Braisted, William. *The United States Navy in the Pacific, 1897–1909.* Austin: University of Texas Press, 1958.

————. *The United States Navy in the Pacific, 1909–1922.* Austin: University of Texas Press, 1971.

Buell, Augustus C. *The Memoirs of Charles H. Cramp.* Philadelphia: Lippincott, 1906.

Chadwick, French E. *The Relations of the United States and Spain: The Spanish-American War.* 2 vols. New York: Scribner, 1911.

Clark, George, et al. *A Short History of the United States Navy.* Philadelphia: J. B. Lippincott, 1911.

Coletta, Paolo E. *Admiral Bradley A. Fiske and the American Navy.* Lawrence, Kansas: Regents Press of Kansas, 1979.

————. *Bowman Hendry McCalla: A Fighting Sailor.* Washington: United Press of America, 1979.

————. *French Ensor Chadwick: Scholarly Warrior.* Washington: United Press of America, 1980.

Cooling, Benjamin F. *Benjamin Franklin Tracy: Father of the Modern American Fighting Navy.* Hamden, Connecticut: Shoe String, 1973.

Coontz, Robert E. *From the Mississippi to the Sea.* Philadelphia: Dorrance, 1930.

Davis, Vincent. *The Admirals Lobby.* Chapel Hill: University of North Carolina Press, 1967.

Evans, Robley D. *An Admiral's Log.* New York: D. Appleton, 1910.

————. *A Sailor's Log: Recollections of Forty Years of Naval Life.* New York: Appleton, 1901.

Fiske, Bradley. *From Midshipman to Rear Admiral.* New York: The Century Company, 1919.

Gleaves, Albert. *A History of the Transport Service.* New York: George H. Doran Co., 1921.

Goode, William A. M. *With Sampson Through the War.* New York: Doubleday and McClure, 1899.

Graham, George E. *Schley and Santiago.* Chicago: Conkey, 1902.

Healy, David F. *Gunboat Diplomacy in the Wilson Era: The U.S. Navy in Haiti, 1915–1916.* Madison: University of Wisconsin Press, 1976.

Herrick, Walter R. *The American Naval Revolution.* Baton Rouge: Louisiana State University Press, 1966.

Hirsch, Mark D. *William C. Whitney: Modern Warwick.* New York: Dodd, Mead, 1948.

Kennan, George. *Russia Leaves the War.* Princeton, N.J.: Princeton University Press, 1956.

Knott, Richard. *The American Flying Boat.* Annapolis: Naval Institute Press, 1979.

Leutze, James. *A Different Kind of Victory.* Annapolis: Naval Institute Press, 1981.

Long, John D. *The New American Navy.* 2 vols. New York: Outlook, 1903.

Love, Robert, ed. *The Chiefs of Naval Operations.* Annapolis: Naval Institute Press, 1980.

Maclay, Edgar. *Life and Adventures of "Jack" Philip, Rear Admiral USN*. New York: Baker and Taylor, 1903.

Mahan, Alfred. *Lessons of the War with Spain*. Boston: Little, Brown, 1899.

Mayo, L. S., ed. *America of Yesterday, as Reflected in the Journal of John Davis Long*. Boston: Atlantic Monthly Press, 1923.

Millis, Walter. *The Martial Spirit: A Study of Our War with Spain*. Cambridge, Massachusetts: Riverside Press, 1931.

Mitchell, Donald. *A History of Russian and Soviet Sea Power*. New York: Macmillan, 1974.

————. *History of the Modern American Navy*. New York: Alfred A. Knopf, 1946.

Morison, Elting E. *Admiral Sims and the Modern American Navy*. Boston: Houghton Mifflin, 1942.

Morris, Charles. *The War with Spain*. Philadelphia: J. B. Lippincott, 1899.

Reynolds, Clark. *Famous American Admirals*. New York: Van Nostrand Reinhold, 1978.

Richardson, Leon B. *William E. Chandler: Republican*. New York: Dodd, Mead, 1940.

Roscoe, Theodore. *On the Seas and in the Skies*. New York: Hawthorn Books, 1970.

Scheina, Robert, and John Reilly, Jr. *American Battleships, 1886–1923*. Annapolis: Naval Institute Press, 1980.

Schley, Winfield S. *Forty-five Years Under the Flag*. New York: Appleton, 1904.

Schroeder, Seaton. *A Half-Century of Naval Service*. New York: D. Appleton, 1923.

Spears, John R. *Our Navy in the War with Spain*. New York: Scribner, 1898.

————. *The History of Our Navy from Its Origin to the End of the War with Spain*. New York: Charles Scribner's Sons, 1899.

Sprout, Harold and Margaret. *The Rise of American Naval Power, 1776–1918*. Annapolis: Naval Institute Press, 1966.

Sprout, Margaret T. "Mahan: Evangelist of Sea Power." In *Makers of Modern Strategy: Military Thought from Machiavelli to Hitler*, edited by Edward M. Earle, pp. 415–45. Princeton: Princeton University Press, 1943.

Stirling, Yates. *Sea Duty: The Memoirs of A Fighting Admiral*. New York: Putnam, 1939.

Tolley, Kemp. *Caviar and Commissars*. Annapolis: Naval Institute Press, 1983.

————. *Yangtze Patrol: The U.S. Navy in China*. Annapolis: Naval Institute Press, 1971.

Turnbull, Archibald, and Clifford Lord. *History of United States Naval Aviation*. New Haven: Yale University Press, 1949.

Watts, A. J., and B. G. Gordon. *The Imperial Japanese Navy*. Garden City, N.Y.: Doubleday, 1971.

West, Richard S. *Admirals of American Empire: The Combined Story of George Dewey, Alfred Thayer Mahan, Winfield Scott Schley, and William Sampson*. Indianapolis: Bobbs-Merrill, 1948.

Wilson, H. W. *Ironclads in Action*. 2 vols. London: Sampson, Low and Marston, 1896.

————. *The Downfall of Spain: Naval History of the Spanish American War*. Boston: Little, Brown, 1900. Reprint. New York: Burt Franklin, 1971.

Periodicals

Ackerman, A. A. "Face Hardened Armor." *USNIP* 21 (1895).

Anderson, M. A., and E. R. Freeman. "The Contract Trial of the U.S.S. *New York*." *ASNE* 5 (1893): 613–35.

Army and Navy Register. Various volumes (Washington, D.C., 1900–1915).

Barry, E. B. "A Modern Fleet." *SNAME* 14 (1906).

Bowles, Francis. "Remarks on the New Designs of Naval Vessels." *SNAME* 10 (1902): 273–87.

Cathcart, W. Ledyard. "Water-Tube vs. Cylindrical Boilers for Naval Vessels." *ASNE* 15 (November 1903).

Chadwick, French. "The *New York* at Santiago." *The Century Magazine* 58 (May–October 1899).

Coffey, R. B. "A Brief History of the Intervention in Haiti." *USNIP* 48 (August 1922): 1325–26.

Cook, Francis. "The *Brooklyn* at Santiago." *The Century Magazine* 58 (May–October 1899).

"Could Admiral Sampson Have Taken Havana?" *USNIP* 34 (1908): 362.

Crank, R. K. "Latest Type of Babcock and Wilcox Marine Boiler." *ASNE* 16 (November 1904).

———. "Notes on Firing of Boilers on Recent Trial Trips." *ASNE* 18 (1906): 931–32.

Danforth, G. W. "U.S.S. *California*." *ASNE* 19 (1907): 2–16.

Dinger, H. C. "Notes for General and Routine Work of Engineer's Division, U.S. Naval Vessel." *ASNE* 16 (November 1904).

———. "Suggestions for the Care and Operation of Naval Machinery in the Engineer Department U.S. Navy." *ASNE* 18 (1906).

Dyson, Charles. "Screw Propellers of U.S. Naval Vessels." *ASNE* 15 (May 1903).

———. "Screw Propeller Criticism and Notes on Screw Propeller Design Based on Actual Standardization Trial Results of U.S. Vessels." *ASNE* 21 (February 1909).

Evans, Robley. "The *Iowa* at Santiago." *The Century Magazine* 58 (May–October 1899).

Gleaves, Albert. "The Howell Torpedo." *USNIP* 21 (1895).

"The Harvey Armor Plate: Results of the Recent Trial at Annapolis." *USNIP* 17 (1891): 387–89.

Herbert, W. C. "Contract Trial of the U.S. Armored Cruiser *Brooklyn*." *ASNE* 13 (1896): 741–62.

Hichborn, Philip. "Recent Designs of Battleships and Cruisers for the United States Navy." *SNAME* 8 (1900): 261–78.

———. "Recent Designs of Vessels for the United States Navy." *SNAME* 3 (1895): 115–38.

Hovgaard, William, "The Cruiser." *SNAME* 13 (1905): 103–44.

———. "On the Speed of Battleships." *SNAME* 15 (1907): 213–42.

Howe, Charles. "The Niclausse Boiler." *ASNE* 15 (November 1903).

Kenney, Lewis. "The U.S.S. *Pennsylvania*." *ASNE* 17 (1905): 1–41.

———. "U.S. Armored Cruiser *Tennessee*." *ASNE* 18 (May 1906): 386–464.

Leavitt, William. "Description and Official Trials of the U.S.S. *Washington*." *ASNE* 18 (May 1906): 761.

"Maneuvering Qualities of Battleships." *ASNE* 15 (May 1903): 433–34.

Meigs, John. "Recent Developments in Armor and Armament." *SNAME* 14 (1906).

Melville, George. "Advantages of the 100-Foot Smoke-Pipes of Armored Cruiser No. 3." *ASNE* 5 (1893).

———. "Notes on the Machinery of the New Vessels of the United States Navy." *SNAME* 1 (1893).

Miller, H. B. "Shooting the Catapult." *USNIP* 59 (April 1933): 548–52.

Niblack, Albert. "Further Tactical Considerations Involved in Warship Design." *SNAME* 15 (1907): 155.

———. "Tactical Considerations Involved in Warship Design." *SNAME* 3 (1895).

"*North Carolina*'s Aeroplane Catapult." *USNIP* 42 (May–June 1916).

O'Neil, Charles. "The Development of Modern Ordnance and Armor in the United States." *SNAME* 10 (1902): 264.

Parks, W. M. "Test of a Niclausse Boiler Under Forced Draft." *ASNE* 16 (1904).

Paullin, Charles. "A Half Century of Naval Administration in America, 1861–1911: The Navy in the Spanish-American War, 1898." *USNIP* 40 (March–April 1914).

———. "The American Navy in the Orient in Recent Years." *USNIP* 37 (1911): 1137–75, and 38 (1912): 87–115.

Philip, John. "The *Texas* at Santiago." *The Century Magazine* 58 (May–October 1899).

Pond, Charles. "Report of the Commanding Officer of the USS *Pennsylvania*." *USNIP* 37 (March 1911): 191–92.

"Professional Notes." *USNIP* 28 (December 1902), 979–80.

Raby, J. J. "U.S.S. *South Dakota*." *ASNE* 19 (1907).

"Report of the Policy Board." *USNIP* 16 (1890): 201–77.

Robinson, R. H. M. "Notes on the Development of Warship Design." *SNAME* 14 (1906).

Rodgers, W. L. "A Study of Attacks Upon Fortified Harbors." *USNIP* 36 (1910).

Ryan, Paul. "Ten Days at Vera Cruz." *USNIP* 98 (July 1972).

Sampson, William. "Present Status of Face Hardened Armor." *SNAME* 2 (1894): 183–203.

Scribner, E. H. "United States Armored Cruiser *Colorado*." *ASNE* 16 (1904).

Sears, W. J. "A General Description of the Whitehead Torpedo." *USNIP* 20 (1896).

Smith, W. Strother. "Propeller Blade Inaccuracies: Proposed Method of Machining and Finishing." *ASNE* 16 (August 1904).

———. "United States Armored Cruisers *West Virginia* and *Maryland*." *ASNE* 17 (1905).

Smith, W. W. "Performance of the Assistant Cylinders of the U.S.S. *Washington*." *ASNE* 18 (1906).

"Speed Trials of the *Brooklyn*." *USNIP* 22 (1896).

Taylor, David W. "Comments on the Size of Battleships as a Function of their Speed." *USNIP* (March 1907).

———. "Our New Battleships and Armored Cruisers." *USNIP* 26 (1900): 593–99.

Taylor, Henry. "American Maritime Development." *SNAME* 3 (1895).

Underwood, E. B. "An International Incident." *USNIP* 41 (January 1925).

Van Deurs, George. "Pete Mitscher and Armored Cruiser Aviation." *USNIP* 95 (November 1969): 152–53.

Very, E. W. "The Howell Automobile Torpedo." *USNIP* 16 (1890).

Washburn, H. C. "The War with Spain: A Study of Past Performance." *USNIP* 43 (July 1917).

White, William. "U.S. Armored Cruiser *Montana*." *ASNE* 20 (August 1908).

Wilson, Theodore. "Steel Ships of the United States Navy." *SNAME* 1 (1893): 116–39.

Withers, Thomas. "The Wreck of the U.S.S. *Memphis*." *USNIP* 44 (July 1918): 1459–60.

Interviews

Donald C. Heath, interview with author, Minneapolis, 27 December 1983.

Index